PAUL SAMUELSON AND MODERN ECONOMIC THEORY

Courtesy of Marnie Samuelson

PAUL SAMUELSON AND MODERN ECONOMIC THEORY

Edited by
E. Cary Brown
Robert M. Solow

Massachusetts Institute of Technology

McGRAW-HILL BOOK COMPANY

New York   St. Louis   San Francisco   Auckland   Bogotá
Hamburg   Johannesburg   London   Madrid   Mexico   Montreal   New Delhi
Panama   Paris   São Paulo   Singapore   Sydney   Tokyo   Toronto

This book was set in Times Roman by The Total Book (GTI).
The editor was Peter J. Dougherty;
the production supervisor was Charles Hess.
The cover was designed by Carla Bauer.
R. R. Donnelley & Sons Company was printer and binder.

PAUL SAMUELSON AND MODERN ECONOMIC THEORY

2 3 4 5 6 7 8 9 0   DOCDOC   8 9 8 7 6 5 4 3

ISBN 0-07-059667-0

Library of Congress Cataloging in Publication Data
Main entry under title:

Paul Samuelson and modern economic theory.

    Includes bibliographies.
    1. Samuelson, Paul Anthony, date   —Addresses, essays, lectures. 2. Economics—Addresses, essays, lectures. I. Brown, E. Cary (Edgar Cary) II. Solow, Robert M.
HB119.S25P38 1983   330   82-20343
ISBN 0-07-059667-0

CONTENTS

LIST OF CONTRIBUTORS

KENNETH J. ARROW
Joan Kenney Professor of Economics and Professor of Operations Research,
  Stanford University

E. CARY BROWN
Professor of Economics, Massachusetts Institute of Technology

F. H. HAHN
Professor of Economics and Fellow of Churchill College, University of Cambridge

HENDRIK S. HOUTHAKKER
Henry Lee Higginson Professor of Economics, Harvard University

RONALD W. JONES
Xerox Professor of Economics, University of Rochester

ROBERT C. MERTON
J. C. Penney Professor of Management, Massachusetts Institute of Technology

RICHARD A. MUSGRAVE
Harold Hitchings Burbank Professor of Political Economy, Emeritus, Harvard
  University and Adjunct Professor of Economics, Crown College, University of
  California, Santa Cruz

DON PATINKIN
Professor of Economics, Hebrew University

PAUL A. SAMUELSON
Institute Professor and Professor of Economics, Massachusetts Institute of
  Technology

ROBERT M. SOLOW
Institute Professor and Professor of Economics, Massachusetts Institute of
  Technology

JAMES TOBIN
Sterling Professor of Economics, Yale University

C. C. VON WEIZSÄCKER
Professor, Institute for Sociology and Economics, Bonn

PREFACE

Paul A. Samuelson has touched the contributors to this volume in many ways: as a scholar who has radically changed economic analysis from the way he found it; as a teacher who enriched many subjects and stimulated research; as a fellow student or, as Samuelson would say, comrade in arms; as a helpful and supportive colleague; and as a warm and generous friend. Because Paul is such a special person, we thought that a set of essays appraising his many contributions to various areas of economic analysis would make a unique and fruitful tribute to him—something for the man who has everything. Despite efforts to cast our net as widely as possible, there are still omissions. The first is an amusing object lesson in Samuelsoniana. In the course of planning the division of labor in this volume, we realized that the famous overlapping-generations consumption-loan model had a foothold all through economics: in the theory of capital, of course, in monetary theory, in general equilibrium, in welfare economics, and even in macrotheory. Only when it was too late to do anything about it did we realize that, though it is mentioned in several places, a full treatment had slipped through the safety net. We comfort ourselves that it was not truly needy. Second, we give little emphasis to his effective and serious efforts to promote public understanding of economics, economic events, and policies, through many vehicles: his consultations with the Congress, the administration and its agencies, public talks and debates, and "the" textbook, now in its eleventh edition. The essays in this volume are, therefore, concerned with Samuelson, the scientist. In this preface, we will speak of his special contribution to the Department of Economics at MIT.

In 1940 Samuelson had just completed a three-year appointment as Harvard junior fellow, a period which he has termed "golden and productive," when he essentially completed the *Foundations*. He had accepted a Harvard instructorship, the standard prize for an outstanding young scholar. He was prepared to settle into what was then the dominant economics department in the country and which had provided a fruitful environment over the previous five years.

The MIT Department of Economics of the 30s was a far cry, indeed, from Harvard: it was strictly a service department supplementary to engineering education, composed of a faculty of modest distinction, plus some remarkable juniors (David Lusher, Phillip Bradley, Lionel McKenzie, Robert Roosa, Leonid Hurwicz, Robert Livernash, Russ Nixon). The arrival of Rupert Maclaurin in 1936 from the Harvard Business School changed the vision of the Department. Rupert, the son of MIT's sixth president, was a restless activist, so full of energy that it sometimes outran his judgment. He gave a major push to what was labeled industrial economics, set up and headed the Industrial Relations Section in 1937, and was to gather a group of young scholars of the economics of technological change in particular industries. To industrial relations came Douglass V. Brown and Charles Myers; to industry studies Arthur Bright (electric light), Robert Bishop (glass container), Warren Scoville (French and US glass industry), Daniel Vandermuelen (paper), and Richard Bissell.

Rupert also had a vision of graduate work and of a broader department. Harold Freeman, a brilliant classical statistician and the most distinguished member of that earlier department, was taking some graduate courses at Harvard. He learned of, and got acquainted with, the Wunderkind of the graduate student body and returned with glowing reports of someone they should try to get. Such an opportunity challenged Rupert's entrepreneurial instincts, and, with Ralph Freeman, the longtime departmental head, he set to work on a congenial offer. MIT was able to come up with an assistant professorship. Continued urging by MIT, whose active interest must have contrasted with Harvard's, finally made the acceptance of the better offer the sensible thing to do. The prospects for advancement were certainly excellent; while there was no graduate program, there was one on the way, and Paul knew that the kind of research that he carried out was not substantially dependent on numbers of students. Moreover, Harvard would be only two subway stops away. So came about one of the smartest things that MIT ever did, a matter of critical importance to the future of the Department.

Paul was the heart of the graduate program started in 1941—a Ph.D. in Industrial Economics. While the inclusion of the word "Industrial," later dropped, was to a large extent motivated by the desire to make the degree fit more comfortably into the MIT ambience, it also represented the major thrust of the original program. Through the next decade, candidates were required to choose four fields from the following eight: economic theory, sociopsychological theory, industrial relations, industrial organization and price policy, economics of technical change, statistical methods, economic history, and the state in relation to industry. Indeed, most of the theses in this period were in industrial relations.

Maclaurin was an effective fund raiser; the fellowships that could be offered in this small program were high in terms of the standards of the time; and the program got off to a modest but good start. The first entering class included Lawrence Klein, later a Clark medalist and Nobel laureate, and George Shultz, later to become Dean of the Chicago Business School, the holder of a variety of cabinet posts under Nixon, President of Bechtel Corporation, and now Secretary of State. Hardly had the program started, however, when our entry into World War II essentially shut it down along with other programs throughout the country. Students were limited in numbers and many of the faculty were involved with the military or in defense work. The extent to which this program was dependent on Samuelson can be seen from the catalog listings of that period: two terms of graduate microtheory; mathematical economics shared with Harold Freeman; business cycles; advanced economic statistics shared with Harold Freeman; and public finance. When he joined the Radiation Laboratory at MIT for the years 1943–1945, the program was more or less suspended.

After the war, the influx and reflux of graduate and undergraduate students started a period of university expansion. The war's disruption of the academic community created great postwar mobility. Many academics shifted academic positions; many others remained in government. In such a fluid situation, it was possible by astute hiring to transform whole departments. The substantial dominance of the Harvard and Chicago departments of the prewar period was challenged by developments in many schools with new stars: MIT had Samuelson, Yale had Tobin, Stanford had Arrow, and Chicago had a renaissance with Friedman. MIT could not at first match the quality of other graduate departments, but Paul was a powerful attraction as a colleague. In the balance of the decade, the Department added Morris Adelman, Cary Brown, Charles Kindleberger, Max Millikan, George Shultz, and Robert Solow. This was the group that determined the character and interests of the Department for the next twenty years. (It was reinforced by Paul Rosenstein-Rodan and Everett Hagen, who joined Millikan's Center for International Studies after its establishment in 1952.)

What role did Samuelson play in all this? Certainly not an administrative one. When Brown was appointed, Ralph Freeman, then department head, was seriously ill and the chore of making the written offer fell to Paul. While there had been no discussion of any rank other than that of assistant professor, the letter from Paul offered an associate professorship (which the recipient did not take seriously) and was followed by several frantic telegrams of demotion. In 1949–50, before the MIT administration had fully perceived Paul's distinctive talents as an academic administrator, he was appointed to the Committee on Undergraduate Courses, and, whenever the Committee met, departmental phones repeatedly jangled as Paul tried to determine what our major required in the way of units, prerequisites, requirements, which he seemed (or wanted) never to get straight. He was not, to our knowledge, ever formally designated an advisor of either undergraduates or graduates. He was terrorized by red tape: Marion shielded him from it in his personal affairs; the rest of us tried to in academic matters. He was not fussy, but he liked things to come out right. Optimal travel guidance, for example, was provided by the balanced portfolio of Domar and Solow.

Paul was, and continues to be, however, an interested and effective academic statesman. He was concerned about the quality and direction of the Department and MIT. He could always be called upon to serve on useful committees—personnel committees in the department, presidential selection committees for the Institute— and was generous in time spent on prospective faculty and students, even on visitors who wanted words with a famous man. He knows the dangers to a department of lack of intellectual public-spiritedness; he is never so preoccupied with his own research and career that he cannot attend to the development of the Department. He has been the best of colleagues to the junior faculty. His door was open to those who wished to drop in, though in later years, as his time became more and more occupied with outside commitments, one might trip over television cables, fall over reporters, or interrupt the *Newsweek* column. His appetite for conversation and pleasure in his colleagues helped the development of a luncheon table where most of us met daily. There was a time when economics was simpler and less specialized, and we were fewer and less specialized; the lunch talk was often about the central ideas of economics and vividly educational. The multiplication of journals and demands on time have, alas, reduced that commonality of experience.

Loyalty is another one of Paul's virtues, and MIT has gained from it. Few universities would not have been overjoyed to induce Samuelson to come there. Famous or not, he felt a responsibility to the Department and to MIT that transcended any modest gains that might arise from such a shift. Indeed, it is remarkable how one so much in demand spent so little time weighing such offers. He believed that if things were going right they should be left alone.

Paul has been more than a role model; he has been the role. He has carried his full share of teaching responsibility and thesis supervision even when he became an Institute Professor. Only in very recent years has he cut down to a half load. His teaching has had extraordinary versatility, as one would expect: introductory economics, graduate theory, macro and micro, international economics, public finance and fiscal policy, business cycles, and money. He has even taught statistics, although never labor economics and industrial organization. But have no doubt that even in these fields he could teach an interesting and stimulating course.

As role model, Paul has set a pattern that the rest of us have fallen into. It created our style for the next few decades that involved caring about the academic program and the students in it, being available to colleagues and students, minimizing competition between students and among faculty, being interested in and supportive of others in their professional and personal problems. The lightness with which he carries his talents and honors makes it difficult for us ordinary mortals to take ourselves very seriously. In short it has made the Department a comfortable place in which to work, as it must also have been as a place in which to study. In the earliest oral defense-of-thesis that one of us remembers, Paul quizzed a student on one side of a major policy issue for awhile, then worked the other side of it, revealing large unreconciled differences in the candidate's position. Expecting to hear an adverse judgment of what appeared to one of us as a shambles, his verdict was—"That was a pretty good performance," and he told us why. Yet he was not a negligent grader in the Schumpeterian mold.

The importance to Paul of a congenial environment is evident from the following story. In the mid or late 50s, Seymour Harris conducted a poll among the Chairman's group of the American Economics Association to determine their view of the outstanding graduate department in the country. Seymour was an extraordinary chauvinist but so good natured and charming about it that one could take no umbrage. He was said to have gleefully reported the results: Harvard first and MIT tenth or fifteenth or twentieth, we forget now. When Paul was told this story, his quick response was: "We may not be the best department, but we certainly are the happiest."

Paul certainly knows his worth, is very self aware, but extraordinarily modest considering his remarkable achievements. Once when we were discussing a person's inability to produce published research, he said that publication was largely a matter of habit! Going to lunch one day, the late Svend Laursen, an old friend of graduate school days and then at Brandeis, jokingly chided Paul that he, Svend, had

had to turn from Paul to Lloyd Metzler for help in working out the problem of flexible exchange rates and employment that later appeared as a joint paper. Paul's prompt reply: "Genius flies where talent plods." He had attributed part of his genius to chemical response and much of his success to hard work [IV, Chap. 278, reprinted in this volume]. And, indeed, he does work long and hard and effectively, his intellectual machinery seeming never to slow down. Substantial as is his volume of publication, there are many more manuscripts that have never been published.

As a companion, Paul is simply superb. His conversational and writing styles are very similar: trenchant, vivid figures of speech, extensive historical references, illuminating comparative situations or ideas. He loves to improve on conventional widsom by rephrasing, sometimes standing it on its head. For example: "The exception that improves the rule."

Alfonso the Wise is supposed to have said that if he had been present at the Creation, he would have done a better job. Paul was, and did. It was only the creation of a little world, though it reached through all of economics. We mean this book as a token of gratitude for that little world.

E. Cary Brown
Robert M. Solow

ECONOMICS IN A GOLDEN AGE: A PERSONAL MEMOIR*

Paul A. Samuelson

On Alfred Nobel's last birthday, in Europe's most beautiful building of this century, Professor Arne Tiselius spoke of a visit he once made to a Scottish chemistry laboratory. Through some failure of communications he did not realize until ushered into a large auditorium that a lecture was expected from him. When he asked what they would like to hear him discuss, someone called out, "How does one go about getting a Nobel Prize?" Professor Tiselius confessed he could not be responsive to the question.

When my turn came for the usual Stockholm remarks of gratitude and humility, I departed from my polished text to say, "I can tell you how to get a Nobel Prize. One condition is to have great teachers." And I enumerated the many great economists whom I had been able to study under both at Chicago and Harvard.

Although necessary, this condition is not by itself sufficient. "One must also have great collaborators." And, again, from Robert Solow down, I was able to count my own blessings. "Of course, one must have great students," following which went a recital of famous names.

Finally, in a crescendo of humility, I said, "And more important than all of these, one must have LUCK."

I stand by all these impromptu remarks. But with the shade of Samuel Johnson hovering over me and warning against all cant, I must add some afterthoughts. In the dark of the late October night, when a reporter phoned my home to ask my reaction to having received the Alfred Nobel Memorial Prize in Economic Science for 1970—and I spell out the title to emphasize that economics is a latecomer at the festive table with an award that is not quite a proper Nobel Prize—my first response

*"Economics in a Golden Age: A Personal Memoir" by Paul A. Samuelson is reprinted from *The Twentieth-Century Sciences*, Studies in the Biography of Ideas, Edited by Gerald Holton, with the permission of W. W. Norton & Company, Inc. Copyright © 1972, 1970 by the American Academy of Arts and Sciences; reprinted in P. A. Samuelson, *Collected Scientific Papers*, IV, Chap. 278.

was, "It's nice to have hard work rewarded." My children told me later it was a conceited remark.[1] Nonetheless one must tell the truth and shame the devil. It has been one of the sad empirical findings of my life: other things equal—with initial endowments and abilities held constant—the man who works the hardest tends to get the most done, and the one who saves the most does, alas, end up richest. To find these copybook maxims valid is as vexing as to learn that the horror stories told in my youth against cigarette smoking are after all true.

One must also tell the truth and shame the angels. So I must add what I might not have felt it necessary to add twenty years ago, namely that one must have been blessed with analytical ability. Great intellects—Newton, Lagrange, Gauss, and Mill will do as examples—have often been accused of false modesty. Newton said that however he may have appeared to others, to himself he appeared like a child playing with pretty pebbles on the beach. Lagrange explained his success in solving difficult problems by "always thinking about them." In similar words, Gauss discounted his superiority over other great mathematicians, saying in effect that, if you had thought as hard as he had about these matters, you too would be a Gauss. Finally, John Stuart Mill, who seems to have had the highest IQ ever observed tells us in his autobiography, in words that are as charming as they are naive, "Aw, shucks, anyone could have learned Greek at three and written a history of Rome at five"—and, I may add, have a nervous breakdown by nineteen—"if only he had the advantage of a teacher like James Mill."

What are we to make of these absurd disclaimers? Certainly Newton, who anonymously led the battle against Leibniz' claims to the calculus and who declared he would go to his grave without writing up the universal law of gravitation if he were required to make acknowledgment that Hooke had also some notions about attraction according to the inverse square of the distance, was anything but a truly modest man. And the record for Gauss is not that of a generous person. (When an old friend wrote to tell that his son had discovered non-Euclidean geometry, Gauss could not forebear from saying that he himself had already done that in unpublished work decades earlier. Worse than to kiss and tell is to not publish and claim.) A truly generous scholar, Euler—who made sense of Maupertuis' mystical principle of least action but refused to take the credit for it, and who delayed his own publications in the calculus of variations so that the youthful Lagrange could publish his novelties first—did not go around belittling himself or his work. Only in the case of Mill was pathological modesty a characteristic feature. (Actually when we read his remarks about (1) his father, (2) that paragon of all intellectual and other virtues, Harriet Taylor, and finally (3) his step-daughter, with whom he lived after Harriet's death, we do not have to be a Freud to recognize that we are in the presence of neurotic

---

[1] They were apparently not alone. In a recent biographical work, W. Breit and R. L. Ransom, *The Academic Scribblers: American Economists in Collision* (New York: Holt, Rinehart and Winston, 1971), the authors quote the remark, with the prefacing words: "He was characteristically brash about his own achievements and prize." Despite some acknowledgments of help from me in personal correspondence on some fine points of doctrine, the authors' account does not jibe with my views on a number of matters.

pathology. Besides, Mill's notions of radical philosophy—utilitarianism, feminism, and much else—required him to have a belief in the environment as the prime determiner of all abilities.)

Properly understood, there is much truth and not merely cant in the disclaimers of these men. A fish has no reason to be aware of the water he has never left. As we live inside our own skulls, our findings become transparently clear. We not only see our discoveries; but, particularly among profound minds, we also see through them. The excitement is in the chase. Once we have conquered the theorem, there is, as Mach has stated, an inevitable feeling of letdown, almost I would say a postorgasmic relaxation. When Newton was asked how he knew that gravitational attraction would lead to Keplerian ellipses for planetary motion, he could say simply, "I calculated it." When one heard the late John von Neumann lecture spontaneously at breakneck speed, one's transcendental wonder was reduced to mere admiration upon realizing that his mind was grinding out the conclusions at rates only twice as fast as what could be done by his average listener. Is it so remarkable that a few leading scholars will again and again lead the pack in the conquering of new territory? If you think of a marathon race in which, for whatever reason, one clique gets ahead, then you will realize that they need subsequently run no faster than the pack in order to cross each milestone first.

But let us make no mistake about it. Although there is much truth in the quoted disclaimers, there is also much nonsense. Mere work will not make a bookkeeper into a Gauss: it will not even make a Jacobi into a Gauss. And John D. Rockefeller did not get that rich by saving more dimes than other people. Talent, natural talent, is a necessary even if not sufficient condition for success in these realms. My old colleague in the Society of Fellows, Stanislaus Ulam, used to tell the story of a mathematician friend who had worked out a wonderful formula for success. Success in life turned out to be a many variable function, which depended *inter alia* on how handsome you were, how wellborn, and a great variety of other matters. "Ability," said Ulam, "did enter into the formula, but after much manipulation it was found to enter both in the numerator and the denominator and could be neatly cancelled out of the final answer." That is a good story to tell at a cocktail party. But, outside the fields of college administration, it is utter poppycock. Ulam himself provides an excellent counterexample: it was not his brown eyes that explain the invention of the hydrogen bomb, the development of the Monte Carlo method, and numerous advances in the area of topology.

As mentioned, twenty years ago I would not have insisted on these trite assertions. However, by pure chance, I was for a time given some medication that excellently treated the symptoms for which it was prescribed. But during that period, I felt that it took the fine edge off my mind. Suddenly I realized how the other half lives! It was not that my performance suffered so visibly to the outer world. During that very period I wrote one of my best articles, but to myself it was clear that I was living on capital. (Paderewski used to say that if he quit practicing for one day, *he* noticed it; if he quit for two days, the critics noticed it; if he quit for three days, the whole world noticed. Luckily I was able to change my diet before the third day.) It was not merely that my ability to discover new truth was lowered; in addition, the zest to discover new truth was diminished by a more passive participation in the struggle against ignorance. In sum, there is a chemical element in intellectual achievement, and one is a fool to take great pride in the chance circumstances that one's chemistry happens to be a favorable one. I may add as a corollary that it would be nice to give Newton and Gauss a potion to show *them* what they were really like.[2]

THE TIME AND THE PLACE: THE MIDWAY

The year 1932 was a good time to come to the study of economics. "May you live in interesting times" may be a curse against happiness, but it is surely a benison for any scientist. Louis Pasteur in Eden would have become merely a brewer of beer.

The University of Chicago was a great place to study economics then. Frank Knight and Jacob Viner were at the top of their form. Henry Schultz, with energy and passion, was introducing the new mysteries of econometrics. Paul Douglas and Henry Simons catered to the needs of the young for relevance and commitment. Outside of the Economics Department, the rest of the university was in its finest hour. The new broom of Hutchins swept in exciting innovations of undergraduate curriculum and had not yet become the wand that paralyzes and destroys.

When I appeared on January 2, 1932, at 8:00 A.M. to hear Louis Wirth lecture on Malthus' theories of population, my mind was literally the tabula rasa of John Locke's psychology. Not yet graduated officially from high school, I had never heard of Adam Smith. (I later discovered that *The Wealth of Nations* had always been in our family library, disguised as a few inches of the five-foot Harvard Classics. But having sampled to my displeasure *Two Years Before the Mast* and being conditioned against the volume on the *Aeneid* which I had used as a trot—or, as we called it in those days, a "pony"—I forewent the pleasures of a liberal education in favor of research on sex in the eleventh edition of the *Encyclopaedia Britannica* and of browsing through the debates on Christianity and socialism that my father had picked up in the second-hand bookstores. For my money, Clarence Darrow and Robert Ingersoll always won the arguments: at fourteen turning the other cheek seemed merely stupid.)

I was prepared to find college difficult. True, I had always been a bright student. Although it was fashionable then to say you hated school, I always secretly liked it as a child and looked forward to the coming of September. Before the sociologists at the university showed me that all differences in performance rest on environmental

---

[2]Reminiscing one night at the Society of Fellows, I. A. Richards told me that the great Cambridge philosopher, Frank Ramsey, whose death at twenty-six was such a tragedy to economics as well as philosophy, found it hard to believe that others could not solve complicated syllogisms of mathematical logic in their heads. "Can't you *see* it? he would ask. No they couldn't. (A good joke about von Neumann is in order. According to legend, when asked the old problem of how much distance a fly traverses in running back and forth between two approaching locomotives, von Neumann is supposed to have given the right answer—by *summing* the series. The other night, instead of counting sheep, I tried to do the same in my head. Although I dislike puzzles, it turned out to be fairly easy—given *all* the time one needs.)

opportunities, I was a naive Francis Galton.[3] To ourselves, my brothers and I seemed perceptibly "smarter" than our cousins, who in turn were definitely smarter than the general run. It was with incredulity that I discovered in the second grade a boy who could add faster than I, but I could rationalize this by the fact that I was always being "skipped" a term, something that was particularly easy to do under the unconventional semester plan which characterized the innovative Gary school system. However, I reached my finest hour just before my hormones changed and turned me into an underachiever. Coming into college a term behind my class, I therefore thought that hard work would be necessary to survive, an agreeable error that launched me into scholarly orbit. As Wirth, himself a distinguished sociologist and excellent lecturer, expounded the 1-2-4- . . . and 1-2-3- . . . arithmetic of Malthus, it was all so simple that I was sure I must be missing the essential point. Since then I have come to realize that Malthus was just as simple as it seemed to me at sixteen, and hence I have never been surprised by the popularity of Malthusian doctrines with the man in the street and Ph.D.s in biology.

Although there was a minute in my sophomore year when I toyed with the notion of becoming a sociologist, my real stimulus came from an old-fashioned course in elementary economics that remained in the curriculum as a fossil from the pre-Hutchins "old plan" days, and which I was put in by virtue of my late arrival. Having missed the cosmic aspects of economics, as expounded by Harry Gideonse and the really excellent staff in Social Science Survey I, I was expected to be able to catch up by learning about marginal cost and elasticity of demand. By luck, my teacher was Aaron Director, a strong libertarian of the Knight-Hayek school. (A local joke was that, later, he used to refer to Milton Friedman as "my radical brother-in-law.") Director was also an analyst and an iconoclast, whose cold stare terrorized the coeds in the class but captivated me. In any case, even if I had had Mr. Squeers for a teacher, the first drink from the economic textbooks of Slichter and Ely would have been like the Prince's kiss to Sleeping Beauty. It was as if I were made for economics.[4] I could not believe that the rest of the class were making heavy weather

---

[3] A few years ago on a plane from Chicago to Washington, conversation with a fellow passenger enabled me to infer that he must be a Chicago professor of sociology. Without identifying myself, I chanced to remark: "At the University of Chicago I was taught to believe that differences in abilities and achievements are almost solely a function of differences in the environment. But now that I have become the father of six children, three of them triplets, I have had to modify my views." This drew down upon my head the following reproof: "Actually, you were right the first time. It *is* environment which is all important. Just to illustrate, take my own case: you may not realize it, but I am a distinguished professor and scholar. Yet I had two uncles who I can assure you were of the caliber to hold a chair in any great university in the world; but being poor immigrant boys, they were deprived of environmental opportunity." I could not resist replying: "Isn't it remarkable that a man who doesn't believe in the importance of heredity could report that no less than three of his immediate family were capable of being great scholars." Fortunately, he never turned his head.

[4] Years ago I heard Boris Goldovsky interviewed on radio. He was asked whether his son had talent, and replied: "Of course both his mother and father are musical, but still it is uncanny. Even at the age of five, when he goes to the piano it is as if his fingers have a wisdom that the little boy himself does not know." Or to vary the analogy, no cat ever took to catnip the way our first-born, Jane, reacted at the age of several months to her first taste of ice cream: her eyes rolled to know that such delights existed, and if she could have climbed a tree or rassled a bear she would have. So with me, on looking into economic books. Possibly I would have done well in any field of applied science or as a writer, but certainly the blend in economics of analytical hardness and humane relevance was tailor-made for me or I for it.

of such problems as the what would be the effect upon the price of kidneys of Minot's discovery that liver cured anemia, or the effect on mutton price if orlon were invented.

Chicago was a good place to learn economics at that time precisely because it was a stronghold of classical economics, a subject which had reached its culmination thirty years earlier in the work of Cambridge's Alfred Marshall. Economics itself was a sleeping princess waiting for the invigorating kiss of Maynard Keynes, and if one had to spend one's undergraduate days marking time before that event, Chicago was a better place to do so than would have been Harvard, Columbia, or the London School. Cambridge University was never within my ken, but since economics was also waiting for the invigorating kiss of mathematical methods, it would have been a personal tragedy if I had become merely a clever First in the Economics Tripos there. (I like to think I might have risen above the tragedy, but as Wellington said of Waterloo, it would have been a "damned close-run thing.")

I have written elsewhere that, for an economic theorist, the last half of the nineteenth century, was a bad time to be born. The really great work in neoclassical economics was all done in the years 1865 to 1910. Jevons, Menger, Walras, Bohm-Bawerk, Marshall, Wicksteed, Wicksell, and Pareto had gone beyond the classical synthesis of Smith, Ricardo, and Mill. Even the Marxian branch of the classical tree, save for one brief period of Indian Summer, shows clear sign of degeneracy after the turn of the century and the demise of Marx and Engels.

I do not say that 1915 was the perfect year to be born. Much as every family thinks that it would be happier with 20 percent more income, every scientist thinks that if he or she had turned up just a bit earlier many of the delays in his or her subject might have been avoided and many more of the victories would have been his or hers alone. Right before my time came the wonder generation of Frisch, Hotelling, Harrod, Myrdal, Tinbergen, Ohlin, Haberler, Hicks, Joan Robinson, Lerner, Leontief, Kaldor, and others too numerous to mention. Still to a person of analytical ability, perceptive enough to realize that mathematical equipment was a powerful sword in economics, the world of economics was his or her oyster in 1935. The terrain was strewn with beautiful theorems begging to be picked up and arranged in unified order. Only the other day I read about the accidental importation into South America of the African honey bee, with a resulting decimation of the local varieties. Precisely this happened in the field of theoretical economics: the people with analytical equipment came to dominate in every dimension of the vector the practitioners of literary economics.[5]

Elsewhere in this volume, Talcott Parsons tells how he moved out of economics

---

[5] That the apparatus of marginal revenue and imperfect competition should have had to be painfully rediscovered at the beginning of the 1930s, almost a century after Cournot's definitive 1838 work, testifies to the decadence of economics at that date. Or to illustrate with a harder problem that my economist readers will understand: in 1936, after I had already taken graduate courses in economic theory from Jacob Viner at Chicago and Joseph Schumpeter at Harvard, I still had to go around the Harvard Yard like Diogenes asking, "Why is it necessary for optimality that price should have to equal marginal cost?" And I was to receive no definitive understanding on the matter until my classmate Abram Bergson gave his 1938 definitive reformulation of modern welfare economics.

and into sociology more or less by chance and the necessity to make a career. It seems to me that this was a great stroke of luck for him. Although his genius might have turned economics in the direction of methodological system building, it would have been the Lord's own work and definitely against the tides of change. What were the major tides of economics in the decades after my 1935 graduation?

Back around 1950, at a Princeton Inn meeting of the American Economic Association's executive committee, Frank Knight once announced in his cracker-barrel Socratic manner: "If there is anything I can't stand it's a Keynesian and a believer in monopolistic competition." Being not much more than half his age at the time, but definitely old enough to behave myself better, I asked, "What about believers in the use of mathematics in economic analysis, Frank?" When told he couldn't stand them either, I realized that the indictment fitted me to a "T." And I thanked my lucky stars once again by chance and necessity, I, like Parsons, had been forced to leave the womb. Having been the usual A student and local bright boy at Chicago, I naturally thought it to be Mecca. Why leave Mecca?

Aside from its genuine excellence as a leading center for economics, Chicago had an additional attraction for me.[6] Although still an undergraduate, I had the opportunity to take Jacob Viner's celebrated course in graduate economic theory—celebrated both for its profundity in analysis and history of thought, but also celebrated for Viner's ferocious manhandling of students, in which he not only reduced women to tears but also on his good days drove returned paratroopers into hysteria and paralysis. I, nineteen-year-old innocent, walked unscathed through the inferno and naively pointed out errors in his blackboard diagramming. These acts of Christian kindness endeared me to the boys in the backroom of the gradute school: George Stigler, Allan Wallis, Albert Gaylord Hart, Milton Friedman, and the rest of the Knight Swiss guards. As I performed various make-work tasks for the department—dusting off the pictures of Bohm-Bawerk, Menger, and Mill in the departmental storage room which Stigler and Wallis had squatted in—we would gossip for hours over the inadequacies of our betters and the follies of princes who try to set right the evils of the marketplace.

Karl Marx, though, was right in his insistence on the economic determinism of

---

[6] It is fashionable to recall how much one hated school days at Eton, and it is subtly self-flattering to state how badly one was educated at college. (Henry Adams even complained that he was never assigned *Das Kapital* in Harvard College, which demonstrates that the faculty there was already up to its tricks of not assigning books not yet written.) I had a great education at the University of Chicago from 1932 to 1935, and one of my resentments against Robert Hutchins is that, by the time of his retirement, he had reduced a thriving college of 5,000 undergraduates into a few hundred under-age neurotics. To be sure the withdrawal of Rockefeller's princely patronage also contributed to the decline. Among the great noneconomist lecturers I heard, and got to know outside of class, were the mathematician Gilbert Bliss, the biologist Anton Carlson, the anthropologists Fay-Cooper Cole and Robert Redfield, the paleontologist Alfred Romer, and nearer to my own field, Frederick Schuman and Harold Lasswell in political science, Louis Wirth in sociology, and W. T. Hutchinson in American history (the single best course lecturer I have heard anywhere). My education was more in width than depth, not a bad way to spend the years sixteen to nineteen prior to specialized research. In a 1972 obituary article of Jacob Viner [*Collected Scientific Papers*, IV, Chap. 282], I include some further recollection of the Chicago scene.

history, including the history of economists. For a few pieces of silver I left Olympus. The Social Science Research Council tried the experiment of picking the eight most promising economic graduates by competitive exam and, in effect, subsidizing their whole graduate training. My comfortable fellowship carried only one stipulation: leave home. As a scholar, I sighed; as an opportunist, I obeyed.

But where to go? Foreign study was frowned on. The choice, and it tells us as much about the state of economic institutions as would a Carnegie or Rosenwald Report, was either Columbia or Harvard. Most of my teachers and friends advised Columbia. Harry Gideonse, whose influence along with that of Eugene Staley on my choice of economics as a major was insufficiently stressed in my earlier remarks, said: "How could anyone give up Morningside Heights in preference for New England?" (How times change!) Wallis, Friedman, and many of the Chicago students of that day and since tended to have Columbia ties as well. They advised me, only too correctly, that I would not learn any modern statistics at Harvard if I passed up the chance to attend Hotelling's Columbia lectures.

The decision was made, as so many important ones, by nonrational processes and miscalculation. I picked Harvard. Why? It was not because of the great Schumpeter. Actually I was warned that he was kind of a brilliant nut who believed that the rate of interest was zero in a stationary state, an impossibility that had been demonstrated at length by our local sage. I had never heard of Leontief or the mathematical physicist Edwin Bidwell Wilson (not to be confused with my Society of Fellows contemporary, E. Bright Wilson, Jr., the physical chemist also at Harvard), two great reasons for studying economics at Harvard. My teacher in money, Lloyd Mints, told me that John Williams was a good man but to watch out for the inflationist Seymour Harris. (Since Harris was still an orthodox protégé of Harold Hitchings Burbank, this judgment says much for Mints's prophetic powers to smell out evil.) I must confess that glances into Edward Chamberlin's recent and great book on *Monopolistic Competition* carried some small weight in the balance in favor of Harvard.

But in the end my decision was made on quite nonscholarly grounds. Gideonse did not know his man. I went to Harvard in search of green ivy. Never having been east (I don't count Florida as east) before the age of twenty, I picked Cambridge over New York in the expectation that the Harvard Yard would look like Dartmouth's Hanover common. Expecting white churches and spacious groves, I almost returned home after my first view of Harvard Square, approached by bad chance from the direction of Central Square. No wonder I annoyed Chairman Burbank at first encounter: I told him that I (1) would not take E. F. Gay's famous (and sterile and dull) course in economic history, but instead would take Chamberlin's course given to second-year graduate students, (2) intended to "skim the cream" of Harvard since it was by no means certain that I would choose to stay more than a year, and (3) had not made advanced application to do graduate study at Harvard for the simple reason that in those days any paying customer, to say nothing of an anointed Social Science Research Council Predoctoral-Training Fellow, could get in anywhere. It was not love at first sight. But it really would not have mattered since Burbank stood for everything in scholarly life for which I had utter contempt and abhorrence.[7]

THE GOLDEN DAYS OF THE HARVARD YARD

"In 1935 a brash young student from the University of Chicago appeared at Harvard."[8] Luck was with me. Harvard was precisely the right place to be in the next half dozen years. When I once told Edward Mason that I proposed to write a memoir on the golden days for economics in the Harvard Yard, he suggested I wait "until we are up again." Well, there will never be a better time than now to sing of the Age of Hansen—and of Schumpeter, and of Leontief, and (for me) of E. B. Wilson. And I can sing for all my comrades at arms—Alan and Paul Sweezy, Kenneth Galbraith, Aaron [R. A.] Gordon, Abram Bergson, Shigeto Tsuru, Richard Musgrave, Wolfgang Stolper, and others who were already established when I arrived in the graduate school, September 1935; and for many yet to come—Lloyd Metzler, Robert Triffin, Joe Bain, James Tobin, Robert Bishop, John Lintner, Richard Goodwin, Henry Wallich, Cary [E. C.] Brown, Emile Despres, Walter and William Salant, Sidney Alexander, Benjamin Higgins, to say nothing of postwar diamonds such as James Duesenberry, Robert Solow, Carl Kaysen. . . .

Harvard made us. Yes, but we made Harvard. By the time of World War II the dominance in economics of Harvard had become almost a scandal. The old-school tie counted for much, too much no doubt—but it does save time to have familiar faces around. (When I came to do mathematical work at the Radiation Lab during the war, I found that the old Princeton tie had a similar role in moving you up the mathematics queue.) When the American Economic Association commissioned an official survey volume on the state of modern economics, George Stigler, in a scholarly review, drew up a statistical matrix of index references and mutual citing of the Harvard constellation in order to document the dominance I speak of. I do not suppose he would have gone to the trouble if he had not thought it a distorted reflection of the intrinsic worth of the barbarians outside the walls: Stigler has always insisted on the old-fashioned distinction between value and market price!

And yet, that this involved more than mutual backscratching was brought home

---

[7] It tells much about the Harvard of President Lowell's days that such men received office space and held power. But to admit the rich texture of life, I repeat a conversation between the late Alfred Conrad, Richard M. Goodwin (Hoosier, Rhodes Scholar, former Harvard don, and now a fellow in Peterhouse College at Cambridge) and me, as we were driving back to Boston from Joseph Schumpeter's funeral in Connecticut. Conrad: "Say what you will about Burbie, knowing that I had tuberculosis at Saranac, never a week went by that he did not ask me about my health. No one else in the huge Harvard environment seemed to know whether I was dead or alive. You were in a human relation with Burbank." Goodwin: "Indeed you were. He once said to me, 'Dick, I'd like to do with you what my father once did to me. Tie you to the wheel of a wagon and apply a long black whip to your back.'" One should add that he was genuinely fond of Goodwin. During the war years a dear friend of ours was Burbank's secretary, but we avoided all strain by not talking about the man she worshiped and I despised.

[8] Breit and Ransom, *Academic Scribblers*, p. 111.

to me by a later event. In 1948 when Alvin Hansen turned sixty, some of his fond students banded together to present him with a *Festschrift*.* Since he had at that time spent no more years teaching at Harvard than he had teaching earlier at Minnesota, our committee naturally thought to invite students from his Minnesota days to contribute. From the Harvard vintages, there was almost an embarrassment of riches to choose from. Yet despite an extra effort the final disproportion was striking. Years later I happened to ask Alvin why that should have been so. He said that he had indeed had some very good students at Minnesota but that, by and large, the very best students had tended to bubble off (with his blessing) to the few largest centers. This confirmed the advice that I used to give young students: If you have any reason to think you are good, beg, borrow, or steal the money to come to the top place. If you go to Rome, it is your classmates who will be the next cardinals and who will be picking popes. I presume that these casual observations from experience confirm the views about "the institutionalization of a discipline" that Edward Shils discusses elsewhere.

Readers who are noneconomists will not wish me to elucidate the many features of graduate study at Harvard in those days. Let me summarize it all by saying that my transfer from Chicago to Harvard put me right in the forefront of the three great waves of modern economics: the Keynesian revolution, of which I shall give an account presently, the monopolistic or imperfect-competition revolution, and finally, the fruitful clarification of the analysis of economic reality resulting from the mathematical and econometric handling of the subject—including an elucidation for the first time of the welfare economics issues that had concerned economists from the days of Adam Smith and Karl Marx to the present.

Much of Harvard analysis was crude and unrigorous, as I discovered to my intense surprise. But it had life and it lacked closure. The mistakes one's teachers made and the gaps they left in their reasonings were there for you to rectify. You were part of the advancing army of science. There was an extra advantage: in that pluralistic environment there was plenty of opposition to every one of the new doctrines. You were not an Uncle Tom if you enlisted in the wave of the future. Schumpeter repudiated Keynes. Williams and Hansen conducted a famous dialogue, the courtesy of which in the face of fundamental disagreement does both men credit. (The greatest capital for undercutting a colleague in asides with students would have accrued to Hansen, and all honor must go to him that never once did he indulge in such personal criticisms. I was one of his favorites and intimates and the farthest I could push him to go was to say, when I praised a colleague long dead, that the man had in effect been a closet-Keynesian who, to curry favor with businessmen, had camouflaged his wisdoms and insights.)

All autobiography loses interest when success arrives. So let me simply say that the years 1935–1940 were good to me. As a junior fellow I was completely happy, turning out paper after paper. I once had a student who told me that he could have

---

*Published as *Income, Employment, and Public Policy* (New York: Norton, 1948).

spent his whole life hitting fungoes to his brother on the farm back in Illinois but he had a suspicion it couldn't last. I could have remained a junior fellow all my life. Indeed it was fortunate that no one offered me a permanent fellowship at Harvard— lecturer was the name given for those with second-class membership in the club— because I would certainly have happily accepted it.

In 1940 I was offered the princely post of instructor in the Department of Economics and tutor in the Division of History, Government and Economics. I gladly took it and continued in my same Leverett House office. When a month later a better offer came from MIT and when I learned that my departure would not cause irreparable grief, I took the offer.[9] My last qualm in doing so was overcome as a result of a long, handwritten letter from my revered teacher of mathematical economics and statistics, E. B. Wilson, about his Hegira from Yale to MIT early in the century. Wilson was the last of the universal mathematicians. He was Willard Gibbs's favorite student, and one of the first to do work in a variety of fields: vector calculus, functionals, mathematical physics, aeronautical engineering, vital statistics, psychometrics, and, most important for me, mathematical economics. He was the only intelligent man I have ever known who loved committee meetings. He also loved to talk and we had hours of conversation following his lectures. What a teacher's pet I have always been! I was also a favorite protégé of his. In the letter he told how his agonizing decision to leave Yale for MIT, which friends had warned him against as a barbarian outpost, had been the beginning of a fruitful and happy epoch. Until you leave home, he said in effect, you are a boy and not the master of your own house. (In Virginia Woolf's diary there is a striking entry, which I quote from imperfect memory: "Father [Leslie Stephen, the biographer, historian, and mountain climber] would have been ninety today. Thank God he died. I could never have realized myself otherwise.")

Since gossip always likes a good story, and since McGeorge Bundy and the cited Breit-Ransom book have commented in print on the fact of my leaving Harvard, a few words on the event may not be out of order. I left Harvard in 1940 for the same reason that James Tobin left it in 1950: I got a better offer. Just as Lord Melbourne said he liked getting the Order of the Garter because there was "no damned merit to it," my parting was eased by the fact that no one, least of all me, thought that it was lack of merit that kept me from a chair in economic theory. Those were the depression days, the days of the Walsh-Sweezy hearings, in which President Conant was rationalizing Harvard's budget and tenure procedures after the benevolent despotism of President Lowell. Even my beloved mentor, Wassily Leontief, did not yet quite have tenure in my time. It was not for another decade that, under the so-called Graustein formula for spacing departmental appointments, a theorist was

---

[9] A couple of months later, Ed Chamberlin, serving as an interregnum Harvard chairman, phoned to ask whether MIT was paying me a full-year's salary despite my late-October recruitment. When I said yes, he asked me whether I would not in that case return my September Harvard check, saying "you wouldn't want to deprive a young scholar of a full-year's income." I meekly returned the check, although it occurred to my wife that perhaps there might have been found a different solution for the poor man's problem.

appointed at Harvard. It is frustrated expectations that make for disappointment and bitterness: from the first day I appeared in Boylston Hall in 1935, I never received any letter, oral promise, or clairvoyant message even hinting that a permanent appointment awaited me. When last year a Harvard Crimson reporter asked why I had not responded to a couple of calls from Harvard in the later days of Bundy and Pusey, I heard myself stating the simple, prosaic truth: "After a cost-benefit analysis, I decided to stay put."

In any case, on a fine October day in 1940 an *enfant terrible emeritus*[10] packed up his pencil and moved three miles down the Charles river, where he lived happily ever after.[11]

WHAT ECONOMICS IS ABOUT

It is easy for the artist to write about himself as a young man, but hard for him to write about his art. Has there ever been even one good novel about a scholar or artist that conveyed any notion of his work? It was Hans Zinsser who said that when any genuine biologist reads Arrowsmith's prayer in the Sinclair Lewis novel, he wants to throw up. (Yet I have seen elsewhere the biography of at least one distinguished scientist who was led into the field by reading that same book.) When my wife was a girl, she thought of her father, a small-town banker, as doing nothing down at work except sitting with his feet upon the desk. That I suspect is every child's view of what his parent does during that hiatus between morning and dusk. If James Joyce were to write the account of a single day in the life of a scientist, that would be unutterably dull except to another scientist.

G. H. Hardy claimed that the one romance of his life as a Cambridge mathematician was his collaboration with Ramanujan, the self-taught Indian genius. The great romance in life of any economist of my generation must necessarily

---

[10] A phrase of Provost Peter Kenen of Columbia, not mine.

[11] A distinguished foreign economist who read this memoir commented to me: "You know, the popular explanation for your leaving Harvard is that you were a victim of antisemitism." I replied, "I suppose that would be the *simplest* explanation." "As a scientist," he added, "aren't you required to accept the simplest explanation?" I do use Occam's Razor to slice away the reasons when they are otiose; but if a simple hypothesis cannot explain all the facts, I don't think it mandatory to embrace it. Lest I be misunderstood, let me state that before World War II American university life was antisemitic in a way that would hardly seem possible to the present generation. And Harvard, along with Yale and Princeton, was a flagrant case of this. So if anyone wants to understand why Jews, in relation to their scholarly abilities, were underrepresented on the Harvard faculty in those days, he can legitimately invoke the factor of antisemitism. (In many of the humanities faculties, bigots genuinely believed that Jews were no good; in science and mathematics, the belief was that they were too good; one could, so to speak, have one's cake and eat it too by believing—as did the eminent mathematician George D. Birkhoff and, to a degree, the eminent economist Joseph Schumpeter—that Jews were "early bloomers" who would unfairly receive more rewards than they deserved in free competition. Again, lest I be misunderstood, let me hasten to add the usual qualification that these two men were among my best friends and, I believe, both had a genuine high regard for my abilities and promise.) To illustrate, though, the failure of any one factor to account for the richness of reality, the following questions can be asked of those who know economists of that period well. (1) Why was Lloyd Metzler not given a tenure post at Harvard, since he suffered only from the disability of being from Kansas? (2) If you contemplate the academic careers in America of three men—Oskar Lange, Jacob Marschak, and Abba Lerner, not all Jewish—how can you cover the facts with the simple theory of antisemitism?

have been the Keynesian revolution. Perhaps the best impression I can convey of its impact is given by the following quoted passage, taken from a eulogy I was invited to write on the occasion of Keynes's death in 1946, less than a decade after the period I have been writing about:

> I have always considered it a priceless advantage to have been born as an economist prior to 1936 and to have received a thorough grounding in classical economics. It is quite impossible for modern students to realize the full effect of what has been advisably called "The Keynesian Revolution" upon those of us brought up in the orthodox tradition. What beginners today often regard as trite and obvious was to us puzzling, novel, and heretical.
>
> To have been born as an economist before 1936 was a boon—yes. But not to have been born too long before!

> "Bliss was it in that dawn to be alive,
> But to be young was very heaven!"

> The *General Theory* caught most economists under the age of 35 with the unexpected virulence of a disease first attacking and decimating an isolated tribe of South Sea islanders. Economists beyond 50 turned out to be quite immune to the ailment. With time, most economists in-between began to run the fever, often without knowing or admitting their condition.
>
> I must confess that my own first reaction to the *General Theory* was not at all like that of Keats on first looking into Chapman's Homer. No silent watcher, I, upon a peak in Darien. My rebellion against its pretensions would have been complete except for an uneasy realization that I did not at all understand what it was about. And I think I am giving away no secrets when I solemnly aver—upon the basis of vivid personal recollection—that no one else in Cambridge, Massachusetts, really knew what it was about for some 12 to 18 months after its publication. Indeed, until the appearance of the mathematical models of [it] there is reason to believe that Keynes himself did not truly understand his own analysis.
>
> Fashion always plays an important role in economic science; new concepts become the *mode* and then are *passé*. A cynic might even be tempted to speculate as to whether academic discussion is itself equilibrating: whether assertion, reply, and rejoinder do not represent an oscillating divergent series, in which—to quote Frank Knight's characterization of sociology—"bad talk drives out good."
>
> In this case, gradually and against heavy resistance, the realization grew that the new analysis of *effective demand* associated with the *General Theory* was not to prove such a passing fad, that here indeed was part of "The wave of the future." This impression was confirmed by the rapidity with which English economists, other than those at Cambridge, took up the new Gospel . . . and still more surprisingly, the young blades at the *London School* . . . who threw off their Hayekian garments and joined in the swim.
>
> In this country it was pretty much the same story. Obviously, exactly the same words cannot be used to describe the analysis of income determination of, say, Lange, Hart, Harris, Ellis, Hansen, Bissell, Haberler, Slichter, J. M. Clark, or myself. And yet the Keynesian taint is unmistakably there upon every one of us. . .
>
> Instead of burning out like a fad, today ten years after its birth the *General Theory* is still gaining adherents and appears to be in business to stay. Many economists who are most vehement in criticism of the specific Keynesian policies—which must always be carefully distinguished from the scientific analysis associated with his name—will never again be the same after passing through his hands.

It has been wisely said that only in terms of a modern theory of effective demand can one understand and defend the so-called "classical" theory of unemployment. . . .

Thus far, I have been discussing the new doctrines without regard to their content or merits, as if they were a religion and nothing else. . . .

The modern saving-investment theory of income determination did not directly displace the old latent belief in Say's Law of Markets (according to which only "frictions" could give rise to unemployment and overproduction). Events of the years following 1929 destroyed the previous economic synthesis. The economists' belief in the orthodox synthesis was not overthrown, but had simply atrophied. . . .

Of course, the Great Depression of the Thirties was not the first to reveal the untenability of the classical synthesis. The classical philosophy always had its ups and downs along with the great swings of business activity. Each time it had come back. But now for the first time, it was confronted by a competing system—a well-reasoned body of thought containing among other things as many equations as unknowns. In short, like itself, a synthesis; and one which could swallow the classical system as a special case.

A new *system*, that is what requires emphasis. Classical economics could withstand isolated criticism. Theorists can always resist facts; for facts are hard to establish and are always changing anyway, and *ceteris paribus* can be made to absorb a good deal of punishment. Inevitably, at the earliest opportunity, the mind slips back into the old grooves of thought since analysis is utterly impossible without a frame of reference, a way of thinking about things, or in short a theory.[12]

The final lines of this quoted passage contain certain notions that have brought fame to Thomas Kuhn, who argues in *The Structure of Scientific Revolutions* (University of Chicago Press, 1962) the importance of scientific paradigms in conditioning the thought of each school of science. This is a seminal idea, but, as expressed in the first edition of that work, one which fails to do justice to the degree to which "better" theories, and I mean intrinsically better theories, come to dominate and replace earlier theories. Now if Dr. Kuhn had been talking about the softer science of economics, I could provide him with much grist for his mill. And yet I must confess to the belief that truth is not merely in the eye of the beholder, and that certain regularities of economic life are as valid for a Marxist as for a classicist, for a post-Keynesian as for a monetarist.

In short, economics is neither astrology nor theology.

---

[12] Quoted, with grateful acknowledgment to the original journal, from "Lord Keynes and the General Theory," *Econometrica* 14 (1946), 187–199, and reprinted in P. A. Samuelson, *Collected Scientific Papers*, II (Cambridge, Mass.: MIT Press, 1966), pp. 1517–1533.

CONTRIBUTIONS TO WELFARE ECONOMICS

Kenneth J. Arrow

THE BERGSONIAN SOCIAL WELFARE FUNCTION: HISTORICAL BACKGROUND

The work of Paul Samuelson on the meaning and foundation of welfare judgments in economics is, as he repeatedly states, indissolubly linked with another's—the formulation of the social welfare function due to Abram Bergson. The analysis of concepts that lie so close to the roots of the social essence of humanity can never be definitive, but certainly the formulation of Bergson and Samuelson profoundly affected the direction of all future thinking, at least by economists. It stated with admirable economy the essence of the problem to be faced. More specifically, it brought us to a confrontation and in certain aspects a reconciliation of two themes in economic thinking about individual economic behavior and the choice of policies: the utilitarian tradition of normative analysis and the much more recent parsimonious description of economic behavior usually referred to as *ordinalism*.

What I will try to exhibit is the extent to which Bergson and Samuelson have developed a formalism or language for expressing social welfare judgments that is in fact neutral with respect to many of the alternative possible interpretations. It might be said to be the broadest language that is compatible with the basic intentions of both utilitarianism and ordinalism. By the same token, it does not take a stand with respect to controversial issues, particularly those which lie at the intersection of ethics and epistemology, that is, the reality of interpersonal comparability of utility in any form.

To some extent, the value of an exposition of Samuelson's ideas on welfare economics has been reduced by the appearance of Samuelson's own account (1981), a thoughtful and vigorous restatement of the Bergson-Samuelson position, with vigorous differentiation of it from other points of view that developed from it subsequently. But it may still be useful to re-present these views with the additional perspective of another's position.

The starting point may be taken as the status of welfare economics in 1938, the date of Bergson's paper (reprinted in 1966, pp. 3–26). What kind of arguments were thought to be logically usable to defend policy measures? After all, economics originated as a defense of certain policies, and the tradition of giving advice has remained strong in the discipline. Even the most austere seeker after truth and logic has found it difficult not to speak out on occasion to make some recommendation or another, and any recommendation must involve a normative statement. "Ought" can never be implied by a series of "is" propositions without at least one "ought" in them. Paul Samuelson has certainly not hesitated to advocate and advise; even the unworldly author of these lines has felt the obligation to speak out. So we must all be talking the prose of normative discourse, though, unlike Moliere's M. Jourdain, we are aware of it.

As far as I can see, there were ultimately only two kinds of argument in the literature that were intellectually coherent: the utilitarian criterion and the concept of Pareto optimality. Utilitarianism in its rigorous formulation states that each individual has a numerically defined utility function defined (in the most general case) over the entire social state and that the aim of economic (or any other) policy is to maximize the sum of these utilities over all individuals. The utilitarian formulation is expressed clearly enough in the scattered works of Jeremy Bentham and, through his influence, in those of John Stuart Mill and many later thinkers, especially economists to whom such ideas were most congenial. Its biggest practical implication has been the consideration that policies should be judged by their consequences, rather than in terms of intrinsic merits. It is precisely this feature that has aroused the scorn of those, like John Ruskin, who thought of themselves as having a feeling for the higher things in life. This aspect has less importance for economists, for most of whom economic policies have little intrinsic value in any case; economic policies are usually judged solely by their consequences. However, as far as I can tell from fairly desultory reading, this is the only application that John Stuart Mill makes of the utilitarian perspective, for all his known advocacy; his applications are typically not to economic problems.

A second application of utilitarianism is to the distribution of income. When coupled with a hypothesis of diminishing marginal utility of income (concavity of the utility function, as we would say today), utilitarianism implies a redistribution of income from the rich to the poor. These implications were drawn more specifically by Henry Sidgwick (1901, originally published in 1874) and especially by Francis Y. Edgeworth (1881, 1897). Edgeworth's contribution is the more remarkable because, unlike Sidgwick, he clearly disliked the egalitarian conclusion and vigorously sought palliatives, but he could not deny the utilitarian logic.

As we all know, utility as the explanation of individual behavior took strong hold with the marginalist revolution of the 1870s. Utility now appeared in a dual role, individually as the explanation of demand functions and collectively, summed over individuals, as the criterion for judging policies and indeed economic systems. This duality clarified the intuitive perception that perfect competition was in some sense a mechanism for insuring social optimality.[1] But this very success proved to be the undoing of utilitarianism. For it became clear to Vilfredo Pareto (1927, originally published in Italian in 1906) that the cardinal concept of a utility function was unnecessary as an explanation of demand behavior; the demand functions were invariant under a monotone transformation of the utility function. Hence, only the indifference surfaces mattered. The indifference surfaces can be thought of (at least ideally) as observable entities. To them can be associated a utility function (Pareto tried to introduce the new term, *ophelimity*, presumably to eliminate the cardinal overtones, but the neologism did not last) that will rationalize the indifference surfaces (that is, the indifference surfaces will coincide with the level surfaces of the utility function).[2] But any strictly monotone transformation of a given utility is also a utility function, in the sense of an index that rationalizes the indifference map.

Pareto then gives his famous definition of optimality, compatible with the ordinal nature of utility functions: A state of the economic system is optimal (yields a "maximum of ophelimity" in his terms) if there is no other feasible state of the system that will make some individuals better off without making anyone worse off. This definition explicitly ignores the distribution of income; it is compatible with running the entire economic system to maximize the well-being of one individual. There is an infinity of positions of the system that are all optimal in the sense of Pareto; whether Pareto himself understood this is not clear from the text.

Pareto's ordinalism was slow in affecting thinking. A few continental writers were concerned, especially in reference to the economics of socialism (Barone, 1935, originally published in 1908). English and American economists were unresponsive until the sudden impact in the 1930s, at the London School of Economics, where Abba Lerner, Lionel Robbins, and John Hicks all reacted, and in the United States, where Harold Hotelling and Henry Schultz assimilated not only the ordinalist view but also Eugene Slutzky's (1915) development of consumer demand theory based on it. Samuelson's work on consumer demand theory pushed the ordinalist viewpoint and its hard-boiled behavioristic essence one step farther. A reconstruction of

---

[1] For a lively and perceptive history of successive refinements of this intuition, see Samuelson's account in *Foundations of Economic Analysis* (1947, pp. 203–219).

[2] It is remarkable how long it took to recognize that the proposition that for a given family of indifference surfaces there necessarily exists a utility function that rationalizes it is not self-evident and requires proof. In fact, the proposition is not true without some continuity conditions. The first proof, as far as I know, is due to H. Wold (1943–44, sections 31, 37). Wold assumes that preference is monotone in each commodity separately. It is then easy to show, by continuity, that every commodity vector is indifferent to a vector all of whose components are equal. The common value of the second vector can be taken to be the utility of the first. Probably the most interesting construction is that of W. Neufeind (1972). Assume the commodity space to be the non-negative orthant. Choose arbitrarily any everywhere-positive function on the commodity space whose integral over the space is finite, for example, a probability density. Then define the utility of any commodity vector to be the integral of that function over the set of points to which the given commodity vector is preferred or indifferent. Another interesting construction is that of Chichilnisky (1980). The last two constructions have the property that they are not only continuous functions of the commodity vector but also continuous functions of the indifference map, when continuity is properly defined.

welfare economics began, trying to base old propositions on the firmer foundation of Pareto optimality, Lerner's (1933) treatment of monopoly and Hotelling's (1938) analysis of decreasing-cost industries being among the best known.

But what was the "old" welfare economics that they were trying to reconstruct? To what extent did it depend upon the utilitarian criterion? Surely, here, if anywhere in economics, we have a classic codification, the very complete statement from the center, A. C. Pigou's *The Economics of Welfare* (1952, but dating primarily from 1920). Surprisingly enough, there is only one mention of summing utilities and that is very incidental. Although the whole work is devoted to optimizing, there is no explicit formulation of a maximand. For the most part, the criterion is increase in the national income ("national dividend" in Pigou's language). But he is at pains to point out national income is itself an imperfect approximation, though I am not clear what it was supposed to approximate.

Nevertheless, summing utilities lies in the background. For Pigou recognizes at several points that changes in the distribution of income might affect welfare: thus a transfer of income from poor to rich would be an adverse change. This proposition is supported by an appeal to "the old 'law' of diminishing utility" (p. 89). Presumably this implies a sum-of-utilities criterion, not stated explicitly.[3] A more open avowal is found, almost in passing, a bit later (pp. 96–97, text and footnote 3) in a cautionary context. Using the variance as a measure of inequality, he states, "it can be proved that, assuming similarity of temperament among the members of the community, a diminution in the inequality of distribution *probably*, though not necessarily, increases the aggregate *sum of satisfaction*" (first emphasis in original, second added). The footnote gives a mathematical argument, which explicitly uses a sum of utilities of income, with each individual having the same utility function, assumed concave.[4] This appears to be the only place in 851 pages in which the utilitarian criterion occurs explicitly.

Thus the situation in 1938 in the foundations of welfare economics was the following: for the most part, economic policy was not defended by an appeal to fundamental principles; to the extent that it was, only two principles existed, the utilitarian and the Pareto. The latter is useless when it comes to decisions affecting income distribution; the former may have provided some predisposition to equalize income but was not used to supply any well-defined conclusions.

As far as applied welfare analysis, even among professional economists, goes, it is not clear that much more can be said even now, though the ability to apply the

---

[3]The opacity of the analysis is increased by the caution of the conclusion drawn: "Any cause which increases the absolute share of real income in the hands of the poor, *provided that it does not lead to a contraction in the size of the national dividend* . . . will . . . increase economic welfare" (emphasis added). The obvious logical conclusion that there is a trade-off between distribution and total size is probably implied but for some reason avoided.

[4]The argument depends upon a Taylor series, in which the first-order terms vanish and the second-order terms are of the right sign, but higher-order terms have unknown signs. The proposition for which Pigou was groping was that a mean-preserving spread of income distribution reduces the sum of utilities; see Rothschild and Stiglitz (1970).

Pareto principle to particular situations has grown greatly and so has its acceptance in political discourse.

THE SOCIAL WELFARE FUNCTION: ITS FORMAL STRUCTURE
AND EPISTEMOLOGICAL ROLE

Bergson's (1938, reprinted in 1966, pp. 3-26) paper was written while he and Paul Samuelson were graduate students. They discussed the paper extensively according to their statements. Bergson (1938, p. 310, fn.) states, "I am grateful to Mr. Paul Samuelson for suggestions on many points." Samuelson (1981, p. 223) speaks with considerable eloquence on his reactions to the paper in light of the then current state of welfare economics, as I have outlined it:

> To one like myself, who before 1938 knew *all* (emphasis in original) the relevant literature on welfare economics and just could not make coherent sense of it, Bergson's work came like a flash of lightning, describable only in the words of the pontifical poet:
>
> Nature and Nature's laws lay hid in night:
> God said, Let Newton be! and there was light.
>
> King Alphonse claimed that if he had been in on the Creation, he could have done a better job. By sheer good luck, as a fellow graduate student and comrade at arms, I *was* in on Bergson's creation: but time has shown that I have not been able to do a better job of it; nor, I believe, has anyone—and this despite the quite confused rumors that Kenneth Arrow's Impossibility Theorem rendered Bergson's "social welfare function" somehow nonexistent or self-contradictory. . . . Mine was the best spectator's seat for Bergson's creative travail. I was the coarse stone against which he honed his sharp axe—the semiabsorbing, semireflecting surface against which he bounced off his ideas.[5]

Samuelson's own exposition of the social welfare function is masterly; it is the content of Chapter VIII of the *Foundations of Economic Analysis* (1947), the only example I know of a doctoral dissertation that is a treatise, or perhaps I should say of a treatise that has so much originality in every part that it is entitled to be accepted as a dissertation. I still assign that chapter in my graduate theory classes; in thirty-five years, there has been no substitute.

Let me try to paraphrase Samuelson's vision and analysis. I will take the most general perspective about the objects of choice, to be termed "social states." A social state may be taken to be a very large vector, describing the private goods received by all individuals, as well as public goods. Each individual is thought of as having an ordering over the set of social states: let R_i be the ordering of the ith individual. Thus "xR_iy" means that individual i regards social state x as at least as good as social state y (either prefers x to y or is indifferent between them). This ordering over social

---

[5] The passage contains some typical features of the Samuelson style: the rhythmic and exciting prose, the allusions to favorite literature (though William Hazlitt appears more often than Alexander Pope or Alfonso el Sabio) incomprehensible to generations of students with successively lower levels of knowledge of the past, the reference to physics, and the sense of personal involvement.

states is the natural extension of the ordering of commodity bundles assumed in the usual theory of demand by the individual. There and here orderings are related to actual choices because orderings are hypothetical choices. That is, "xR_iy" can be interpreted to mean that *if* x and y were the only social states available and *if* individual i were to make the choice, he/she would either choose x or be willing to choose either.

This understanding can be extended to choice when there are not two but many alternative social states: If individual i were to make the choice, x would be among those chosen (there may be more than one) if and only if x is available and xR_iy for all available alternatives y. (In economic analysis, we usually think of the range of alternatives available as all those that could possibly be produced from given amounts of primary factors with the technology in existence; hence, the vague term "available" can be replaced by the term "feasible.")[6]

Bergson and Samuelson now argue that any system of social judgments should have the form of an ordering. It should specify the set of chosen alternatives from any feasible set (more precisely, any feasible set with reasonable topological properties, such as closure or compactness), and the choices should have the consistency properties we associate with an ordering (completeness, that is, some alternative will be chosen out of every pair, and transitivity, that is, if x is at least as good as y and y at least as good as z, then x is at least as good as z). Preferences for one policy over another are expressed in these systems of judgment.

They wanted to preserve the common tradition of the utilitarians and of Pareto in making any social judgment reflect in some measure individual judgments and preferences. In particular, the Pareto principle must surely be maintained: If *every* individual prefers social state x to social state y, then y is not to be chosen if both are feasible.

Let then R be the relation, "socially judged at least as good as"; that is, xRy means that society would (or should) choose x if those two are the only ones available. Just as for the individual, if there are many feasible alternatives, then x is chosen if and only if x is feasible and xRy for all feasible y.

To state the Pareto principle, which expresses the responsiveness of the social ordering to individual preferences, define the following relation among pairs of social states: xR^Uy, read "x is unanimously judged at least as good as y," is defined to hold whenever xR_iy for all individuals i. The *Pareto relation* R^U is not an ordering, for it is not a complete relation. It is of course perfectly possible that, for a given pair of alternatives x and y, some individuals strictly prefer one and others strictly prefer the other, and so neither xR^Uy nor yR^Ux. But the relation R^U is transitive; if everyone regards x as at least as good as y and y at least as good as z, then if each individual's preferences are transitive, as we are assuming, every individual regards x as at least as good as z.

---

[6]Samuelson himself in his study of consumer choice went further, replacing the primitive notion of an ordering by that of choice itself, assumed to obey certain rationality conditions (the revealed preference approach). A vast literature has followed these remarks; the parts most closely associated with social choice theory are surveyed in Sen (1970, Chapters 1 and 1*); for allied developments in consumer demand theory, see Chipman, Hurwicz, Richter, and Sonnenschein (1971).

The relation R^U then is an incomplete transitive relation. We can always find a complete ordering R that agrees with R^U, in the sense that for any pair x, y for which $x R^U y$, it is true that $x R y$. But for some pairs for which R^U is uninformative, that is, for which neither $x R^U y$ nor $y R^U x$, R is informative, with either $x R y$ or $y R x$ (or both). For example, if x, y, and z are three alternatives, it may be that $x R^U y$, but nothing is specified about any pair containing z. This will happen if there are two individuals, individual 1 ranking the alternatives z, x, y, and individual 2 having the ranking x, y, z. Then any of the following complete orderings, R, agrees with R^U: x, y, z; x, z, y; z, x, y.

To state the matter a little more formally, let R and S be any two relations. Then we will say that S is an *extension* of R if, whenever $x R y$, it is also true that $x S y$, but there may be pairs x, y for which $x S y$ but not $x R y$. Then the following theorem is true: For any transitive relation R, there is a complete ordering S, which is an extension of R (Szpilrajn, 1930). Then the Bergson-Samuelson social welfare function approach is embodied in the following condition.

(*Bergson-Samuelson*): *The social ordering R that judges the desirability of alternative social states is an extension of the Pareto relation, R^U.*

Is there any problem of existence? As is clear from the discussion, the answer is no. If there are "rumors that Kenneth Arrow's Impossibility Theorem rendered Bergson's 'social welfare function' somehow nonexistent or self-contradictory," they are indeed "quite confused."

One consequence of the Bergson-Samuelson construction is that if everyone is indifferent between two alternatives, then so is society. For if $x R_i y$ and $y R_i x$ for all i, then $x R^U y$ and $y R^U x$, and therefore, both $x R y$ and $y R x$. Hence, in comparing two social states, only the indifference classes in which the states are located in each individual's preference map are relevant.

I have stated the Bergson-Samuelson position without any use of utility functions, either individual or social. This approach has the merit of emphasizing the extent to which this approach is compatible with ordinalism, indeed, might be said to be dictated by an ordinalist viewpoint. I will, however, argue shortly that in fact the Bergson-Samuelson position is more neutral with respect to cardinality and, indeed, interpersonal comparability than the account so far suggests.

Before going on to alternative interpretations and realizations, let me restate Bergson-Samuelson social ordering in a language that uses the concept of a utility function, if only as an index function for a preference ordering. Represent the preference ordering of the ith individual by a utility function, $U_i(x)$, defined over social states. Let $U(x)$ be a utility function that represents the social ordering R. Now consider two states, x and y, for which each individual is indifferent. As just seen, the social ordering must indicate indifference. Indifference between x and y for individual i means that $U_i(x) = U_i(y)$. Social indifference means that $U(x) = U(y)$. Hence, we can say that

$$\text{if } U_i(x) = U_i(y) \text{ for all } i, \text{ then } U(x) = U(y)$$

This means that if we know the values of $U_i(x)$ for all i, we know the value of

$U(x)$. It is not necessary to know x itself. We may say that there is a function whose arguments are the utility levels of the individual members of society and whose values are the social utilities determined by those individual utilities. In symbols, there is a function, $W(u_1, \ldots, u_n)$, such that, for all x,

$$U(x) = W[U_1(x), \ldots, U_n(x)]$$

and this is the form used by Bergson and by Samuelson, which they term the *social welfare function*.

The further condition of the Pareto principle, that x is socially preferred to y if everyone prefers x to y (or, if everyone regards x as at least as good as y and at least one person strictly prefers x), can be stated in social-welfare-function language by the requirement that W be a strictly increasing function of each of its arguments.

Despite the use of utility functions rather than orderings, the social welfare function can be given a purely ordinal interpretation. Any given individual utility function can be replaced by another, which represents the same indifference map; then the second utility function must be a monotone increasing function of the first. Let $U_i (i = 1, \ldots, n)$ be a set of utility functions, and $U_i' (i = 1, \ldots, n)$ a second set, where for each i, U_i and U_i' both represent the indifference map (preference ordering) of individual i. Then there exist strictly increasing functions, $F_i(u)$, of one variable such that

$$U_i'(x) = F_i[U_i(x)] \text{ for all } x$$

Since F_i is strictly increasing it has an inverse function, $F_i^{-1}(u')$, which is the solution of the equation in u,

$$u' = F_i(u)$$

Now define a function, W', of the variables, $u_i', \ldots, u_n'$,

$$W'(u_i', \ldots, u_n') = W[F_1^{-1}(u_i'), \ldots, F_n^{-1}(u_n')]$$

Since by definition,

$$U_i(x) = F_i^{-1}[U_i'(x)] \text{ for all } x$$

we have clearly,

$$W'[U_1'(x), \ldots, U_n'(x)] = W[F_1^{-1}(U_1'(x)), \ldots, F_n^{-1}(U_n'(x))]$$
$$= W[U_1(x), \ldots, U_n(x)] = U(x)$$

Hence, a change from one index of utility to another for each individual, accompanied by a corresponding change in the social welfare function that "undoes" the transformations of individual utility functions leaves the social ordering unchanged. It is in this sense that the social-welfare-function language is compatible with ordinalism.

Samuelson offers an explicit construction to make this compatibility clear (1981). Take any one of the methods referred to in footnote 2 for assigning a utility function to an indifference map (Samuelson himself uses the construction due to Wold). Then simply take the sum of the utility functions. This is proof, if such be needed, that the Bergson-Samuelson social welfare function can be constructed with the simple property of compatibility with the Pareto criterion and with the further property of using only ordinal properties. It is in effect an exemplification of Szpilrajn's theorem in a context in which continuity assumptions are made on the inputs (the individual preference orderings) and continuity requirements are imposed on the output (the social welfare function).

Hence, we can say that the strictly circumscribed aim of Bergson and Samuelson can be achieved. It is logically consistent to have a social ordering which is utilitarian in the broad sense that social preference between two alternatives depends on the utility levels (or, equivalently, indifference classes) of the alternatives for all individuals, reflects individual preferences positively, and is at least compatible with a strictly ordinal view that no meaning attaches to any indication of individual values other than the indifference map.

Before raising questions of interpretation, there are a few supplementary remarks.

1   From a technical viewpoint, the multilevel form of the social welfare function permits some choice in the formulation of a social optimization problem. We can start with a feasible set in the space of social states and then maximize according to the social ordering over social states, which is indexed by

$$U(x) = W[U_1(x), \ldots, U_n(x)]$$

Alternatively (Samuelson, 1947, pp. 244–245), we can associate with each social state the vector whose components are the utilities of each individual under that state, $U_1(x), \ldots, U_n(x)$. As x varies over feasible social states, the vector of individual utilities varies over a set in the space of n dimensions. The set so traced out might be called the *utility possibility set* (a variation of Samuelson's terminology). Given this set, whose definition does not use any social judgments, an optimal point can be found by maximizing $W(u_1, \ldots, u_n)$ over it. Thus the social judgments come in only at the last stage. This division is frequently clarifying.

2   Samuelson (1981, footnote 1, p. 262) has referred to the "quantum jump of progress in modern welfare economics," the argument of John Harsanyi (1955) that if both the individual preference orderings and the social ordering are applied to uncertainties, that is, probability distributions over social states, and if they both obey the von Neumann-Morgenstern axioms, then it can easily be shown that the social welfare function can be written as a positive linear combination of the individual von Neumann-Morgenstern utility functions. Thus, let $U_i(x)$ be a von Neumann-Morgenstern utility function for individual i, so that one probability distribution over social states is preferred to i to another if and only if $E[U_i(x)]$ is

greater for the first distribution than for the second. Such choices of utility functions are invariant up to positive linear transformations but not up to all monotone transformations. The von Neumann-Morgenstern axioms are stated in impeccably behavioristic terms and so are completely ordinal. Then Harsanyi argues if the social ordering over probability distributions also satisfies the von Neumann-Morgenstern axioms, the social welfare function can always be written in the form

$$W(x) = \sum_i \lambda_i U_i(x)$$

where $\lambda_i > 0$, all i. If we replace U_i by $U'_i = a_i U_i + b_i$, we will get the same choices by dividing λ_i by a_i.

Harsanyi's theorem remarkably points back to classical utilitarianism, though with an entirely new significance.

3   Has the social welfare function played any practical role, whether in actual analysis of concrete social choices or in exposition? It has served as a way of legitimating arguments that could be deduced from a sum-of-utilities assumption in a wider context where interpersonal comparisons of utility are rejected as meaningless and only ordinal comparisons are permissible. For example, I have found very clarifying Samuelson's brief remark on p. 225: "However, it is easy to show that the rule of equality of income (measured in dollars, numeraire, abstract purchasing power) applied to individuals of different tastes, but made to hold in all circumstances, is actually inconsistent with any determinate, definite W function. Equality becomes a fetish or shibboleth, albeit a useful one, in that the means becomes the end, and the letter of the law takes precedence over the spirit." One is accustomed, when dealing with issues of distribution, to assume one commodity and identical utility functions. What Samuelson argues is that as "circumstances" (which I take to mean "endowments of goods in the economy," since utility functions are taken as given) change, the distribution of incomes needed to make sure that the competitive equilibrium yields the optimal social state will change, when individuals have different utility functions for two or more goods.[7] Such an insight would be hard to describe in any other language.

Similarly the social welfare function can be used to describe the conditions under which distributional considerations are or are not important in judging a marginal change; see Bergson (1966, pp. 25–26), Lesourne (1975, pp. 27–31).[8]

---

[7]While this statement is *generally* true, it is not *universally* valid. If each individual has a linear-logarithmic utility function for own consumption,

$$U_i(x_{i1}, x_{i2}) = a_i \log x_{i1} + (1 - a_i) \log x_{i2}$$

where x_{ij} is the consumption of commodity j ($= 1, 2$) by individual i and the coefficients a_i differ from individual to individual, if the totals for each commodity are given, and if $W = \Sigma_i U_i$, then the optimal social state (distribution of the commodities among individuals) can be found by giving equal incomes to all individuals and then allocating goods according to the resulting competitive equilibrium, regardless of the total amounts of all commodities. This proposition ceases to be true if the logarithms are replaced by square roots, for example.

[8]Lesourne has been perhaps the most consistent in using the social welfare function to justify benefit-cost analysis; the cited pages clarify the familiar proposition that benefit-cost analysis presupposes that the distribution of income is optimal.

SOME QUESTIONS OF INTERPRETATION OF THE SOCIAL WELFARE FUNCTION

The social welfare function, especially in Samuelson's hands, is a very austere device, making as few commitments as possible. This inevitably raises the possibility of alternative interpretations, which might extend its usefulness but at the same time increase intellectual risks. I will make only brief comments on a few critical points, especially in view of the subsequent development of social choice theory and impossibility theorems.

a *Relation to cardinal utility*: Samuelson seems not to take the notion of cardinal utility and especially of interpersonally comparable cardinal utility seriously enough to engage in a refutation. Thus, in discussing the social welfare function, he observes:

> It might be thought that our ethical observer, even if the individuals themselves had no unique cardinal indexes of utility, would have to find cardinal indicators. But this would be quite incorrect. Of course if utilities are to be added, one would have to catch hold of them first, but there is no need to add utilities (1947, p. 228).

More recently, he refers in passing to "trucking with the devil of *adding inter*personal utilities" (1981, p. 251; emphasis in original).

Nevertheless, it is worth pointing out that the social welfare function is compatible with a cardinal interpretation. Suppose there are interpersonally meaningful cardinal utilities. Then we would expect to use the sum of utilities. But for each individual the cardinal utility function is an index of the indifference map, and the sum is certainly strictly increasing in each utility. Hence, the sum of utilities is certainly an admissible Bergson-Samuelson social welfare function.

Given the individual orderings, there is a very large number of social orderings compatible with the Pareto relation. We are certainly free to use other information, such as any interpersonal comparisons we may believe in, to choose among this large array.

b *The identity of the social orderer*: The individual orderings are associated with definite individuals who choose or could in principle choose. Whose ordering is the social ordering? Equivalently, whose welfare is being maximized when we maximize the social welfare function? Samuelson clearly regards the question as uninteresting. A social welfare function is a way of expressing any ethical belief:

> Without inquiring into its origins, we take as a starting point for our discussion a function of all the economic magnitudes of a system which is *supposed to characterize some ethical belief*—that of a benevolent despot, or a complete egotist, or 'all men of good will,' a misanthrope, the state, race or group mind, God, etc. (1947, p. 221; emphasis added).

Some of this generality must be modified to take account of the Pareto principle, of course. More recently, he has been still more explicit in his lack of interest in the origins of the social welfare function:

> In my writing on the subject, here and elsewhere, the reader will notice that I have not shown much interest in the process by which particular social welfare functions arise and are deemed to be of interest or relevance." (1981, p. 228).

In some sense, his later paper on social indifference curves, to be discussed in the next section, could be regarded as interpreting the social welfare function as an empirical description of the behavior of a society in its redistributive roles.

c *The social welfare function as functional*: Samuelson is very emphatic that the social welfare function is drawn up for a given society, the members of which have given preferences.

The point of view of social choice theory is very different. It imagines all possible societies in the sense of all possible sets of individuals, each of whom may have any possible individual ordering (or whatever expression of individual values is considered meaningful, up to interpersonally comparable utilities). Social choice theory takes from Bergson and Samuelson the concept that any such society can have a social welfare function. (More modest versions urge only that social welfare functions be defined for a subclass of such societies, with preferences satisfying certain restrictions. But I ignore this development here.)

Social choice theory seeks a rule or correspondence which assigns to each possible society a corresponding social welfare function. Although this is not Samuelson's concept, it does not seem very removed from it. After all, he wants any society to have a social welfare function. Hence, treating the function as itself defined by some characteristics of the society, including its individual preference orderings but possibly also using other information, is not by itself a very large deviation from the Bergson-Samuelson program. In mathematical language, the social welfare function is itself determined by the individual utility functions (as well as possibly other variables) and therefore is, in mathematical language, a *functional*, a function whose independent variables are themselves functions rather than numbers.

What gives the discussion its bite is the assumption that there are or should be some consistency conditions between the social orderings associated with different societies. This is not the place to develop these criteria in detail; they differ among different authors and lead to impossibility theorems and possibility theorems according to different presuppositions, especially about the possible degrees of interpersonal comparability.

What does deserve stressing is the sense in which social choice theory was a child, if unwanted, of the Bergson-Samuelson social welfare function viewpoint.[9]

It may be worth remarking that Samuelson's construction of a social welfare function from individual orderings, by using some rule assigning utility functions to orderings and then adding them up, certainly could be interpreted as a particular

---

[9] For what it may be worth, the beginnings of my work on social choice theory were very explicitly an attempt to operationalize the social welfare function. During the summer of 1948, I was part of the research group at the Rand Corporation in the exciting days when game theory was having an explosive development there. One of the staff members, Olaf Helmer, raised to me a conceptual question: The intended application of Rand's work in game theory was to international conflict, diplomatic and military. The "players" were therefore nations. But what was the meaning of a utility function for a nation? Being well-read and up-to-date, I immediately replied that Bergson and Samuelson had settled that question. He suggested I write a memorandum explaining the relevance of their work to his problem. I had already been thinking about the theory of voting and identified that process with ordinalism, in political choice, which I took to be essential to the social welfare function. My attempt to write a memorandum combining these ideas turned out to be subversive.

functional. Unfortunately, all of the constructions of utility functions now in the literature are not invariant under changes in the units of measurement of the individual commodities. Even if we had but a single commodity, a requirement of invariance under unit changes is very restrictive; the utility function must be a power function, with the same power for all individuals (for a proof, see Blinder, 1982, pp. 323–326). I conjecture the restrictions imposed by invariance under changes of units in the case of two or more commodities are even more severe.

SOCIAL INDIFFERENCE CURVES

I have kept the objects of choice, social states, in the most general form in the preceding exposition. Samuelson, like everyone else, frequently makes the private goods assumption: Each individual receives a vector of commodities, the social state is simply the specification of the commodity vector for each individual, and each individual's ordering of social states is simply his/her ordering of private commodity vectors. Let x^i be the commodity vector for individual i, $x = (x^i, \ldots, x^n)$ is the social state, and $U_i(x)$ depends only on x^i, so that we can write $U_i(x) = U_i(x^i)$.

Samuelson (1956, II, pp. 1073–1094) considers a society that is maximizing its social welfare function,

$$W[U_1(x^1), \ldots, U_n(x^n)]$$

Suppose that it can buy the commodities at fixed prices so that the society as a whole is in effect a consumer. This might be interpreted as reflecting a nation engaged in foreign trade, which clearly was Samuelson's primary motivation, or it might be interpreted to model a society in its aspect as a consumer buying goods from its productive sector. The society also has a given income, possibly derived from the sale of its endowments. Then society chooses the individual commodity vectors x^i to maximize social welfare subject to the budget constraint,

$$p \cdot \sum_i x^i = I$$

where p is the price vector and I, the income of society. The optimization yields each vector x^i as a function, $x^i(p, I)$, depending on prices and income (the optimum might not be unique; see below). We can in turn sum these vectors over individuals to get an overall demand by society for each commodity,

$$x(p, I) = \sum x^i(p, I)$$

Can this be interpreted as the demand function satisfying the Slutzky conditions? Yes, as Samuelson shows. For a given vector of commodities for society as a whole, we can find the optimum allocation among the members and therefore the maximum attainable social welfare with that social total of commodities.

$$V(x) = \underset{\substack{\sum x^i \\ i}}{\text{Max}} \qquad W[U_1(x^1), \ldots, U_n(x^n)]$$

This is a well-defined function of the social commodity vector and therefore defines a *social utility function*. The level curves of this function are the *social indifference curves*. It is obvious that the value of x that maximizes $V(x)$ subject to the budget contraints with prices p and income I is precisely $x(p, I)$.

Further, the social demand function $x(p, I)$ can be realized in a decentralized manner. Given p and I, the chosen individual commodity vectors are necessarily a Pareto optimal distribution of the bundle $x(p, I)$. Hence, if society makes an appropriate distribution of money, individuals will in fact choose $x^i(p, I)$ at the appropriate prices. It must of course be verified that the prices that accomplish the decentralization are the same as those which society faces. I refrain from further details, since I find they have been admirably developed by Chipman (1982).

One last remark. We ordinarily assume that a utility function is quasi-concave, that is, the indifference curves are boundaries of convex sets. As Samuelson made clear in his original paper, it is not so easy to state reasonable conditions for quasi-concavity, even if it is assumed that each individual's utility function is quasi-concave. To be sure, if we assume that each individual utility function is *concave and* if the social welfare function $W(u_1, \ldots, u_n)$ is *concave*, then it is easy to see that $V(x)$ is concave and therefore quasi-concave. But concavity assumptions are not invariant under monotone transformations, so the ordinal spirit is violated. It is true that quasi-concave functions with suitable regularity conditions can be transformed monotonically into concave functions (Kannai, 1977), but there is no obvious reason why the social welfare function appropriate after the transformation should be concave.

However, the assumption of quasi-concavity does not have a very strong foundation even for individuals (see the remarks in Arrow and Hahn, 1971, pp. 172–173). In fact, the derivation of the demand function is not affected by dropping this condition. The social demand function does become multivalued at certain points, but the decentralization property holds for each choice. In a certain sense, demand becomes discontinuous; more technically, it is still an upper semicontinuous correspondence, but it is not a convex set at the price vectors for which it is multivalued. That is, the individual or society in Samuelson's case is indifferent at certain price vectors between two or more bundles but prefers either to a convex combination of them.[10]

CONCLUDING UNSCIENTIFIC POSTSCRIPT

I have tried to convey the sense of vision, precision of accomplishment, and clarity of thought that have characterized one area of Paul Samuelson's work. His accomplishments both close chapters and open new vistas. I have not conveyed some other aspects of his influence: his striking sense of history, so that his works are

---

[10] Like any other utility function, the social utility function may serve as a basis for reasoning about consumer's price index numbers. For an interesting application, see Pollak (1981).

to such a great extent the clear perception of immanent tendencies struggling for release, his fair-mindedness and respect for others even when they disagree, his exemplification of the compleat economist—at home simultaneously in mathematical rigor and probing of foundations and in practical policy formation with a full realization of their underlying unity—, and his warmth as a human being and friend.

REFERENCES

Arrow, K. J., and F. Hahn (1971): *General Competitive Analysis*, San Francisco and Edinburgh, Holden-Day and Oliver & Boyd.

Barone, E. (1935): "The Ministry of Production in the Collectivist State," in F. von Hayek, ed., *Collectivist Economic Planning*, London, Routledge & Kegan Paul, pp. 245–290.

Bergson (Burk), A. (1938): "A Reformulation of Certain Aspects of Welfare Economics," *Quarterly Journal of Economics* 53 (Feb.) pp. 310–334.

—— (1966): *Essays in Normative Economics*, Cambridge, Mass., Harvard.

Blinder, A. (1982): "On Making the Tradeoff between Equality and Efficiency Operational," in G. Feiwel ed., *Samuelson and Neoclassical Economics*, Boston, The Hague, and London, Kluwer-Nijhoff, pp. 317–328.

Chichilnisky, G. (1980): "Continuous Representation of Preferences," *Review of Economic Studies* 47 (Oct.) pp. 959–963.

Chipman, J., L. Hurwicz, M. Richter, and H. Sonnenschein (1971): *Preferences, Utility and Demand*, New York, Harcourt Brace Jovanovich.

Chipman, J. (1982): "Samuelson and Welfare Economics," in G. Feiwel (ed.), *Samuelson and Neoclassical Economics*, Boston, The Hague, and London, Kluwer-Nijhoff, pp. 152–184.

Edgeworth, F. Y. (1881): *Mathematical Psychics: An Essay on the Application of Mathematics to the Moral Sciences*, New York, Kelley 1953.

—— (1897): "The Pure Theory of Taxation," *Economic Journal* 7 (March, June, Dec.), reprinted in F. Y. Edgeworth, *Papers Relating to Political Economy*, London, Royal Economic Society, 1925, Vol. II, pp. 100–122, and, in relevant part, in R. A. Musgrave and A. T. Peacock eds., *Classics in the Theory of Public Finance*, London and New York, Macmillan, 1958, pp. 119–136.

Harsanyi, J. (1955): "Cardinal Welfare, Individualistic Ethics, and Interpersonal Comparisons of Utility," *Journal of Political Economy* 63 (Aug.) pp. 309–321.

Hotelling, H. (1938): "The General Welfare in Relation to Problems of Taxation and of Railway and Utility Rates," *Econometrica* 6 (July) pp. 242–269.

Kannai, Y. (1977): "Concavifiability and Constructions of Concave Utility Functions," *Journal of Mathematical Economics* 4 (March) pp. 1–56.

Lerner, A. P. (1934): "The Concept of Monopoly and the Measurement of Monopoly Power," *Review of Economic Studies* 1 (June) pp. 157–175.

Lesourne, J. (1975): *Cost-Benefit Analysis and Economic Theory*, Amsterdam, North-Holland.

Neuefeind, W. (1972): "On Continuous Utility," *Journal of Economic Theory* 5 (Aug.) pp. 174–176.

Pareto, V. (1927): *Manuel d'économie politique*, 2e édition, Paris, Giard.

Pigou, A. C. (1952): *The Economics of Welfare*, 4th edition, London, Macmillan.

Pollak, R. (1981): "The Social Cost of Living Index," *Journal of Public Economics* 15 (June) pp. 311–336.

Rothschild, M., and J. Stiglitz (1970): "Increasing Risk I: A Definition," *Journal of Economic Theory* 2 (Sept.) pp. 225–243.

Samuelson, P. A. (1947): *Foundations of Economic Analysis*, Cambridge, Mass., Harvard.

—— (1956): "Social Indifference Curves." *Quarterly Journal of Economics* 71 (Feb.) pp. 1–22; *Collected Scientific Papers*, II, Chap. 78.

—— (1981): "Bergsonian Welfare Economics," in S. Rosefielde, ed., *Economic Welfare and* Mass., and London, The M.I.T. Press.

——(1981): "Bergsonian Welfare Economics," in S. Rosefielde ed., *Economic Welfare and the Economics of Soviet Socialism*, Cambridge, U. K., London, and New York, Cambridge University Press, Chap. 9, pp. 223–266.

Sen, A. K. (1970): *Collective Choice and Social Welfare*, San Francisco, Edinburgh, and London, Holden-Day and Oliver & Boyd.

Sidgwick, H. (1901): *The Methods of Ethics*, 6th ed., London, Macmillan.

Slutzky, E. (1915): "Sulla teoria del bilancio del consumatore," *Giornale degli economisti*, 3rd Series, 51, pp. 1–26.

Szpilrajn, E. (1930): "Sur l'extension de l'ordre partiel," *Fundamenta Mathematicae* 16, pp. 386–389.

Wold, H. (1943–44): "A Synthesis of Demand Analysis, I–III," *Skandinavisk Aktuarietidschrift* 26, pp. 85–118, 220–263, and 27, pp. 69–120.

ON
GENERAL EQUILIBRIUM
AND STABILITY

F. H. Hahn

INTRODUCTION

Samuelson has made fundamental contributions to a remarkable variety of fields in economic theory, and general equilibrium analysis and the study of stability are no exception. Certainly in the latter field, Samuelson took the decisive step of the proper formulation of a class of problems that made all subsequent work possible. In general equilibrium analysis he has been more interested in particular applications and in special problems than in the more abstract foundations.[1] But thcsc special cases and these particular applications have been of first-rate importance. One need only think of the nonsubstitution theorem [1951, I, Chap. 36][2] and of his work on factor-price equalisation [1953, II, Chap. 70] to recognize that.

In what follows, some of Samuelson's work in these two areas is recalled and discussed. No claim can be made that this discussion is exhaustive. A Samuelson scholar needs to have a truly vast literature at his fingertips and I can lay no claim to that.

METHODOLOGY

Although Samuelson wrote (he said in jest) that "soft sciences spend time in talking about method because Satan finds tasks for idle hands to do [1963, II, Chap. 129, p. 1772], he seems to have been more conscious than many other economists of carrying out a methodological programme. This methodology is, of course, most

---

[1] But it should be noted that he coauthored an existence proof of competitive equilibrium in 1958.
[2] Citations of Samuelson's Collected Scientific Papers give year of original publication, volume in roman numerals, chapter, and sometimes specific pages.

clear and explicit in the *Foundations*, but it seems to me detectable in much of his subsequent work as well. In a nutshell, he brings economic theorising to a point at which it yields empirically falsifiable propositions. For instance: "Simply to know that there are efficacious 'laws' determining equilibrium tells us nothing of the character of these laws. In order for analysis to be useful, it must provide information concerning the way in which our equilibrium quantities will change as a result of changes in *the parameters taken as independent data*" (*Foundations*, p. 257). Or again "Merely to state . . . that there exists a final functional relationship between all variables and parameters . . . is bare and formal, containing no hypothesis on the empirical data" (*Foundations*, p. 12). The task of wringing "meaningful" propositions out of economic theory was to be made possible by the use of two principles: the principle of maximisation and the correspondence principle.

One ought perhaps to note that this approach, so congenial to a generation brought up on Ayer and Popper, may be unduly narrow. Indeed, Samuelson himself has often departed from it. For one need not be a Weberian to hold the view that there is also a role for understanding. Of course, this is not a simple or self-explanatory notion and it may be that under careful scrutiny *understanding* and *predicting* are in some sense equivalent. But consider the proposition that under certain well-specified conditions an Arrow-Debreu competitive equilibrium exists, is Pareto-efficient, and cannot be upset by any coalition. Moreover for large economies, these equilibrium allocations are the only ones that cannot be blocked by any coalition. As such, Samuelson would argue, these equilibrium results do not constitute falsifiable predictions. Yet I would urge that they are of great importance to our understanding of decentralised economies. We learn that indeed the claim that self-seeking agents guided by sparse market signals are consistent with coherence rather than chaos is at least a logically possible claim. We understand why substantial increasing returns, externalities, few agents, and missing markets can upset these propositions. We are not engaged in predicting the effects of this or that policy or of a change in technology or taste; we are engaged in an argument about economic systems. In such an argument just to achieve some sort of logical consistency is a major achievement. Of course in the final analysis, we must appeal to the world, but there is much to be achieved before this can be done coherently. And when we do appeal, we need not always appeal to Samuelsonian changes in parameters; for instance, the pure Arrow-Debreu model predicts that there is no money and that there is no Stock Exchange. My case is that notwithstanding this false prediction, the model does help us understand money and the Stock Exchange. For instance, it alerts us to look for inefficiencies in any model accommodating these two institutions.

Samuelson's positivism has often made him kindly disposed to special models and perhaps not so kindly disposed to more abstract constructions. "After all generality is not an end in itself. A theory may be so general as to be useless. It is to simple theories that have wide applicability that we must look" (*Foundations*, p. 33). In this view he has been followed by many of his colleagues at M.I.T., and the approach is both attractive and fruitful. That it has its dangers is perhaps best exemplified by the simple monetarist models of "wide applicability." It must also be noted that the notion of *simple* is not simple, and that it is also the case that such models are always tempting economists to advocate policies where a more general approach might have shown them that their advocacy is wildly premature. Indeed, sometimes the *uselessness* of the general model is simply a frank statement of ignorance. The urge to say something definite often overcomes the commandment to speak the truth. Nonetheless, provided it leads to neither philistinism nor self-delusions of realism and relevance, Samuelson's admonition has much to recommend it. Certainly it is possible to make fundamental discoveries by means of very simple models; Samuelson's pure consumption loan model [1958, II, Chap. 21] is a good example.

One of the great virtues of Samuelson's approach is that it gives a very clear understanding of what general equilibrium theory is not about.

> Within the framework of any system, the relationships between our variables are stricly those of mutual interdependence. It is sterile and misleading to speak of one variable as causing or determining another. Once the conditions of equilibrium are imposed, all variables are simultaneously determined. Indeed, from the standpoint of comparative statics, equilibrium is not something which is attained; it is something which if attained, displays certain properties (*Foundations*, p. 9).

Nothing could be more lucid or just than this approach. It has, alas, not prevented the continuance of profound misunderstandings. For instance, in Italy, Cambridge, New York, and who knows where else, there are still those who maintain that neoclassical theory claims that the real wage of labour is *determined* by its marginal product.

While Samuelson has on occasion formulated full general equilibrium models he has never, as far as I can discover, worked with the full Arrow-Debreu construction. In particular, when he has been interested in intertemporal matters, he has quite naturally worked in the context of period analysis, or sequence economies, as we should now say. I am not referring to his studies (with Solow) and elsewhere (1956) on efficient paths of capital accumulation but rather to descriptive or positive theory. The result has been that except for descriptions of steady states, Samuelson does not appear to have committed himself to a formal description of what we are to understand by intertemporal equilibrium. In the *Foundations* he regards the question of which processes to call equilibrium processes as "purely verbal" (p. 330) and argues that there are many options, for example, short run versus long run, all equally legitimate. In particular, he maintains that in general there is no privileged motion of the economy (no sequence) that we want to designate as equilibrium and the stability of which deserves particular attention. Rather it is the asymptotes of "each and every motion of the system" (p. 330) that he proposes to study.

Although I cannot be certain that my interpretation is correct, it seems that Samuelson held (holds?) the view that once the structure and motions of the system have been specified there is no further analytic gain of designating some particular state or motion as an equilibrium. In this he seems to have been followed recently by Lucas (1977), who argues that only equilibrium theories are viable, so that in any theoretical construct we are always and everywhere only concerned with equilibrium states. In this view then, there is no sense in distinguishing theoretically between equilibrium and disequilibrium states. The argument is that in the specification of the actions of agents, whether it be buying, selling, learning, or price setting, we must appeal to what the agent wishes to do in the light of what he or she can do. In other words, the agent is always doing as well as he or she can. In that sense, he or she is always in equilibrium. Similarly, if markets do not *clear*, it is so as a result of an equilibrium decision of agents not to change price or to change inventories, and so on.

Even though the argument is clear, I am not convinced that it is fruitful to drain the equilibrium notion of special significance in this manner. No doubt definitions of concepts are always to some extent a matter of convention, and no doubt it is important to note that actions in much of economic theory are always equilibrium actions in the sense that they are the outcome of rational calculations. Nonetheless, there are considerable gains in clarity and understanding to be had from a much narrower (and more conventional) view of equilibrium. For instance, I think there are important differences between states in which agents are still learning (albeit rationally) from market signals and those in which they are not. It is convenient and insightful to call the latter an equilibrium and deny that designation to the former. But of course Samuelson is right when he argues that no fundamental issues are raised by this piece of methodology.

Let us now turn to the two principles of maximisation and correspondence. We owe it to Samuelson more than to anyone else that at the level of the individual agent, the maximisation hypothesis has been fruitfully put to work. Although there are many more bordered Hessians in the *Foundations* than one would now want, Samuelson squeezed as many *meaningful* propositions out of maximisation as there are. Moreover, he has since been a virtuoso performer in the more satisfying duality approach. In all of this, his methodology has been fully vindicated: maximisation indeed does yield falsifiable propositions. Nor are there propositions always accessible to common sense; for example, the symmetry of the substitution terms.

But our main interest here is the economy as a whole, or at least in market predictions. Here matters are less satisfactory.

Certainly, there are economywide features, especially in the sphere of pure production models, that allow the maximisation principle to perform as desired. For instance, under perfect competition, total profits are maximised over the aggregate production set. The resulting prediction, in obvious notation, is $(p' - p)(y(p') - y(p)) \geqq 0$, and very useful it is, too. The Von-Neumann equilibrium, it will be recalled, can also be cast into maximisation (and dual minimisation) mode. Certain problems in the theory of location also lend themselves to such treatment [1952, II, Chap. 72]. But when households are brought into the picture, then generally things fall apart unless we can abstract from income effects; that is, unless agents have identical homothetic utility functions (Gorman, 1953). In that rather special case, the economy can be viewed *as if* a single maximising household were involved, and so the maximisation hypothesis can deliver at full power. In general, however, the equilibrium cannot be converted into the solution of an *as if* maximisation.

To this rule, there are a number of interesting exceptions. For instance, Meade's model (1968) of philanthropic overlapping generations is one such case. If in the background there actually is a maximiser, for example, a government with a nice

Bergson social welfare function that keeps the distribution of utilities at a desired level, such maximisation may leave us only with substitution, that is, predictable, effects. Lastly, of course, recent work by Bewley (1977) suggests that in the context of models of infinitely long-lived individuals, income effects may be ignorable. Yet the main conclusion stands: In many equilibrium models that interest us, the maximisation hypothesis is not powerful enough to deliver comparative statics results.

Indeed, recent work suggests that matters are even worse. For it has been shown (Pearce and Wise, 1973; Sonnenschein 1973; Mantel 1974; McFadden et al., 1974) that arbitrary excess demand functions that obey Walras' law and are continuous over the interior of the simplex can always be generated as the consequence of the maximixing behaviour of n agents with particular utility functions and endowments. Thus, Walras' law apart, maximisation cannot in general yield any comparative statics results.

Samuelson certainly has always realised that maximisation on its own is not enough for the given task, although neither he nor anyone else foresaw the result that I have just mentioned. In any case, as is well known, he proposed to supplement maximisation with the correspondence principle. The latter is the claim that the hypothesis that an equilibrium is stable yields extra restrictions which can be used to supplement whatever restrictions were yielded by the (second order) conditions of maximisation to help one in deducing propositions in comparative statics. It should be noted right at the outset that Samuelson did not claim that the two principles combined would be of sufficient power in all, or even in most, cases: "The restrictions imposed by our hypotheses on our equilibrium equations (stability and maximum conditions, etc.) are not always sufficient to indicate *definite* restrictions as to algebraic sign of the rates of change of our variables with respect to any parameter" (*Foundations*, p. 19). On the other hand, in the *Foundations* he thought that only equilibrium would be observed. But more recently he has modified this view by saying that it is an empirical question "which cannot be answered by dividing dichotomously the world's possibilities into categories of stable and unstable and inferring that our observed world by its not having exploded away is necessarily in the stable category" [1955, II, Ch. 128, p. 1770].

In my own view, the correspondence principle was always a nonstarter. It was motivated by the right reasons and it was in some sense natural, but it never had a chance of bearing much fruit for the simple reason that economic theory when the principle was first stated, just as now, has no accepted propositions on disequilibrium dynamics and thus no necessary stability conditions of equilibrium. Less important, it is also true that if our ad hoc dynamic adjustment model is of any order higher than two, the necessary conditions for (local) stability are not powerful enough to deliver the desired comparative statics predictions.

I return to stability below; here I am concerned with methodology. Samuelson's positivism led him to view comparative statics theorems as "the sole *raison d'être* of equilibrium analysis" [1946-47, I, Chap. 6, p. 56]. I have already argued that this view seems to me too strong. But of course, taken purely as a methodological point, this may be debatable. More serious perhaps is the fact that this programme in general will bear few fruits. At the level of the individual agent or indeed in considering the effects of parameter changes on maximising or minimising magnitudes in any maximum (or minimum) problem, the method works like a charm and Samuelson has given a virtuoso performance of it in many applications. But in much of theory and certainly in much of theory directed to policy, we are interested in the whole economy. There, most of the time, Samuelson's two principles cannot deliver. This suggests that in most cases, we cannot have prediction without measurement—for instance, we need to estimate a Jacobian. The virtue of theory is that it tells us what we ought to measure and to this important role, Samuelson attaches (attached?) too little significance. In all of this, we do not seem very differently placed from the natural sciences. Newtonian mechanics will not give us a planet's orbit without measurement of distances, and so forth.

On a somewhat more technical level, it is also worth noting that when considering the economy (but not the individual agent), Samuelson seems mainly to have been concerned with infinitesimal parameter changes. But that is very restrictive for comparative statics. Once *discrete* comparative statics is attempted, the question of whether or not equilibrium is unique becomes important. Also, there are not available for nonlinear dynamic equations any powerful necessary conditions known for convergence to some equilibrium. But it is such conditions that are needed for the correspondence principle. All this suggests that we cannot look to the two principles for much help in the discrete cases. I myself now find this a perfectly acceptable state of affairs. It seems satisfactory that we should have detailed empirical knowledge before we can go into the prediction business. This circumstance, as I have already noted, in no way reduces the importance of theory.

GENERAL EQUILIBRIUM

There are general equilibrium aspects to much of Samuelson's work and it is clear that he has always had Walrasian insights and methods at his fingertips. But it seems to me that in his nonsubstitution theorem [1951, I, Chap. 36; 1961, I, Chap. 37][3] and in his studies of factor-price equalisation, the general equilibrium aspect is at the centre of the stage and it is with this aspect that I shall be mainly concerned.

Now that we know it, the nonsubstitution theorem seems natural and almost obvious. It was not always so, as can be verified by looking at earlier discussions of Marxian values or the Leontief input-output system. The theorem has two forms. As first stated, it applied to an economy with timeless production and implicitly no durable inputs. In its second (and later) formulation, it took account of inputs preceding outputs and really applied to economies in steady state. Samuelson, for the differentiable case, provided a complete proof of the timeless situation and he stated the correct result for the time-using production process. However, a general proof (and formulation) of this latter case is due to Mirrlees (1969). In both versions, one is studying a special case in which relative general equilibrium prices are independent of the composition of demand or on certain assumptions of the scale of demand. It is important to understand that these are theorems of general equilibrium theory applied to a special kind of economy. One would have thought

---

[3] It seems that this theorem was also independently enunciated by Georgescu-Roegen. (See Koopmans, 1951).

that Marxists and Sraffa followers would have been delighted with a result that gave them a relative price proposition which they want without either assuming that there is no choice of technique or that capitalists are not greedy for profits. But this has not been the case, probably because rational choice that underlies the theorem can be reformulated in terms of the much-hated marginal products of inputs.

In the *Foundations* (p. 234), we read for the two-goods case: "If constant returns to scale and only one factor . . . are assumed, we have the classical case of a straight line transformation curve." This occurs in the context of a discussion of the Pareto-efficiency of competitive equilibrium. Samuelson was nearly there; all that was needed was the generalisation to higher dimensions. This, however, had to wait a few more years.

Let x_i be the $(n + 1)$ vector of inputs in the production of good i ($i = 1 \ldots n$). The $(n + 1)$th input is the nonproduced factor. There is not joint production and the production functions $F^i(x_i)$ exhibit constant returns to scale. Given a finite amount of the nonproduced input, it is possible to produce positive net outputs of every good. Let C_i be the net output of good i, then $C_i = F^i(x_i) - \Sigma_j x_{ji}$, where x_{ji} is the ith component of x_j. For any production efficient net output $(C_1^* \ldots C_n^*)$, it must be true that this vector solves the problem

$$\max [F^1(x_1) - \Sigma x_{j1}]$$

$$\text{subject to } F^i(x_i) - \sum_j x_{ji} \geqq C_i^* \quad i = 2 \ldots n$$

$$\Sigma x_{jn+1} \leqq 1$$

where I have assumed that there is one unit of the nonproduced input available to the economy. Samuelson considers the case $C_i^* > 0$ all i. The necessary (because of convexity) and sufficient condition for a solution to this problem is

$$F_1^1 = 1, F_i^1 F_j^i - F_j^1 = 0 \ (i = 2 \ldots n), (j = 1 \ldots n + 1).$$

where $F_j^k = \partial F^k / \partial x_{kj}$. Because of constant returns to scale, each of these expressions is homogeneous of degree zero in its arguments. Hence the ratio of inputs in the production of any good (the technique), is independent of $(C_1 \ldots C_n)$ and independent also of the scale of production. Thus there is only one (efficient) technique for the production of each good, and the transformation locus is a hyperplane. Since competitive equilibrium is production-efficient, it now follows that relative equilibrium prices are independent of the scale and composition of final demand. In fact, these prices can be read off from the normal to the hyperplane of production-efficient net outputs. If one thinks of the nonproduced inputs as *labour time*, then the relative prices just derived are Marxian values. Evidently full use has been made of *marginal productivity conditions*.

In the paper I am surveying, Samuelson also considered the nondifferentiable case. In the same volume in which Samuelson's contribution appears, this case had also been studied by Koopmans (1951) and Arrow (1951). The latter considered the general case and showed that the intersection of the economy's production set with the positive orthant is a hyperplane. He paid careful attention to the *end points* of this hyperplane, that is, where the net output of some good was zero. The most satisfying proof is due to Mirrlees (1969). He showed (by very simple means) that there was only one hyperplane that separates every production-efficient net output vector from the set of outputs that Pareto-dominate it.

Samuelson's own proof is the shortest of all of these, and it is very ingenious. It makes no direct appeal to separation theorems, although if all his arguments are spelled out formally, such an appeal is implied. The argument goes as follows. Consider any efficient net production vector. Through this vector there must pass a hyperplane of feasible net production vectors. For, if we keep the coefficients of production constant at the levels they have at the efficient point, the Leontief system with these coefficients gives us the hyperplane we want. But the set of feasible net production vectors is convex and there is a hyperplane of production feasible points through any efficient point. "It must follow that the frontier locus is itself a linear hyperplane, for if it anywhere had a corner or curved surface, it would be impossible for us to find a hyperplane of feasible points going on all sides of the efficient point in question" [1951, I, Chap. 36, p. 518].

This "sketch of a brief but rigorous proof" [Ibid.] shows Samuelson at his most characteristic and best. He lays out the essential argument and leaves it to others to dot the i's and to cross the t's. Certainly some crossing and dotting remains to be done. For instance, Samuelson does not consider the end points, he does not show that the assumptions suffice for the Leontief hyperplane to be meaningfully derivable, and in the last resort he appeals to our geometrical intuition, which may not be well developed in higher dimensions. Nonetheless, he clearly hits the nail right on the head.

In later papers [1959, I, Chap. 31, 32] he used his theorem to discuss the classics and particularly Ricardo. He noted that in the classical world, labour was *producible* at a constant subsistence wage represented by a fixed basket of goods. The single nonproduced input was land. If the latter is taken of homogeneous quality, then the resulting Samuelson prices are *land prices* in the sense that the price of any good is equal to the sum of direct and indirect land embodied in it.

In the case so far discussed, preferences over goods or between goods and leisure—indeed any kind of preferences—are irrelevant to the determination of (normalised) equilibrium prices. One has here the general equilibrium equivalent of the Marshallian scissors with one blade always in a fixed position. The ordinary general equilibrium requirement that profit-maximising supplies of goods and demand for labour should equal preference-maximising demand for goods and supply of labour are here needed to determine the composition and scale of output where it is assumed that labour is the sole nonproduced input. The whole constitutes a general equilibrium system where production efficiency conditions suffice to determine all prices.

It is clear that this result is bought at considerable cost; in particular, the assumption of a single nonproduced input and the absence of joint production is unpalatable. This shortcoming is obvious if production takes time and if there are durable (produced) inputs. Since goods at different dates are, from the point of view of economic theory, different goods, it is immediate that one will now have differently dated primary inputs (even if there is only one physical type) and hence more than one nonproduced input. If there are durable inputs, then the output of the produced good must be augmented by the "output" of used durable input and in that sense there is joint production. Of course, even in the absence of this time dimension to production, there may be many different nonproduced inputs (different sorts of labour, land, and so on). However, this case is most conveniently discussed when we turn to Samuelson's general equilibrium approach to factor-price equalisation.

Samuelson considered the time problem in "A New Theorem on Nonsubstitution" [1961, I, Chap. 37]. He states the

> . . . following theorem: Although it be rigorously impossible in a labor and multicapital-good model to reduce matters to a two-factor labor and capital model, it is nonetheless completely possible to reduce everything rigorously down to a real wage and single interest-rate model. While capital goods involve millions of different dimensions, the whole problem yet can be rigorously boiled down to the two-dimensional realm of wage and interest (p. 526).

As statements of theorems go, this must certainly be judged to be among the more informal. From what follows and from what we have learned since about these matters, we deduce that Samuelson's theorem tells us that given a rate of interest in a closed bounded interval, all long-run (steady state) equilibrium prices in terms of the nonproduced input (labour) are determined. Although in the paper of this theorem Samuelson gives only an example and docs not really prove what he asserts, thus providing no proof of the theorem, it is quite clear tht he had the correct insight. It is as if having seen the point, it seemed too obvious to him to require more than a sketch.

He may also have had in mind his work on Ricardo [1959, I, Chap. 31, 32] where the generalized nonsubstitution theorem is used and stated in a rather special context. But even here, at a rather crucial moment, we are referred to "a sketchy proof" [1959, I, Chap. 32, p. 420] in his paper on factor-prices and general equilibrium [1953, II, Chap. 70]. This proof, as we shall see below, has certain difficulties, and I am not clear how it is to be applied to the Ricardian example.

There are two ways of going about the business of proof of a generalised nonsubstitution theorem, and they correspond to the two parts of the fundamental theorem of welfare economics. One way is to utilise the special market equilibrium conditions that apply under constant returns to scale. The other is to calculate the shadow prices of a Pareto-efficient allocation and then show that these prices correspond to equilibrium prices. In both cases, the aim is to show the independence of the (normalised) prices of the composition of final demand and in both cases, the rate of interest (uniform rate of profit) is taken as exogenous. In some ways, the first route is easier than the second because there are certain problems with the appropriate definition of Pareto-efficiency in the intertemporal setting with a given interest rate. On the other hand, the second route is the more satisfying.

To proceed along either route requires one to concentrate on special equilibria, or special allocations, namely, steady states. This is obvious when one recalls that when relative prices are changing over time, one cannot talk of a uniform profit rate. Indeed, Samuelson and Solow [1956, I, Chap. 25] and Dorfman, Samuelson, and Solow (1958) have given a definitive account of these matters. It is therefore a little surprising that there is no reference to the steady state in Samuelson's discussion of the generalised nonsubstitution theorem. This omission also makes the interpretation of Ricardo in the time-using production case a little suspect since, for Ricardo, the steady state was also the end of capitalism.

The simplest case arises when there are no durable inputs. If the time interval between the application of input and the appearance of output varies, we can define sufficient goods in progress so that all goods have a delay of one period. (Of course, one-year-old wine appears as an input in two-year-old wine). We are only interested in steady states so that relative prices can be written without time subscript. There is no joint production. If r is the uniform interest (profit) rate, w is the wage of labour, the only nonproduced input, and if wages are paid at the end of the period, we get the equilibrium conditions

$$\frac{1}{1+r}\, P_i = C_i\left(p, \frac{w}{1+r}\right) \quad i = 1, \ldots, n \tag{1}$$

when there are n goods produced and $p = (p_1 \ldots p_n)$ is the vector of their prices, and $C_i(\cdot\ j\ \cdot)$ is the minimum unit cost function. Of course the partial derivatives of C_i, as Samuelson taught us, are the a_{ij} coefficients of the Leontief matrix. They themselves clearly depend on $[p, (w/1 + r)]$.

Since the unit cost functions are homogeneous of degree one in (p, w) the system (1) contains only $(n + 1)$ unknowns: $(1/w)p$ and r. But there are only n equations and hence one degree of freedom. In principle then, we could try and solve for n of the unknowns in terms of any remaining one. But Samuelson and most other writers want to solve for $q \equiv (1/w)p$ in terms of r.

There are now the following questions:

1 Does a solution $q(r)$ to (1) exist for given r with $q(r) > 0$?
2 Is that solution unique?
3 How is the general equilibrium system completed?

The answers to the first two questions were provided by Morishima (1964). If over the domain of prices the Jacobian (C_{ij}) is semipositive and indecomposable and if labour is an indispensable input, then if a solution $q(r)$ exists, it is unique and strictly positive. Moreover, if r lies in a certain bounded interval when the economy is productive, then a solution exists. These two results together give a generalised nonsubstitution theorem. As a bonus, using Samuelson's envelope results, one obtains $q'(r) > 0$, that is, a downward-sloping factor-price frontier [recall $q_i = (1/w)p_i$]. The proof of uniqueness is easy; that of existence requires some technical machinery.

But this method of proof does not go to the heart of the matter, which is the linearity of the relevant transformation locus. Here we must turn to Mirrlees (1969) although Samuelson clearly had some elements of this approach in mind [1961, I, Chap. 37]

Let (x^i, x_0^i) be the vector of inputs of sector i where x^i stands for the vector of goods and x_0^i for the input of labour, both non-negative. Let y^i be the vector of output that appears one period later. In the present simple case of no durable inputs, y^i had zeros everywhere except in the ith place. Let $R = (1/1 + r)$. The set of possible activities (y^i, x^i, x_0^i) is such that $Ry^i - x^i$ has at most one positive component in the ith place. However, we assume that there exist sectoral activities such that $\Sigma_i Ry^i - x^i \gg 0$.

Let $y = \Sigma y^i$, $x = \Sigma x^i$, $x_0 = \Sigma x_0^i$. Then Mirrlees says that (y^*, x^*, x_0^*) in the economy's production set is *R-efficient* if there exists no distinct (y, x, x_0) in this production set such that $Ry - x > Ry^* - x^*$ and $x_0 \leq x_0^*$. Since there are constant returns to scale everywhere, the set $\{(z, -x_0)/(y, x, x_0) \in T\}$ is a convex cone where $z = Ry - x$ and T is the economy's production set. By assumption there is $z \gg 0$ in this set and one can show that there is an R-efficient z^*, x_0^* with $z^* \gg 0$. The usual separation argument ensures the existence of (p, w) such that $(p, w)(z^*, - x_0^*) = 0$ and $(p, w)(z, - x_0) \leq 0$ all $(z, - x_0)$ in our set. Now $z^* = Ae$ where A is the matrix with columns $Ry^{*i} - x^{*i}$ and e is the unit vector. By assumption $z^* \gg 0$ and only the diagonal elements of A are positive. Hence by a well-known theorem $A^{-1} > 0$. Let $x_0^* = (x_0^{*i})e = a_0 e$. Then separation now yields[4]

$$pA = wa_0$$

and $p = wa_0 A^{-1}$ so that $w = 0$ implies $p = 0$ which is impossible. Hence $w > 0$ and $q(r) = a_0 A^{-1} \gg 0$.

Clearly $q(r)$ decentralises the R-efficient allocation. That is, $(Ry^{*i} - x_*^{*i} - x_0^{*i})$ maximises $(q(r), 1)(Ry^i - x^i, - x_0^i)$ each i. But $q(r)$ decentralises every R-efficient allocation. Suppose not, and that some other R-efficient allocation is decentralised by $q'(r) \neq q(r)$. Let (B, b_0) correspond to this other allocation. Then from separation:

$$0 = pA - wa_0 \geq pB - wb_0 \Rrightarrow q(r) \leq b_0 B^{-1} = q'(r)$$
$$0 = p'B - w'b_0 \geq p'A - w'a_0 \Rrightarrow q'(r) \leq a_0 A^{-1} = q(r),$$

a contradiction. Lastly it is obvious that every competitive equilibrium is R-efficient. Hence $q(r)$ is the unique competitive equilibrium vector of relative prices.

Mirrlees does not discuss the meaning of R efficiency; it is simply a characterisation of the steady state equilibrium. But it may be useful to remark that an interpretation of the result is that competitive equilibrium is golden rule efficient for the growth factor R^{-1}. That is so because $y - R^{-1}x$ is the steady state consumption vector when the growth factor is R^{-1}. In general the actual growth rate will not exceed the interest rate.

When there are durable inputs, matters are harder and one needs more

---

[4]Notice that here wages are paid in advance.

assumptions. The joint production aspect of the transfer of used machines from one period to the next causes no intrinsic difficulties. But as Mirrlees has noted, a long-lived machine can be the source of indirect joint production if it is transferable between processes. A machine capable of producing two different goods can be used in a single process to produce the two goods at different dates. but this process is not the convex combination of two processes, each using the machine to produce just one of the goods. That observation leads to the conclusion that we cannot get the desired result unless it is assumed that machines once installed cannot be shifted.

It is clear that if machines are not altered by use, we could proceed much as before when looking at long-lived inputs. The vector y^i would now have components denoting machines transferred from one period to the next. But we retain the assumption that $Ry^i - x^i$ has only one positive component, all i. However, $y = \Sigma y^i \gg 0$ does not now imply that every industry is operating at a positive level at an R-efficient production. This causes trouble. For we might now have, say, two R-efficient allocations with $y \gg 0$, in one of which one industry is operating while it is not doing so in the other. The separation argument would then fail us. Mirrlees introduces assumptions to exclude this possibility. They are that if G is the growth factor of the economy, $y^j - Gx^j$ should have only one positive component and if the kth component is zero, then $y_k^j = x_k^j = 0$. This is not a strong requirement. Together with the natural $RG \leq 1$ it implies that $Ry^i - x^i$ has only one positive component and it implies that when a steady state is feasible, that is, $y \geq Gx$, that every industry must be used.

When machines are altered by use, we proceed by redefining production activities. Suppose machines last for T periods (the case of different lifetimes for different machines can also be handled). Then in steady state when the growth factor (of the labour force) is G, output will be made up of production on T vintages as follows. Let Y_t be the net output vector of the economy on vintage t machines. Then at $t = 1$, the net output vector of the economy $Y(1)$ is given by:

$$Y(1) = \sum_1^T G^{T-i} Y_i.$$

If $n_t \leq 0$ is the labour input on vintage t production, then

$$n(1) = \sum_1^T G^{T-i} n_i$$

is the economy's labour input at $t = 1$. We say that $(Y_1 \ldots Y_T)$, $(n_1 \ldots n_T)$ is feasible if $Y(1) \geq 0, n(1) \geq \bar{n}$, where $\bar{n}$ is the available labour force. In analogy with earlier assumptions we postulate that there exists a feasible programme with $Y(1) \gg 0$, that in all feasible programmes $n(1) < 0$ if anything is produced, and lastly that $Y(1)$ can be spanned by as many industry activities $y^i(1)$ as there are goods where for each i, $y^i(1)$ has at most one positive component. Notice that in steady state, we need only be interested in a single T-cycle of production.

One now redefines R-efficient production as a feasible $(Y_1 \ldots Y_T)$ such that $Y(R) = \Sigma \, R^{i-1} Y_i$ cannot be Pareto-dominated by any other feasible production process. Lastly one now needs $R \, G \leqq 1$ and the existence of $[Y(R) \gg 0]$. With these modifications one can proceed as before. Looking at the set of feasible $[Y(R), n]$ we find an efficient one with strictly positive net outputs $[Y(R) \gg 0]$. Since the convex cone properties have been preserved, we find (p, w) as the coefficients of the separating hyperplane. These are now obviously equilibrium prices. To show that $q = (1/w)p$ is invariant for other R-efficient productions, we proceed exactly as before using the fact that the matrix $[y^i(R)]$ has a positive inverse. Lastly it is clear that every steady state equilibrium is R-efficient.

The above is an account of the proof given by Mirrlees (1969) and very elegant it is, too. Samuelson saw that this result is true (see especially his Ricardo piece [1959, I, Chap. 31, 32]), but on this occasion he did not firmly establish his findings.

The various nonsubstitution theorems that Samuelson originated are a notable contribution to general equilibrium analysis and they are of obvious relevance to problems discussed by classical economists and by Marx. They also have positive uses. For instance, if the technological assumptions fit and if rates of return are equalised internationally, then so should be real wages [1965, II, Chap. 71]. But it must be admitted that the assumptions are pretty strong. In particular, if one thinks of the heterogeneity of labour, the prevalence of genuine joint production and the variety of nonproduced inputs quite apart from the evidence of increasing returns, one hesitates to make this sort of model the prime vehicle of theorising. On the other hand, Leontief input-output analysis is widely used and knowledge of these results should save one from the horrors of neo-Ricardianism.

All this still leaves unanswered one of the questions that I posed at the outset: How is the model to be closed? The answer to this question has been the occasion of tiresome controversy that would be uninstructive to rehearse. Let us therefore content ourselves with simply stating the general equilibrium route.

As has been stressed repeatedly above, the dynamic nonsubstitution theorem applies to an economy in steady state and hence to a special sort of equilibrium. In general, the factor-price frontier $q(R)$ gives prices in different steady states, and of course, in different techniques of production. If we think of R as the *free* variable yet to be determined, it is clear that this cannot be done by invoking any marginal productivity relationship. The reason for this is that we have already used (implicitly) all the marginal productivity relations that there are in determining $q(R)$. Also we must note that at $q(R)$ supply of every good is a correspondence: Firms do not care how much or how little they supply. So it is simplest to postulate that at $q(R)$ every sector is willing to supply whatever is demanded.

But at any t this is a willingness to supply goods at $t + 1$ (we now revert for simplicity's sake to the one-period production process). The goods available at t are the outcome of previous decisions. To analyse the steady state case, we must assume that for every R these past decisions were such that the ratio in which the goods are available is consistent with a steady state at R when the technology is appropriate to $q(R)$. That is, the vector of endowments must, except for scale, be determined by R. Of course, this must not be interpreted as *determining* the past (decisions at $t - 1$) in the present (at t). One is looking for those decisions that would have had to be taken at $t - 1$ if R is to be consistent with a steady state at t.

For every R we can thus think of a *composite good* made up in the appropriate (steady state) ratios. For equilibrium, the excess demand for that composite good must be zero, which is another way of saying savings must equal investment. Since the Walras Law makes the sum of the value of the excess demand for the composite good plus the value of the excess demand for labour zero, we must just as well use the equation: zero excess demand for labour to complete the model. In any case, the whole model consists of

1 the equations telling us that maximal unit profits everywhere are zero.

2 the equations giving us the steady state composition of endowment (and output for $t + 1$).

3 the condition that either the excess demand for labour or composite good is equal to zero.

If we count up, we have enough for $q(R)$, R, and the $(n - 1)$ ratios of goods. That leaves the usual existence problems that can be answered on conventional lines.

This seems to be all that needs to be said. It makes it quite clear that we are concerned with a special general equilibrium case. The fact that we must restrict ourselves to steady states further reduces the descriptive power of the theory. As already noted, it seems not a hopeful way of doing nineteenth century value theory, whether Ricardo or Marx. On the other hand, there may be no correct way of doing this theory at all. The Sraffian literature to which Samuelson has been surprisingly kind simply avoids discussion of these matters.

GENERAL EQUILIBRIUM (FACTOR-PRICE EQUALISATION)

Elsewhere in this volume, Samuelson's remarkable contributions to the pure theory of international trade are discussed, so here I restrict myself to remarks on certain general equilibrium aspects.

In a recent impressive account of the factor-price issue in international trade, Dixit and Norman (1980, p. 125) write "the most important contribution is clearly that of Samuelson [1953, II, Chap. 70]. He saw through the whole problem and we think that if he had filled in some of the asides and terse remarks he makes, he would have developed the argument much as we have done here." And that is correct. Samuelson's 1953 paper is a landmark in the integration of the international trade and general equilibrium theory. His later emendations and supplementations [1967, III, Chap. 161] are also most useful.

Historically, the problem seems to have rapidly become a purely mathematical one. Suppose there are m factors and n goods, constant returns to scale, and no joint production. Consider the case $m = n$ where all goods are produced in both of two countries. If p is the price vector of goods common to both countries, w the price vector of factors in one country, then under the assumptions equilibrium requires $p = C(w)$ where $C(w)$ is the vector of minimum unit cost functions. If this map is one to one over the domain of factor prices so that $C^{-1}(p)$ is a singleton, then the two countries can be in equilibrium only if (for a given normalisation) w is the same in both countries. Factor-price equalisation thus seemed to turn on the global univalence of the map $C(w)$. Surprisingly, the mathematical literature until recently seems to have had no theorems on globally univalent maps and economists had to supply their own.

In 1953, Samuelson proposed a theorem to which Nikaido produced a counterexample. In a note to this paper published later [1965, II, p. 908] he proposed an amendment. This required that a naturally ordered set of principal minors of the Jacobian $[C_{ij}(w)]$ be each positive and bounded above and below on the domain. This theorem was proved by Nikaido (1972) and can be applied to the present problem by the transformation $C_i = \log c_i$ and $w_i = e^{x_i}$. Before that Gale and Nikaido (1965) had shown that a sufficient univalence condition on a rectangular domain was that $[C_{ij}(w)]$ be a P-matrix and McKenzie (1967) had shown the sufficiency of diagonal dominance of the Jacobian.[5]

More recent work on univalence (Dierker, 1972; Varian, 1975; Mas-Colell, 1975; Nishimura, 1976) has made use of the rather powerful tools of differential topology. A fundamental result is the Poincaré-Hopf Index Theorem (for example, Milnor, 1965 and Varian, 1975).

Let $f: A \to TA$ be a smooth vector field on the disk that points outward on the boundary of A and has a finite number of isolated zeros at $a^1 \ldots a^n$ with $|Df(a^i)| \neq 0$ for $i = 1 \ldots n$. Then one can define an index $\lambda(a^i)$ such that $\lambda(a^i) = +1$, if $|Df(a^i)| > 0$, $\lambda(a^i) = -1$ if $|Df(a^i)| < 0$ and $\Sigma_i \lambda(a^i) = 1$.

To apply this to the present case (recall that I am taking $n = m$), one defines $f(p, w) = C(w) - p$ where the map is from the space of factor prices with p fixed. One bounds the set of w by (0) below and takes a large upper bound. This rectangle can be smoothed into a disk. One now needs to assume that for w with w_i small enough one cannot have $f(p, w) = 0$. For w large enough (near the boundary) we can (by homogeneity) assume $f(p, w) > 0$. It is then possible to construct a vector field $g(p, w)$ that points out on the boundary of the wage space and always points in the same direction as $f(p, w)$. Hence if the determinant of the Jacobian $|Df(p, w)| > 0$, (really never changes sign), then the above theorem ensures that there is only a single w that solves $f(p, w) = 0$ (Nishimura, 1976). This result is more satisfactory than any earlier ones, including those of Pearce and Wise (1973). The condition on the Jacobian can be interpreted as a kind of generalised nonreversal of factor intensities. But the other conditions needed to ensure that the vector field points outward on the boundary are also crucial. Counterexamples to the Jacobian condition have violated these boundary conditions.

So far, we have been concerned with only a part of the general equilibrium system, concentrating only on the production conditions. That this will not do becomes clear when we drop the assumption of there being as many goods as factors. For then, looking only at the unit cost, equal price equations, we have either an over- or underdetermined system. Samuelson [1953, II, Chap. 70] saw this clearly

---

[5] An $n \times m$ matrix is a P-matrix if all its principal minors are positive. A matrix has diagonal dominance if there exists a vector $(h_1 \ldots h_n) > 0$ such that $[h_i a_{ii}] > \Sigma_{j \neq i} a_{ij} h_i$ all i.

and in his discussion of over- and underdeterminacy, he pointed in the right direction—the completion of the full general equilibrium systems. But he did not, at least not formally, complete the model to derive a general equilibrium construction for both countries trading with each other.

The first step was to take note of the endowments of the country. Samuelson [1953, II, Chap. 70] pointed the way but the decisive step was taken by McKenzie (1955) and further illuminated by Samuelson [1967, III, Chap. 161]. Suppose there are at least as many goods (n) as factors (m). Then we want at least m goods to be produced in each country. Is that possible at the given p and if so do we get factor-price equalisation?

Suppose goods labelled $i = 1 \ldots m$ are produced in both countries. By the envelope theorem, the normal to $C_i(w)$ at the point w^* where $C_i(w^*) = p_i$ is the unit input vector in the production of good i. Taking these normals for each i at w^* we generate a cone that McKenzie calls the diversification cone. If this production combination is to be feasible, then the country's endowment must be spanned by the input vectors, that is, be in the diversification cone. There may, of course, be another w, say w^{**}, such that $C_i(w^{**}) = p_i$. It, too, will have a diversification cone. However, if the endowments of each country lie in the same diversification cone, then there must also be factor-price equalisation when the m goods are being produced. Notice that in this result, factor-intensity reversal that may occur as we pass from w^* to w^{**} does not cause a problem.

But equilibrium does cause a problem. For we don't know whether the outputs that we calculate from the full employment of factors condition will also be demanded, and we have said nothing about the remaining ($n - m$) goods. All this was clear to Samuelson in 1953:

> However if commodity prices are not given to us arbitrarily, but are determined by international trading between countries with the same production function as ours and with factor endowments not too different from ours, then there is a *presumption* that the international commodity prices will be such as to allow us to produce something of at least r goods (p. 893).

Samuelson's r is our m. Moreover, he saw clearly that if that were so, there would be ($n - m$) degrees of freedom on the world pattern of goods produced.

Samuelson, therefore, had the general equilibrium resolution in the hollow of his hand but never formally displayed it. Uzawa (1959) took a further step in doing so, indeed an essential step. But a really satisfactory treatment has only been given recently by Dixit and Norman (1980).

Let the two countries be distinguished by the subscript k, let x be an output vector, e, an endowment vector, d( ), a vector of demand functions. Then the full general equilibrium system for two countries with internationally immobile factors is:

$$p_i - C_i(w_i) \leqq 0, [p_i - C_i(w)]x_i = 0 \qquad i = 1 \ldots n, k = 1, 2 \qquad (1)$$
$$[DC(w_k)]x_k = e_k \qquad k = 1, 2 \qquad (2)$$
$$x \equiv \Sigma x_k = \Sigma d_k(p, w_k, e_k) \qquad (3)$$

On usual assumptions this has a solution $(p^*, w_1^*, w_2^*, x_1^*, x_2^*)$. Suppose $w_1^* = w_2^*$. Then (p^*, w^*, x^*) with $x^* = x_1^* + x_2^*$ is also the solution to the general equilibrium system for the internationally mobile factor case:

$$p_i - C_i(w) \leqq 0 \, [\, p_i - C_i(w)]x_i^* = 0 \qquad i = 1 \ldots n \tag{1'}$$

$$[DC(w)]x = \Sigma \, e_k \tag{2'}$$

$$x = \Sigma \, d_k(p, w, e_k) \tag{3'}$$

This was first noted by Uzawa (1959).

Now reverse the question. If (p^*, w^*, x^*) solves (1'), (2'), (3'), is there an allocation x_1^*, x_2^* so that (p^*, w^*, x_1^*, x_2^*) solves (1), (2), (3)? Answer: If and only if there exists $0 < x_1 < x^*$ such that

$$[DC(w^*)]x_1 = e_k \tag{4}$$

If that holds, then necessarily $x^* - x_1^* = x_2^*$ satisfies the endowment equation of country (2). If it does not hold there cannot be factor-price equalisation. Formally, then, we have the following result. Assume that (1'), (2'), (3') have a unique solution (p^*, w^*, x^*). Let

$$K = \{e \| DC(w^*) \| x = e \text{ for } 0 \leqq x \leqq x^*\}$$

Then there will be factor-price equalisation if $e_1 \, \epsilon \, K$ (Dixit and Norman, 1980).

The cases $n > m$ and $m > n$ now resolve themselves easily and indeed require no special analysis. For instance, if the dimension of x^* is greater than the number of factors and the conditions of the theorem are met, we get an indeterminateness in the composition of output (as Samuelson noted) that is inessential. There is no overdeterminacy. If $m > n$, since K can be at most n-dimensional while the factor space is m-dimensional, it is clear that it is unlikely (one can make this into a precise generic statement) that the conditions of the theorem will be met.

We can end as we started. Samuelson not only invented the question[6] of factor-price equalisation but he saw also early on that it would require general equilibrium analysis for its answer. In his 1953 paper he went almost all the way. I agree with Dixit and Norman when they argue that it was a pity, at least from the point of view of the specific question, that the whole matter thereafter turned on the univalence problem. In concentrating entirely on the $p \equiv C(w)$ equations, a good deal of general equilibrium information is lost. On the other hand, the univalence question is of interest in its own right and Samuelson's ventures have stimulated a good deal of work (and controversy). It is only very recently, however, that the mathematical tools known to economists were available and adequate.

Lastly we should note that Samuelson also put the dynamic nonsubstitution theorem to work on this problem. He assumes exponential decay for each capital good and supposes there to be no trade across frontiers. We are implicitly looking at

---

[6]A. P. Lerner must share this honour (1952).

steady states where relative prices remain constant. If there are m capital goods, all being produced, we get the equations

$$p_i = C_i((r - \delta_1)p_1 \ldots (r - \delta_m)p_m, 1) \qquad i = 1 \ldots m$$

where r = interest rate, δ_i the depreciation rate of the ith capital good, and p_i is the price of a new machine in terms of labour. In this formulation, the dynamic nonsubstitution theorem can be proved rather easily. Anyway, if r is in a certain interval then the above equations determine a unique $p(r)$. Since consumption goods are produced by labour and capital goods, we can readily determine the consumption goods price vector $q(r)$ also in terms of labour. It is easy to check that if there are no factor-intensity reversals, the relative prices of any two consumption goods will be monotone in r. It follows that if in world equilibrium any two goods are produced in and traded by both countries, r must be equalised. But then $q(r)$ is equalised, that is, the real wage is also equalised.

Should there be free (financial) capital movements leading to the direct equalisation of r, then, of course, real wages would also be equalised. Although such free movements of financial capital obtains, say in the European Economic Community (E.E.C.), one must note that British real wages are sadly far below those of most other E.E.C. members. One of the problems among many is that the real rate of interest is not the same as the rate of profit and that a British car is not a Volkswagen. The applicability of the theory must be in some doubt.

GENERAL EQUILIBRIUM: A FINAL REMARK

In his review of Mosak [1945, II, Chap. 63] Samuelson wrote: "No more than one-third of the book is concerned with international trade, which is probably as it should be, as the subject—aside from its traditions and policy aspects—constitutes an analytical special case of general economic theory" (p. 802). Precisely so, and although in the literature of this subject this specialness is often lost sight of, Samuelson made much of international trade theory an integral part of general equilibrium theory. By so doing he not only advanced the former but also advanced the latter.

The various nonsubstitution theorems constitute interesting special cases. Certainly Samuelson made a decisive difference in our understanding of constant returns to scale economies. He was also one of the pioneers of the dual approach and made good use of the envelope theorem, which, I suspect, was unknown to economists before the *Foundations*.

In much of his writings in this area, Samuelson made good use of the maximising principle, in particular, the maximisation of an economy's profits under perfect competition.

STABILITY

Part II of the *Foundations* treats dynamics. Together with the appendices it provided to economics the first comprehensive application of classical mathematical results in the theory of difference and differential equations. In the process Samuelson transformed the way in which dynamic economic theory was formulated and studied. He also taught a good many economists the mathematics needed.

Samuelson has, of course, studied a great variety of dynamic systems, both before and after the *Foundations*, from the famous multiplier-accelerator model [1939, II, Chap. 82] to predator-prey Volterra equations applied to economics [1971, III, Chap. 171]. In this account, however, I shall mainly deal with his contributions to the classical price-stability problem, although some notice will be taken of some macroeconomic models as well.

A number of the most significant contributions in Part II of the *Foundations* were first published in *Econometrica* [1941, 1942, 1944, I, Chap. 38, 39, 40]. In particular, it was not long after the publication of *Value and Capital* that Samuelson wrote the important paper noting that the Hicksian stability analysis lacked a true dynamics. Samuelson showed that neither *perfect* nor *imperfect* stability as defined by Hicks was necessary or sufficient for true dynamic stability.[7] In this paper Samuelson formulated the price adjustment model that dominated the next twenty years of stability analysis. This model was given by

$$\dot{p}_i = H_i(Z_i) \qquad i = 1 \ldots n$$

where H_i is a sign preserving function of excess demand Z_i with $H_i' > 0$ and $H_i(0) = 0$.

It was implicitly assumed that this was a numeraire process, that is, there are $n + 1$ goods with $\dot{p}_{n+1} \equiv 0$. Since in the event Samuelson only dealt with local (asymptotic) stability and since he took equilibrium prices to be strictly positive, he did not worry about the behaviour of the system when some price was zero. But rather surprisingly, he gave no economic account of this model of the price-mechanism. Tâtonnement is not listed in the index of the *Foundations* and is, as far as I have been able to discover, nowhere discussed by Samuelson. The excess demands are written as functions of prices only, that is, endowments are not included. And so it came about that he did not consider processes in which endowments are changing in the process of exchange, nor did he discuss this matter.

It is clear—especially with the hindsight of 1980—that imperfect stability is a nonstarter for true dynamic stability. If we work with excess supplies, the condition can be translated into the requirement that the principal minors of order $(n - 1)$ of the excess supply Jacobian should be of the same sign as the full Jacobian determinant. Clearly this is neither necessary nor sufficient for the real parts of the roots of the Jacobian to be positive (recall that we are dealing with excess supplies). Perfect stability, on the other hand, requires all the principal minors of the Jacobian to be positive. That this is not necessary for the local stability of Samuelson's price system is clear. Samuelson produced an example [1942, I, Chap. 40] to show that it was not sufficient either. The stage was set for the search of sufficient conditions that culminated in the famous papers by Arrow, Hurwicz, and Block (1958, 1959, 1960, 1962).

---

[7]The demonstration that perfect stability was not sufficient for true stability appeared after the main article in which Samuelson had conjectured a contrary result.

In his discussion of Hicks, Samuelson noted that in the absence of income effects, when the Jacobian is symmetric, the dynamic system will have asymptotic stability and also be perfectly stable in the sense of Hicks. In a footnote [1941, I, Chap. 38, p. 551], he argues that in a productive economy where households sell factors and buy goods a "cancelling of income effects" between buyers and sellers leads to absurdity. But here he seems to have made a mistake due to neglecting the payment of profits to households. If households have parallel linear Engel curves through the origin, then we can treat the economy as *if* it had only one household. Suppose, for simplicity, that labour is the only factor and that $\overline{L}$ is the maximum amount of leisure that households can consume. The budget constraint is: $p.x + wL \leqq w\overline{L} + \pi(w,p)$ where $\pi(\ )$ is the usual profit function. The income term, say, for a change in w is now $[(\overline{L} - L) + \pi_w] \times$ marginal propensity to consume the good in question. Recalling that π_w is the negative of the demand for labour and that we are interested in differentiation at an equilibrium, we see that the term in square brackets is zero.

Samuelson's command over the classical theory of differential and difference equations has always been very impressive. His very early treatment of the linearisation of nonlinear differential equation systems is a case in point. Even now when we come to this method, most of us simply say that we are dealing with cases where the deviation from equilibrium is small enough to allow us to ignore higher order terms in a Taylor expansion. This, of course, begs a number of questions. Samuelson did not proceed in this way. As an example, consider the single variable system $\dot{x} = f(x)$ with $f(0) = 0$ as the unique critical point and f analytic. The Taylor expansion yields $f(x) = \Sigma a_i x^i$. Samuelson now appealed to the following result in mathematical analysis. The solution to the differential equation satisfies:

$$x(t) = \sum_{o}^{\infty} C_i(\alpha e^{a_1 t})^i$$

where α depends on initial conditions and the C_i can be calculated by substituting back into the Taylor expansion and equating coefficients. It is now clear that if $a_1 < 0$, the power series converges for t large enough and that $x(t) \rightarrow 0$. But this now means that the stability of the first order approximation $\dot{x} = a_1 x$ is indeed sufficient for stability in the small.[8] Samuelson notes that "this is an *exact* solution in which no terms are considered to be of an order of smallness and ignorable" [1942, I, Chap. 40, p. 571].

There are many examples where Samuelson's wide knowledge of the mathematics illuminated a problem in economic dynamics. But of special interest from the point of view of what followed is the fact that on one occasion he used the methods of Lyapounov [1942, I, Chap. 40, p. 582] without naming them as such. He was here within a hair's breadth of a development that did not occur for another ten years.

The problem at issue was what we would now call a gradient process:

$$\dot{x}_i = F_i(x_1 \ldots x_n)$$

---

[8]This result was extended to more variables and to difference equations.

where $F_i(\cdot) = [\partial F(\cdot)/\partial x_i]$. Samuelson normalised so that F attained its maximum at $x_i = 0$ all i. Hence for x sufficiently close to zero $\Sigma F_i(0 \ldots 0) x_i < 0$. He then noted that this implied that the function $\frac{1}{2}\Sigma x_i^2$ was monotone declining for $x \neq 0$ and used this to establish stability in the small. Concavity and boundedness could have been used to give stability in the large. Boundedness and using $F(x)$ as a Lyapounov function would have shown convergence to some critical value. But he certainly provided here an important clue that was not taken up for a considerable time. No other economist, as far as I know, had employed a Euclidean norm in stability analysis before Samuelson. His technical mastery and insights make it a pleasure to reread these early and vital contributions.

Samuelson's outstanding contributions to trade cycle theory are beyond the scope of this paper. However rereading them now leaves one with two salient impressions: Samuelson (and Frisch and later Goodwin) was streets ahead of other contemporary work on this subject and provided the technical framework of much of the best subsequent research. But also Samuelson, like all his contemporaries, and indeed most of his successors, never seems to have found it necessary to provide a link between his general equilibrium (value) theory and his macroeconomic modelling. One may be a little wary of the contemporary search for microeconomic foundations of macroeconomics and yet find it astonishing that for so long these two modes of theorising were not only kept quite apart but also were not seen to be logically inconsistent. For instance, in a world where agents can buy and sell as much as they wish at going prices, there is no meaning to "lack of effective demand." It is quite impossible to suppose that Samuelson did not see these problems. Perhaps he refrained from discussing them because he, like everyone today, did not know how to proceed to a resolution. But it must be admitted that trade cycle theory without prices now seems inconclusive.

Some of these difficulties are seen in Samuelson dynamisation of the IS-LM model that he used to illustrate the correspondence principle. For instance, he concludes "that an increase in the amount of money must *ceteris paribus* lower interest rates" [1941, I, Chap. 38, p. 559]. Of course, Samuelson knew all about homogeneity of excess demand functions in money and money prices and one can only guess whether the *ceteris paribus* was meant to denote fixed money prices. But one can see why the initial monetarist tide was so successful—no one had thought of building any dykes.

The dynamisation of IS-LM is of the type

$$\dot{y} = G(y, i, \alpha)$$
$$0 = L(y, i, M)$$

where y is income, i, the interest rate, M, the stock of money, G, the excess demand for goods (investment minus saving), and L, the excess demand for money. Here α is a shift parameter with $G_\alpha > 0$ so that an increase in α denotes an increase in the propensity to invest relatively to the propensity to save. If this system is locally stable, then one must have $\Delta > 0$ where Δ is the determinant of the Jacobian. But when we look at the comparative statics consequence of a change in α we find for instance

$$\frac{dy}{d\alpha} = -\frac{L_i G_\alpha}{\Delta}$$

Since on general grounds $L_i < 0$ and since, as we have seen, stability requires $\Delta > 0$, we conclude that $(dy/d\alpha) > 0$ for stable systems. The correspondence principle implies that, indeed, the equilibria we observe are stable. Other models of this kind and other assumptions are discussed. Samuelson is careful to note cases where the principle is insufficient to sign the comparative statics differential.

But as already noted, he gives perhaps insufficient attention to the dependence of the principle on the dynamic formulation. He does show that a difference equation formalisation of the IS-LM dynamisation may lead to different comparative statics prediction than does the differential equation systems [1941, I, Chap. 38, p. 562]. But he draws no moral for the principle itself from this observation. Consistency between a comparative statics proposition and stability of a particular process undoubtedly yields some extra restrictions of a logical kind. But until we have a *true* dynamics or at least an axiomatic dynamics, the predictions are in fact still anyone's guess.

To this must now be added the fact that in large systems of equations the necessary and sufficient conditions for a matrix to have roots with negative real parts do not seem to lead to any comparative-statics results at all.

ENVOI

To write this piece, I reread much of the *Foundations* and a good number of Samuelson's papers. This turned out not only to be an extremely enjoyable undertaking but also a very instructive one. The verve, the intelligence, and the wit provided the enjoyment. The deep insight into the economics of a problem and some of the technical apparatus yielded instruction. In general equilibrium analysis, Samuelson provided one of the most interesting applications (factor-price equalisation) and laid the foundations for one of the most interesting special cases (nonsubstitution theorems). He was responsible for formulating and precisely specifying the (tâtonnement) version of price adjustment that is more or less all we have now. He taught a generation of economists the necessary mathematics for this and related dynamic tasks. If I have expressed reservations about an aspect of Samuelson's methodology or here and there allowed a critical note of this or that construction, it is at least partly to avoid the pitfalls of hagiography into which any student of Samuelson's work is only too apt to fall.

REFERENCES

Arrow, K. J. (1951): "Alternative Proof of the Substitution Theorem for Leontief Models in the General Case" in T. Koopmans, ed.: *Activity Analysis of Production and Allocation*, New York, Wiley.

—— and L. Hurwicz. (1958): "On the Stability of Competitive Equilibrium I," *Econometrica* 26 (Oct.).

——, L. Hurwicz, and H. D. Bloch. (1959): "On the Stability of Competitive Equilibrium II," *Econometrica* 27 (Jan.).

—— and L. Hurwicz. (1960): "Competitive Stability under Weak Gross Substitutability: The 'Euclidean Distance' Approach," *International Economic Review* 1 (Jan.).

—— and L. Hurwicz. (1962): "Competitive Equilibrium under Weak Gross Substitutability: Non-linear Price Adjustment and Adaptive Expectations," *International Economic Review* 3 (May).

Bewley, T. (1977): "The Permanent Income Hypothesis: A Theoretical Formulation," *Journal of Economic Theory* 16 (Dec.).

Debreu, G. (1970): "Economies with a Finite Set of Equilibria," *Econometrica* 38 (May).

——. (1970): "Excess Demand Functions," *Journal of Mathematical Economics* 1.

Dierker, E. (1972): "Two Remarks on the Number of Equilibria of an Economy," *Econometrica* 40 (Sept.).

Dixit, A. K. and V. Norman. (1980): *Theory of International Trade*, Nisbet and Cambridge.

Dorfman, R., P. A. Samuelson, and R. M. Solow. (1958): *Linear Programming and Economic Analysis*, New York, McGraw-Hill.

Gale, D. and H. Nikaido. (1965): "The Jacobian Matrix and Global Univalence of Mappings," *Mathematische Annalen* 159.

Gorman, W. M. (1953): "Community Preference Fields," *Econometrica* 21 (Jan.).

Koopmans, T., ed. (1951): *Activity Analysis of Production and Allocation*, New York, Wiley.

——. (1951): "Alternative Proof of the Substitution Theorem for Leontief Models in the Case of Three Industries," in *Activity Analysis of Production and Allocation*, New York, Wiley.

Lerner, A. P. (1952): "Factor Prices and International Trade," *Economica* 19 (Feb.).

Lucas, R. E. (1977): "Understanding Business Cycles," *Journal of Monetary Economics* 5 (Supplementary Series).

Mantel, R. (1974): "On the Characterization of Aggregate Demand," *Journal of Economic Theory* 7 (Mar.).

Mas-Colell, A. (1975): "On The Equilibrium Price Set of a Pure Exchange Economy," University of California mimeo.

McFadden, D., A. Mas-Colell, R. Mantel, and M. K. Richter. (1974): "A Characterization of Community Excess Demand Functions," *Journal of Economic Theory* 9 (Dec.).

McKenzie, L. (1955): "Equality of Factor Prices in World Trade," *Econometrica* 23 (July).

——. (1967): "The Inversion of Cost Functions: A Counterexample," *International Economic Review* 8 (Oct.).

——. (1967): "Theorem and Counterexample," *International Economic Review* 8 (Oct.).

Meade, J. E. (1968): *The Growing Economy*, Noted to Chapter 3, London, Allen & Unwin.

Milnor, J. W. (1965): *Topology from the Differentiable Viewpoint*, Charlottesville, University Press of Virginia.

Mirrlees, J. (1969): "The Dynamic Non-substitution Theorem," *Review of Economic Studies* 36 (Jan.).

Morishima, M. (1964): *Equilibrium Stability and Growth*, Oxford, Oxford University Press.

——. (1973): *Marx's Economics: A Dual Theory of Value and Growth*, Cambridge, England, Cambridge University Press.

Mosak, J. (1944): *General Equilibrium Theory in International Trade*, Bloomington, Ind., Principia Press.

Nikaido, H. (1972): "Relative Shares and Factor Price Equalization," *Journal of International Economics* 2 (Aug.).

Nishimura, K. (1976): "Factor Price Equalisation," University of Rochester mimeo.

Pearce, I. F. (1967): "More about Factor Price Equalisation," *International Economic Review* 8 (Oct.).

Pearce, I. F. and J. Wise. (1973): "On The Uniqueness of Competitive Equilibrium," *Econometrica* 41 (Sept.).

Samuelson, P. A. (1939): "Interactions between the Multiplier Analysis and the Principle of Acceleration," *Review of Economics and Statistics* 21 (May); *Collected Scientific Papers*, II, Chap. 82.

———. (1941): "The Stability of Equilibrium: Comparative Statics and Dynamics," *Econometrica* 9 (April); *Collected Scientific Papers*, I, Chap. 38.

———. (1942): "The Stability of Equilibrium: Linear and Non-Linear Systems," *Econometrica* 10 (Jan.); *Collected Scientific Papers*, I. Chap. 40.

———. (1944): "The Relation between Hicksian Stability and True Dynamic Stability," *Econometrica* 12 (July-Oct.); *Collected Scientific Papers*, I, Chap. 39.

———. (1945): Review of J. L. Mosak: *General Equilibrium Theory in International Trade*, in *American Economic Review* 35 (Dec.); *Collected Scientific Papers*, II, Chap. 63.

———. (1946–47): "Comparative Statics and the Logic of Economic Maximizing," *Review of Economic Studies* 14 (No. 1); *Collected Scientific Papers*, I, Chap. 6.

———. (1947): *Foundations of Economic Analysis*, Cambridge, Harvard University Press.

———. (1951): "Abstract of a Theorem Concerning Substitutability in Open Leontief Models," in T. C. Koopmans, ed.: *Activity Analysis of Production and Allocation*, New York, Wiley; *Collected Scientific Papers*, I, Chap. 36.

———. (1952): "Spatial Price Equilibrium and Linear Programming," *American Economic Review* 42 (June); *Collected Scientific Papers*, II, Chap. 72.

———. (1953): "Prices of Factors and Goods in General Equilibrium," *Review of Economic Studies* 21(1); *Collected Scientific Papers*, II, Chap. 70.

———.(1955): "Comment on Professor Samuelson on Operationalism in Economic Theory," by Donald F. Gordon, *Quarterly Journal of Economics* 69 (May); *Collected Scientific Papers*, II, Chap. 128.

———, and R. M. Solow (1956): "A Complete Capital Model Involving Heterogeneous Capital Goods," *Quarterly Journal of Economics* 70 (Nov.); *Collected Scientific Papers*, I, Chap. 25.

———. (1958): "An Exact Consumption-Loan Model With or Without the Social Contrivance of Money," *Journal of Political Economy* 66 (Dec.); *Collected Scientific Papers*, I, Chap. 21.

———. (1959): "A Modern Treatment of the Ricardian Economy: I. The Pricing of Goods and Labour and Land Services," *Quarterly Journal of Economics* 73 (Feb.); *Collected Scientific Papers*, I, Chap. 31.

———. (1959): "A Modern Treatment of the Ricardian Economy: II. Capital and Interest Aspects of the Pricing Process," *Quarterly Journal of Economics* 73 (May); *Collected Scientific Papers*, I, Chap. 32.

———. (1961): "A New Theorem on Nonsubstitution," in *Monetary Growth and Methodology* in honour of Johan Åkerman, Lund Social Science Studies, vol. 20 (March); *Collected Scientific Papers*, I, Chap. 37.

———. (1963): "Comment on Ernest Nagel's Assumptions in Economic Theory," *American Economic Review, Papers and Proceedings* 53 (May); *Collected Scientific Papers*, II, Chap. 129.

———. (1965): "Equalization by Trade of the Interest Rate Along with the Real Wage" in

Trade, Growth and the Balance of Payments, essays in honor of Gottfried Haberler, Chicago, Rand McNally; *Collected Scientific Papers*,II, Chap. 71.

———. (1967): "Summary on Factor Price Equalisation," *International Economic Review* 8 (Oct.); *Collected Scientific Papers*, III, Chap. 161.

———. (1971): "Generalised Predator-Prey Oscillations in Ecological and Economic Equilibrium," *Proceedings of the National Academy of Sciences* 68 (May); *Collected Scientific Papers*, III, Chap. 171.

——— and C. C. von Weizsäcker (1971): "A New Labour Theory of Value for Rational Planning Through Use of the Bourgeois Profit Rate," *Proceedings of the National Academy of Sciences* 68 (June); *Collected Scientific Papers*, III, Chap. 155.

———.(1971): "Maximum Principles in Analytical Economics," *Les Prix Nobel in 1970*, Stockholm, The Nobel Foundation; *Collected Scientific Papers*, III, Chap. 130.

Sonnenschein, H. (1973): "Do Walras' Identity and Continuity Characterize the Class of Community Excess Demand Functions?" *Journal of Economic Theory* 6 (Aug.).

Uzawa, H. (1959): "Prices of the Factors of Production in International Trade," *Econometrica* 27 (July).

Varian, H. R. (1975): "A Third Remark on The Number of Equilibria of an Economy," *Econometrica* 43 (Sept.-Nov.).

ON CONSUMPTION THEORY

Hendrik S. Houthakker

Paul Samuelson's earliest publications, written when he had barely entered his twenties, already show the versatility that has characterized his work ever since. Instead of specializing in any branch of economic theory, he has made fundamental contributions to virtually every branch, at the same time staying clear of the hairsplitting to which specialists are prone. One should therefore not read much into the fact that among his writings of the late 1930s consumption theory loomed large. This prominence may have reflected no more than a natural desire to start at the beginning, where the theory of choice is located relative to economics as a whole.

However this may be, Samuelson's first professional publication did deal with consumption. So did the slightly later article that was to become Chapter 1 in his *Collected Scientific Papers*. Thus began a long string of contributions to the subject, among which may be mentioned:

1 the "revealed preference" approach;
2 the Le Chatelier principle;
3 the analysis of spending and saving in relation to the life cycle (1958, I, Ch. 21)[1];
4 the elucidation of Marshall's assumption of a constant marginal utility of income (1942, I, Ch. 5);
5 the theoretical foundation of the Linear Expenditure System (1947–48, I, Ch. 8);
6 a theory of the allocation of expenditures within the household (1956, II, Ch. 78).

Only the first two subjects can be discussed here, not necessarily in historical order.

---

[1] References in this form are to Samuelson's own writings; the *Collected Scientific Papers* are referred to by year of original publication, volume in roman numerals, followed by chapters.

REVEALED PREFERENCE

Although not his first publication, it was an eleven-page paper in *Economica* (1938a, I, Ch. 1) that established Samuelson as a major economic theorist. Clear yet rigorous, original yet scholarly, it reads as well now as when it first caught my fancy shortly after World War II. Its opening sentence puts his contribution firmly in a historical perspective:

> From its very beginning the theory of consumer's choice has marched steadily towards greater generality, sloughing off at successive stages unnecessarily restrictive conditions.

His aim was to determine how far this march could go. Was the replacement of marginal utility by the marginal rate of substitution—as proposed by Hicks and Allen (1934)—the final step? Samuelson did not think so; he detected "vestigial traces of the utility concept" even in that famous pair of papers, and undertook to "start anew in direct attack upon the problem, dropping off the last vestiges of the "utility analysis."[2]

After this introduction the approach was axiomatic. Three postulates were formulated. The first asserted the existence of single-valued demand functions

$$q_i = q_i(p_1, \ldots, p_n, y) \qquad i = 1, \ldots, n \tag{1}$$

such that

$$\sum_{i=1}^{n} p_i q_i = y \tag{2}$$

where the q_i are quantities bought, the p_i prices, and y is money income.[3] The second postulate declared the functions in (1) to be homogeneous of degree zero in prices and income. Both these postulates are standard. Subsequently Samuelson (in an addendum also published in the 1938 volume of *Economica*) showed the first two postulates to be consequences of the third.

This third postulate, which later became known as the "Weak Axiom of Revealed Preference," was the main contribution of this paper. It refers to a consumer who faces two different price-income situations. In situation A his income is y_A and prices are $p_{A1}, \ldots, p_{An}$; in accordance with the (unspecified) functions (1) he buys quantities $q_{A1}, \ldots, q_{An}$. In situation B income is y_B and prices are $p_{B1}, \ldots, p_{Bn}$. If the theory of consumer's choice is to be meaningful (that is, to have empirically verifiable implications) it must impose some restriction on the quantities $q_{B1}, \ldots, q_{Bn}$ bought in situation B. Samuelson assumes the following restriction:

Weak Axiom of Revealed Preference

$$\text{If } \Sigma p_{Ai} q_{Bi} \leqslant \Sigma p_{Ai} q_{Ai} \tag{3a}$$

---

[2] All these quotes are from pp. 62–63 of the 1938a paper. The author was careful—presumably in view of his 1937 paper (I, Ch. 20)—that he did not "preclude the introduction of utility by any who care to do so." His essentially conservative approach to economic theory also led him to assure the reader that his analysis would not "contradict the results attained by the use of related constructs."

[3] This is not the original notation.

$$\text{then } \Sigma p_{Bi} q_{Bi} < \Sigma p_{Bi} q_{Ai} \tag{3b}$$

where all summations are over i from 1 to n.

The inequality (3a) says that in situation A the bundle q_B *could* have been bought since it cost no more, at the prevailing prices p_A, than the bundle q_A that *was* bought.[4] The fact that q_B was not bought when it could have been reveals that the consumer preferred q_A to q_B, hence the (later) term "revealed preference."[5] The first inequality in the Weak Axiom therefore says that q_A is revealed to be preferred to q_B.

If the other inequality (3b) were false (that is, if $\Sigma p_{Bi} q_{Ai} \le \Sigma p_{Bi} q_{Bi}$) then q_B would be revealed to be preferred to q_A, contradicting the interpretation given to (3a). Thus the Weak Axiom postulates consistency (more precisely, irreversibility) in the relation of revealed preference.[6]

After laying the axiomatic foundations Samuelson proceeded without further ado to the derivation of their observable implication. To begin with, if we put $\Delta q_i = q_{Bi} - q_{Ai}$, and drop the subscript A, then the Weak Axiom implies that

$$\text{if } \Sigma p_i \, \Delta q_i = 0 \text{ (not all } \Delta q_i = 0) \tag{4a}$$

$$\text{then } \Sigma \Delta p_i \, \Delta q_i \le 0 \tag{4b}$$

a generalized version of Marshall's Law of Demand that had earlier been derived by Georgescu-Roegen (1936) from utility theory. This in turn can be translated into various inequalities involving differentials of prices and quantities. Another implication of the Weak Axiom is that if the Laspeyres index equals one, then the Paasche index must be less than one.

Thus Samuelson fulfilled his promise of demonstrating that most of the general theorems on consumer's choice followed from his postulate(s) without even invoking the concept of utility. The main exception, as he recognized, was the Slutsky equation

$$\frac{\partial q_i}{\partial p_j} + q_j \frac{\partial q_i}{\partial y} = \frac{\partial q_j}{\partial p_i} + q_i \frac{\partial q_j}{\partial y} \tag{5}$$

which is equivalent to the integrability of the system of demand functions (1). His brief remarks on this subject (1938, I, Ch. 1, p. 10) are hard to reconcile with the

---

[4]It is tacitly assumed that the bundles q_A and q_B are not identical.

[5]Apparently this term was first used in the *Foundations of Economic Analysis* (1947, pp. 151–152.)

[6]The Weak Axiom was originally formulated by Abraham Wald (1936) in his analysis of general equilibrium. However, Wald applied it to market demand rather than to a single individual. As Samuelson showed in a companion paper in *Econometrica* (1938b, Ch. 3), the Weak Axiom does not in general hold for market demand. Neither of the two 1938 papers refers to Wald; in view of Samuelson's habitual scrupulousness—indeed, generosity—in referring to precursors, it must be assumed that at the time he was not conscious of Wald's contribution. He did discuss Wald's use of the Weak Axiom in a much later article (1955, Ch. 34).

overall thrust of the *Economica* paper[7] and represent one of the few blemishes in an otherwise masterly performance. Later developments make it clear that these confusing remarks did not express his considered opinion.

Before discussing the subsequent history a few comments on the Weak Axiom may be in order. Its significance in capturing the essence of the theory of choice is evident from its equivalence, in a slightly generalized form, to a seemingly quite different basic proposition concerning rational behavior, namely the Independence of Irrelevant Alternatives (Arrow, 1951).[8] But that leaves us in the realm of pure theory. What is the empirical importance of the Weak Axiom? That question is not fully answered in the *Econometrica* paper (1938b, I, Ch. 3), despite its title. Suppose, then, that the purchasing history of a consumer contradicts the Weak Axiom. Does this mean that economic theory belongs in the trash can? Hardly; all it means is that the consumer has changed his mind, or more exactly, his preference ordering. The Weak Axiom in fact, is a test for the invariance of preferences, and has been used as such by Koo (1963). Houthakker (1963), and others. Its usefulness for this purpose stems from its nonparametric nature: there is no need to specify the demand functions. Tests for invariance that do postulate particular demand function may appear more powerful, but they are subject to misspecification and therefore tend to beg the question.

The immediate impact of Samuelson's two 1938 papers on the study of consumption was minimal, but the appearance of the *Foundations of Economic Analysis* in 1947 served to focus interest on the subject. There Samuelson raised the problem whether, by repeated application of the Weak Axiom, one could reconstruct an individual's preference ordering by observing purchases in different price-income situations. His tentative conclusion was that this could not be done and that a "zone of darkness" would remain.

It did not take long for Little (1949) to show that, at least in the case of two commodities, the zone of darkness could be shrunk to a smooth curve that is indistinguishable from the traditional indifference curve. However, the points on this pseudo-indifference curve are not necessarily indifferent to each other, since there is no such thing as "revealed indifference." Little's insightful analysis was confirmed and restated by Samuelson (1948, I, Ch. 9).[9]

After Little's contribution, the principal unsolved problem facing the revealed

---

[7] Specifically he said that (5) "makes [integrability] doubtful and subject to refutation. . . ." (I, Ch. 1, p. 10). Yet the early parts of this article suggest that its main purpose was to obtain refutable propositions, so why suddenly balk at this one? There also appears to be a veiled slap at Henry Schultz ("I have little faith in any attempts to verify [the Slutsky equation] statistically [p. 10].") Schultz reported such an attempt in his *Theory & Measurement of Demand* (1938), a landmark in the early history of econometrics. Samuelson (possibly reflecting the views of his early mentor, Jacob Viner) once told me that Schultz was not taken very seriously at the University of Chicago, where he taught until his accidental death in 1938. The only reason for bringing this up is that is may explain a certain lack of interest in econometric research on Samuelson's part.

[8] For a proof of this equivalence, see Houthakker (1965). It is interesting to note that all three authors involved were much influenced by modern logic, especially the logic of relations. Samuelson participated in W.V.O. Quine's seminar at Harvard, Arrow while still in his teens assisted Alfred Tarski, and I took several courses with the late E. W. Beth at the University of Amsterdam.

[9] The publication dates of these two articles do not reflect the order in which they were written.

preference approach was the ancient question of integrability. In the prevailing context it amounted to asking under what conditions (if any) a consumer of three or more commodities would reveal his preferences if there were enough observations on his purchases. The two-good case considered by Little was too special to shed much light on this point, but his success in treating it was encouraging.

Although usually viewed as a strictly mathematical problem, integrability (it transpired) could be more usefully investigated by means of the logic of relations.[10] Revealed preference, like "ordinary" preference, belongs to the class of (strong) ordering relations. This class has two defining characteristics: any relation R belonging to it must be irreflexive (that is, aRb excludes bRa) and transitive (aRb and bRc imply aRc). The irreflexivity of revealed preference, as defined by (3), is asserted by the Weak Axiom.

However, the transitivity of revealed preference according to this definition would be equivalent to the algebraic proposition

$$\text{if } \Sigma\, p_{Ai}q_{Bi} \leqslant \Sigma\, p_{Ai}q_{Ai} \text{ and } \Sigma\, p_{Bi}q_{Ci} \leqslant \Sigma\, p_{Bi}q_{Bi}, \qquad (6)$$
$$\text{then } \Sigma\, p_{Ai}q_{Ci} \leqslant \Sigma\, p_{Ai}q_{Ai}$$

whose truth is not obvious even if the Weak Axiom holds for each of the three comparisons in (6). After all attempts to derive (6) from the Weak Axiom had failed, it became apparent that the definition of revealed preference had to be extended.

Let us rename the original concept, defined by (3), "explicitly revealed preference," and let us define the new concept of "implicitly revealed preference" by

q_A is implicitly revealed to be preferred to q_B if there are price vectors $p_A, p_C, \ldots,$
$$p_Y, p_Z \text{ such that} \qquad (7)$$
$$p_A q_C \leqslant p_A q_A$$
$$p_C q_D \leqslant p_C q_C$$
$$p_Y q_Z \leqslant p_Y q_Y$$
$$p_Z q_B \leqslant p_Z q_Z$$

where the number of vectors $p_C, p_D, \ldots, p_Z$ is arbitrary (including zero, in which case there is explicitly revealed preference). Since the Weak Axiom refers to explicitly rather than implicitly revealed preference, the question now is whether implicitly revealed preference is also irreflexive, as a strong ordering relation should be. After a protracted search a counterexample was found, demonstrating that the Weak Axiom was not sufficient to make implicitly revealed preference irreflexive. One such counterexample[11] is the following

---

[10]The following account, while historical in its essentials, has been simplified by using a certain amount of hindsight.

[11]Due to Sir John Hicks, who presented it in an unpublished (1951) lecture incorporated in his *Revision of Demand Theory* (Hicks, 1956). The original counterexample, derived in the summer of 1949 and referred to in Houthakker (1950), is lost. It is unfortunate that neither of these counterexamples was immediately published, for they might have prevented several futile efforts to prove that the Weak and Strong Axioms are equivalent.

$$p_A = \begin{bmatrix} 1 \\ 1 \\ 2 \end{bmatrix} \quad q_A = \begin{bmatrix} 5 \\ 19 \\ 9 \end{bmatrix} \quad p_B = \begin{bmatrix} 1 \\ 1 \\ 1 \end{bmatrix} \quad q_B = \begin{bmatrix} 12 \\ 12 \\ 12 \end{bmatrix} \quad p_C = \begin{bmatrix} 1 \\ 2 \\ 1 \end{bmatrix} \quad q_C = \begin{bmatrix} 27 \\ 11 \\ 1 \end{bmatrix}$$

to which corresponds a matrix of value sums

$$\begin{bmatrix} p_A'q_A & p_A'q_B & p_A'q_C \\ p_B'q_A & p_B'q_B & p_B'q_C \\ p_C'q_A & p_C'q_B & p_C'q_C \end{bmatrix} = \begin{bmatrix} 42 & 48 & 40 \\ 33 & 36 & 39 \\ 52 & 38 & 50 \end{bmatrix}$$

From the first two elements in the second row we see that q_B is (explicitly) revealed to be preferred to q_A, and the corresponding elements in the first row do not contradict this (that is, q_A and q_B satisfy the Weak Axiom). Similarly q_C is revealed to be preferred to q_B, and again the Weak Axiom holds. Consequently, q_C is implicitly revealed to be preferred to q_A. But the first and last element of the first row show that q_A is explicitly revealed to be preferred to q_C, with the corresponding elements in the third row satisfying the Weak Axiom. Consequently, revealed preference is not irreflexive.

To overcome this difficulty another axiom is needed. It reads, *in extenso*: *Strong Axiom of Revealed Preference*:

If $\Sigma p_A q_B \leqq \Sigma p_A q_A$, and $\Sigma p_B q_C \leqq \Sigma p_B q_B$, and . . . $\Sigma p_Y q_Z \leqq \Sigma p_Y q_Y$ then $\Sigma p_Z q_A > \Sigma p_Z q_Z$

In words, the last element in a chain of commodity bundles, each of which is (explicitly) revealed to be preferred to its successor in the chain, cannot be explicitly revealed to be preferred to the first element.[12] In combination with suitable continuity assumptions the Strong Axiom permits the reconstruction of a consumer's (ordinary) preference ordering regardless of the number of commodities, thus generalizing the result obtained by Little (1949) and Samuelson (1948, I, Ch. 9).

In his comprehensive commentary on these developments Samuelson (1950, I, Ch. 10) started out by declaring that "[a] chapter in the history of utility theory has now been brought to a close . . ." Maybe so, but after 1950 much more was written about the foundations of consumption theory than before. The main reason for this increased interest was insufficient attention to mathematical subtleties in the initial stages of revealed preference theory. Samuelson and his early followers focused on the economic logic of the subject and tended to be cavalier about continuity assumptions and the like. Once the principal propositions concerning revealed preference had been discovered it was natural and proper to worry about mathematical rigor. The efforts along these lines culminated in a book by Chipman and others (1971). It is neither possible nor necessary to report on these efforts, in

---

[12]This formulation was proposed by Houthakker (1950) independently of a rather similar axiom formulated by Ville (1946), though not in the context of revealed preference.

which Samuelson did not participate. Suffice it to say that the early achievements discussed above appear to have survived the later scrutiny without damage, and indeed to have been more firmly established.

A final word about the significance of the revealed preference approach. Did it succeed in "develop[ing] the theory of consumer's behavior *freed from any vestigial traces of the utility concept*," to quote the closing paragraph of Samuelson (1938a, I, Ch. 1, italics added)? Or did something happen on the way? One is tempted to conclude that something did happen, for in 1950 Samuelson restated "the program begun a dozen years ago" as one of "arriving at the full empirical implications for demand behavior of the most *general ordinal utility analysis*" (I, Ch. 10, p. 89, italics partly suppressed). The stone the builder rejected in 1938 seemed to have become a cornerstone in 1950.

Actually these programmatic statements should not be read too literally. Other, less quotable statements in the same writings suggest a better interpretation of the revealed preference approach. Its real aim was to find necessary and sufficient conditions describing the choices made by a consumer endowed with a preference ordering. Before the introduction of the ordinal utility concept, for instance, the consumer was assumed to maximize his or her cardinal utility function. It was discovered by Irving Fisher and Pareto that the cardinality of utility cannot be demonstrated from market behavior under certainty. Hence cardinality is not a necessary condition for such behavior. On the other hand, Gustav Cassel wanted to do away with assumptions about utility altogether. This is not sufficient to account for such phenomena as the Law of Demand. During the 1930s the question of necessity and sufficiency was again raised by the reliance of Hicks and Allen (1934) on the "marginal rate of substitution." Allen, in particular, presented this concept rather than the ordinal preference ordering as the foundation of consumer's choice. The existence of a preference ordering implies the existence of marginal rates of substitution, but not the other way around; is the weaker assumption sufficient to lead to the usual properties of demand function?

It is questions like these that the revealed preference approach was designed to answer, and on the whole did answer. More specifically, the necessary and sufficient conditions relevant to static consumer behavior under certainty are now well known. Compared to this achievement, animadversions about utility are of secondary importance.[13] On the other hand it is disappointing that the revealed preference theory has not been extended to problems beyond the narrow classical framework. For instance, it would be interesting to apply it to dynamic models with habit formation and/or inventory adjustment. Now that the mathematical aspects of revealed preference have been thoroughly explored, we may perhaps look forward to a revival involving more realistic descriptions of consumer behavior.

---

[13]Debreu (1954) clarified the connection between preference orderings and utility functions, and incidentally showed the primary importance of the former. Previously there had been a confusing tendency—as in the title of Houthakker (1950)—to use the two concepts interchangeably. The combined effect of the revealed preference approach and Debreu's work was to downgrade the indifference concept. There is no such thing as "revealed indifference," and consequently a preference ordering revealed by purchasing decisions may not admit a utility function.

THE LE CHATELIER PRINCIPLE

Of Samuelson's many contributions to the theory of the consumer, the only other one that can be discussed here was described by him as the generalized Le Chatelier principle. First stated in the *Foundations of Economic Analysis* (1947, pp. 36–46),[14] it applies to maximizing behavior in general, not just to demand. However, its most important applications are probably in the field of consumption.

Henri Le Chatelier (1850–1936) was a French scientist who in the context of chemical equilibrium formulated certain inequalities concerning the interrelations of changes in volume, in pressure, and in temperature. It is indicative of Samuelson's wide and deep acquaintance with the natural sciences that he was able to see the relevance of this seemingly foreign idea to economic theory. At the same time he thus illustrated his belief[15] that progress in one discipline often consists of borrowing ideas from other disciplines, but that such borrowing should rely on a common mathematical or logical background rather than on superficial analogy.[16]

To understand the Le Chatelier principle there is no need to go back to its chemical origins; instead I shall restate it in the context of consumption theory. Suppose a consumer maximizes a utility function for three commodities $\phi\,(q_1, q_2, q_3)$ subject to a budget constraint.

$$p_1q_1 + p_2q_2 + p_3q_3 = y \tag{1}$$

According to the fundamental theorem of consumption theory we then have

$$\frac{\partial q_1}{\partial p_1} + q_1\,\frac{\partial q_1}{\partial y} < 0 \tag{2}$$

Now suppose that in addition to the budget constraint there is an additional constraint

$$r_1q_1 + r_2q_2 + r_3q_3 = z \tag{3}$$

where the r_i are not proportional to the p_i. What effect will the imposition of (3) have on the compensated own-price effect (2)? The answer turns out to be unambiguous: (2) cannot be smaller (that is, larger in absolute value) when (3) holds than when it does not hold; explicitly

$$0 > \left[\frac{\partial q_1}{\partial p_1} + q_1\,\frac{\partial q_1}{\partial y}\right]_{\Sigma r_i q_i = z} \geqq \frac{\partial q_1}{\partial p_1} + q_1\,\frac{\partial q_1}{\partial y} \tag{4}$$

---

[14]Some errors in the original derivation were corrected in later printings.

[15]Expressed orally; I have not found any written reference.

[16]Actually a close but purely mathematical parallel to the Le Chatelier principle is proved by Courant and Hilbert (1957, Vol. 1, pp. 31–34; the German original was published in 1931) as the "minimum-maximum property" of the eigenvalues of a symmetric matrix. Courant and Hilbert do not refer to Le Chatelier or to anybody else (suggesting that the property was either "well-known" or original with them), nor does Samuelson refer to Courant and Hilbert. In fact the discussion of eigenvalues in Mathematical Appendix A of the *Foundations* stops just short of deriving the minimum-maximum property.

Before considering why this inequality is true, it is of interest to push the principle one step further by imposing yet another constraint, supposed to be independent of (1) and (3):

$$s_1q_1 + s_2q_2 + s_3q_3 = t \tag{5}$$

The three linear equations (1), (3), and (5) then determine the three unknowns q_1, q_2, and q_3, so there is nothing left to maximize. Consequently

$$\left[\frac{\partial q_1}{\partial p_1} + q_1 \frac{\partial q_1}{\partial y}\right]_{\Sigma r_i q_i = z,\ \Sigma s_i q_i = t} = 0 \tag{6}$$

and the LHS of (6) is evidently larger than its counterpart in (4). The generalization to any number of goods is obvious: the more constraints there are, the smaller in absolute value is each compensated own-price derivative (except for occasional instances of equality) until these derivatives reach zero, when there are as many constraints as commodities.

The basic inequality (4) can be proved by a straightforward application of Jacobi's theorem on determinantal minors, which need not be repeated here.[17] What should be noted, however, is the strictly infinitesimal nature of the Le Chatelier principle; the derivatives in (4) cannot in general be replaced by finite differences, such as appear naturally in revealed preference theory. The principle does not hold "in the large."

For a more intuitive demonstration of the principle it may first be pointed out that in practice the additional constraints (3) or (5) often involve only one commodity, so that (3) can, for instance, be written

$$q_2 = z_2 \tag{7}$$

This means that the second good is "rationed" at a level z_2; moreover, it will be assumed that the ration z_2 is equal to the q_2 that would be bought in the absence of rationing. Now suppose that p_1 is increased with a compensating increase in y. Two cases can be distinguished, corresponding to either substitution or complementarity between goods 1 and 2. If 1 and 2 are substitutes[18] an increase in p_1 would, in the absence of rationing, lead the consumer to substitute some of 2 for 1, but that is not possible under rationing, so the decrease in q_1 will be smaller (in absolute value) when (7) holds. If, on the other hand, 1 and 2 are complements, q_2 would be reduced in the absence of rationing and if this is not possible, q_1 will also be decreased by a smaller absolute amount than in the free market. This reasoning suggests that the equality sign in (4) holds only if goods 1 and 2 are neither substitutes nor complements. The main weakness of this intuitive argument is that it may suggest that the Le Chatelier principle holds in the large, which is not the case; in fact the

---

[17] See *Foundations*, p. 38. The same technique was later used by Tobin & Houthakker (1951) to derive various other theorems on rationing.

[18] Substitution and complementarity are defined according to Hicks and Allen (1934).

classification of pairs of goods into substitutes and complements does not hold in the large either.

The most immediate application of the Le Chatelier principle in the area of consumption was to rationing, a matter of considerable policy interest in the 1940s and early 1950s (especially in the United Kingdom) but fortunately not in recent years. The literature on this topic, which also was discussed at some length in the *Foundations* (pp. 163–171), was surveyed by Tobin (1952). It is fair to say that propositions such as (4) are of less practical importance in the analysis of rationing than the method used to derive them, which yields many more useful results.

Nevertheless the Le Chatelier principle is of fundamental importance in optimization theory because it gives precision to the Marshallian distinction between the short run and the long run. This distinction, cited as Samuelson's motivation for the introduction of the principle (*Foundations*, pp. 36–38), is now seen to involve the set of constraints under which a household or firm operates: There are more constraints in the short run than in the long run. In the theory of the firm this distinction has long been prominent, but its application to the consumer is more recent. As econometric demand studies accumulated in the 1940s and 1950s, serial correlation in the residuals (usually positive) turned out to be widespread in the static models that were standard at the time. It also became clear that this was not a merely statistical problem but reflected features of consumer behavior that could not be captured by static demand equations. Various attempts at a dynamic formulation, particularly by Stone and Rowe (1957, 1958) and Nerlove (1960), led to a stock-adjustment model for durable goods. This model was extended to nondurable goods in Houthakker and Taylor (1966), making the distinction between the short run and the long run central to demand analysis.[19] In accordance with the Le Chatelier principle, compensated own-price elasticities for nondurable goods are smaller in absolute value in the short run than in the long run. The opposite is true for durable goods, whence the absence of well-developed second-hand markets changes the time pattern of the constraints.

CONCLUSION

The two examples discussed here do not adequately cover the wide range of Samuelson's contributions to consumption theory; they were selected merely because they had the strongest influence on my own research. Going beyond those specific contributions, let me finish by acknowledging my more general debt to Paul Samuelson for his wisdom, erudition, stimulation, criticism, and (not least) friendship over many years.

REFERENCES

Arrow, Kenneth (1951): *Social Choice and Individual Values*, New York, Wiley.
Chipman, John S., L. Hurwicz, M. K. Richter and H. F. Sonnenschein (1971): *Preferences Utility and Demand*, New York, Harcourt, Brace, Jovanovich.

---

[19]The underlying theory is not fully stated in that book; an abstract (Houthakker, 1962) is currently being expanded for publication.

Courant, Richard and D. Hilbert (1957): *Methods of Mathematical Physics*, New York, Wiley Interscience.

Debreu, Gerard (1954): "Numerical Representations of Technological Change," *Metroeconomica* 6 (Aug.).

Georgescu-Roegen, Nicholas (1936): "The Pure Theory of Consumer's Behavior," *Quarterly Journal of Economics* 50 (Aug.).

Hicks, John R. and R. G. D. Allen (1934) "A Reconsideration of the Theory of Value, Pt. I-II," *Economica* N.S.1 (Feb, May).

Hicks, John R. (1956): *A Revision of Demand Theory*, London, Oxford University Press.

Houthakker, Hendrik S. (1950): "Revealed Preference and the Utility Function," *Economica* N.S.17 (May).

——— (1962): "On a Class of Dynamic Demand Functions," *Econometrica* 30 (No. 3).

——— (1963): "Some Problems in the International Comparison of Consumption Patterns," *Les Besoins de Biens de Consommation*, Colloques Internationaux du Centre National de la Recherche Scientifique, (Grenoble, Sept. 1961) Paris.

——— (1965) "On the Logic of Preference and Choice," in Tymieniecka, A-T. & C. Parsons (eds.): *Contributions to Logic and Methodology in Honor of J. M. Bochénski*, Amsterdam, North-Holland.

——— and Lester Taylor (1966, 1970): *Consumer Demand in the United States*, Cambridge, Harvard University Press.

Koo, Anthony Ying Chang (1963): "An Empirical Test of Revealed Preference Theory," *Econometrica* 31 (Oct.).

Little, Ian Malcolm David (1949): "A Reformulation of the Theory of Consumer's Behavior," *Oxford Economic Papers* N.S.1 (Jan.).

Nerlove, Marc L. (1960): "The Market Demand for Durable Goods: A Comment," *Econometrica* 28 (No. 1).

Samuelson, Paul A. (1937): "A Note on Measurement of Utility," *Review of Economic Studies* IV (Feb.); *Collected Scientific Papers*, I, Ch. 20.

——— (1938a): "A Note on the Pure Theory of Consumer's Behaviour: An Addendum," *Economica* V (Aug.); *Collected Scientific Papers*, I, Ch. 1.

——— (1938b): "The Empirical Implications of Utility Analysis, *Econometrica* 6 (Oct.); *Collected Scientific Papers*, I, Ch. 3.

——— (1942): "Constancy of the Marginal Utility of Income," in Lange *et al*, (eds.) *Studies in Mathematical Economics and Econometrics in Memory of Henry Schultz*, Chicago: University of Chicago Press; *Collected Scientific Papers*, I, Ch. 5.

——— (1947–48): "Some Implications of 'Linearity'," *Review of Economic Studies* XV(2), No. 38; *Collected Scientific Papers*, I, Ch. 8.

——— (1948): "Consumption Theory in Terms of Revealed Preference," *Economica* XV (Nov.); *Collected Scientific Papers*, I, Ch. 9.

——— (1950): "The Problem of Integrability in Utility Theory," *Economica* XVII (Nov.); *Collected Scientific Papers*, I, Ch. 10.

——— (1956): "Social Indifference Curves," *Quarterly Journal of Economics* LXX (Feb.); *Collected Scientific Papers*, II, Ch. 78.

——— (1958): "An Exact Consumption-Loan Model of Interest with or without the Social Contrivance of Money," *Journal of Political Economy* LXVI (Dec.); *Collected Scientific Papers*, I, Ch. 21.

Schultz, Henry (1938): *The Theory and Measurement of Demand*, Chicago, University of Chicago Press, Social Science Studies.

Stone, Richard and D. A. Rowe (1957): "The Market Demand for Durable Goods," *Econometrica* 25 (July).

────── and D. A. Rowe (1958): "Dynamic Demand Functions: Some Econometric Results," *Economic Journal* 68 (June).

Tobin, James and H. S. Houthakker (1951): "The Effects of Rationing on Demand Elasticities," *Review of Economic Studies* 18 (No. 3).

────── (1952): "A Survey of the Theory of Rationing," *Econometrica* 20 (Oct.).

Ville, Jean (1946): "Sur les conditions d'existence d'une ophelimité totale et d'un indice du niveau des prix," *Annales de l'Université de Lyon*, Vol. 9, Sec. A(3); English translation by P. K. Newman, (1951–52): "The Existence Conditions of a Total Utility Function," *Review of Economic Studies* 19.

Wald, Abraham (1936): "Uber einige Gleichungssysteme der mathematischen Okonomie," *Zeitschrift fur Nationalokonomie* 7 (No. 5); English translation by Otto Eckstein (1951): "On Some Systems of Equations of Mathematical Economics," *Econometrica* 19 (Oct.).

INTERNATIONAL
TRADE THEORY

Ronald W. Jones*

"Historically the development of economic theory owes much to the theory of international trade." This, the opening sentence of Paul Samuelson's first article on trade theory in 1938, [81], serves autobiographically to forecast the impact of much of the new work on trade theory that he can rightfully claim in the succeeding forty-two years. And, of course, it is a two-way street; the theory of international trade has benefited significantly from developments in general theory—many of them thrusting Samuelson in joint roles as author and messenger.

If this volume attempts to cut the man to fit ten separate strips of cloth, I think trade theorists would claim that the relative imprint that Samuelson has made on the fabric of the theory of international trade may, in the best traditions of David Ricardo's theory of comparative advantage, be judged the most indelible. With his deep care for developments in modern welfare economics, Samuelson might eschew such interfield comparisons, but those of us on the ground in trade theory find it difficult to discover areas of research in which his insights and basic theorems have not illuminated the way.

In the matrix of economic knowledge the field of international trade represents only one row, but it has many columns. In surveying Samuelson's contributions in this area I have been forced by limitations of space to aggregate into five categories: (1) the gains from international trade, (2) the transfer problem, (3) the Ricardian model of trade, (4) the Heckscher-Ohlin theory, and (5) the sector-specific (or Ricardo-Viner) model of trade. This ordering serves to highlight Samuelson's

*I am indebted to the National Science Foundation for research support in Grant No. SES-7806 59 and, for useful conversations, to Steve Easton, Ron Findlay, Peter Neary, Kalyan Sanyal, Michael Schmid, and Makoto Yano.

interest in basic models of trading communities and, as well, allows us to begin at the beginning.

1 THE GAINS FROM TRADE

Samuelson's first two articles in the trade area, [81] and [82], concern the welfare propositions it is possible to prove about the status of a free-trade equilibrium. For the world as a whole he stresses that free trade represents only one point on a locus of distributions that is optimal in the (Paretian) sense that no country could be made better off without forcing at least one other country to worsen its situation. However, his principal focus is on the properties of the free-trade position from the viewpoint of an individual country. In particular, two explicit questions are raised: (1) Is free trade superior to autarky? and (2) Does free trade represent the optimal position for an individual country?

The second question is easier to handle. If a country can monopolistically affect the prices of what it buys and sells on world markets, free trade would not represent the optimal policy. Instead,

> The monopolistic country will move the other along its offer curve up to a point of tangency of that locus with the monopolist's indifference curve [81, p. 266].

This passing footnote remark on the geometric depiction of the optimal tariff picks up the older Mill-Bickerdike-Edgeworth arguments but casts them in modern dress two years before Kaldor's famous article [40] setting out the geometry explicitly.

In the 1938 article Samuelson deals somewhat casually with the argument that free trade is superior to autarky:

> The very fact that any trade takes place is an indication that both individuals are better off, since each can at the very worst refuse to trade [81, p. 265].

But the 1939 article lays out the argument in a form almost universally adopted by later writers in this area. He first establishes the consequences of maximizing competitive behavior within an economy in which production exhibits constant returns to scale and in which factor supplies may respond to changes in factor prices.[1] For any set of commodity prices (and a corresponding consistent set of factor prices), the quantities of commodities produced (and factor services provided) maximize the difference between the value of output and total factor cost, compared with any other feasible set of outputs and inputs. Thus if the vectors x' of production and a' of factor services correspond to the price vector (p', w') for commodities and factors,

$$p' \cdot x' - w' \cdot a' \geqslant p' \cdot \bar{x} - w' \cdot a \qquad (1)$$

for any feasible $(\bar{x}, a)$ satisfying the technological constraints. This condition, of course, reflects and imposes the usual curvature properties of the technology.

---

[1]Samuelson was careful to base his argument on very broad assumptions as to the nature of factor supplies so as to avoid the real-cost, opportunity-cost dispute between Viner and Haberler. See his opening remarks in [97, p. 820].

The argument then proceeds upon the assumption that the community consists of individuals with identical tastes and ownership of productive factors. He neatly sidesteps the question of determining equilibrium world commodity prices by adopting what is now known as the "small country" assumption, namely that the country faces a fixed set of world prices. Let p' represent these world prices, with corresponding vectors of outputs supplied, x', consumption demands, $\bar{x}'$, factor supplies, a', and factor prices, w'. These will generally be different from those prevailing in a state of autarky: p^o, a^o, w^o, x^o, and $\bar{x}^o$. In autarky consumption and production balance item by item so that x^o equals $\bar{x}^o$. Trade allows the composition of consumption to differ from that of production but imposes a balance of trade constraint on aggregate values:

$$p' \cdot x' = p' \cdot \bar{x}' \tag{2}$$

Inequality (1) is now used to compare $(\bar{x}', a')$ with a particular output, factor supply combination—that prevailing in autarky. Thus:

$$p' \cdot x' - w' \cdot a' \geqq p' \cdot x^o - w' \cdot a^o \tag{3}$$

The vector of autarky production, x^o, can be replaced by autarky consumption, $\bar{x}^o$, while the value of trade output, $p'x'$, can, by (2), be replaced by the value of trade consumption. These alterations in (3) lead to:

$$p' \cdot \bar{x}' - w' \cdot a' \geqq p' \cdot \bar{x}^o - w' \cdot a^o \tag{4}$$

At this stage of the argument Samuelson applies to this problem the reasoning underlying his new theory of revealed preference, as expounded in [80]: The inequality in (4) shows that at trade prices the cost of the original autarky bundle is less than that of the bundle actually chosen with trade. Therefore each of the community's identical individuals reveals a preference for the bundle actually chosen, $(\bar{x}', a')$. Trade is revealed to be preferred to a state of autarky.

Does this argument establish that every individual is made better off (or at least not worse off) by trade? Yes, in the special case in which all individuals are identical in every respect. But Samuelson obviously could not and did not stop there. If individuals differ, some may be made worse off by the change in market prices involved in going from autarky to trade. It would still be possible to rank the two regimes if a social preference ordering were imposed. Instead, Samuelson asks the question: *Could* all individuals be made better off by some scheme of redistribution? In the 1939 article Samuelson argues that such a redistribution scheme is possible,[2] but the details awaited his later 1962 paper [97] and the application to this problem of utility possibility curves as developed in his basic 1950 paper on the "Evaluation of Real National Income" [87] and further extended in his piece on social indifference curves in 1956 [93].

---

[2]A redistribution scheme is outlined in the Caves and Jones textbook [4, Chap. 2]. In the autarky situation some internal trade takes place. Redistribute ownership patterns locally so that at autarky prices internal trade vanishes, with no individual's real income affected at those prices. With trade, everyone gains.

Any bundle of commodities available to a community may be distributed in a number of different ways. Each distribution yields a measure of each individual's utility, u^i. For any prescribed level of utility for all but one individual, there will generally be some unique allocation of the fixed bundle of goods that maximizes utility for the remaining individual. These maximum positions would correspond to allocations along the contract curve of a consumption box-diagram whose dimensions reflect the fixed totals of commodities. Suppose the economy consists of two individuals with different taste patterns. Then any prescribed totals for commodities (for example, the autarky levels) support a *point* utility-possibility frontier in $u^1 - u^2$ space. This locus will generally be downward sloping, but with arbitrary curvature since utility is not assumed to be cardinal (so that the axes can be stretched).

In making welfare comparisons, it is more relevant to examine the *situation* utility-possibility curve corresponding not to a particular bundle of goods, but to the locus of commodities available for consumption in any given situation. For example, points along the transformation curve represent all the consumption choices for an economy closed to trade. Each such choice supports a point utility-possibility frontier for individuals 1 and 2; the situation utility-possibility frontier for autarky represents the outer envelope of all these point frontiers. In his 1962 article Samuelson re-examines his earlier work on the gains from trade. He considers both the small-country case dealt with in his 1939 article and the case of a country large enough to influence world prices of traded commodities.

For the small-country case, free trade allows consumption choices anywhere along line *EUF* in Figure 1.[3] Autarky, by contrast, restricts consumption to the

---

[3]This diagram reproduces Figure 1 of the 1962 article [97, p. 821].

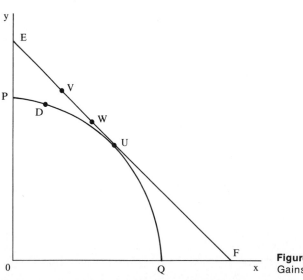

Figure 1
Gains from trade.

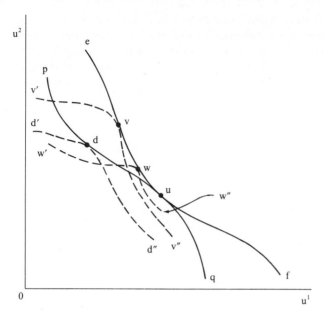

Figure 2
Utility possibility frontier.

transformation curve, PUQ. The corresponding situation utility-possibility curves are illustrated in Figure 2 by euf for trade, and puq for autarky. In Figure 1 points D and W represent two possible autarky and free-trade aggregate consumption points, respectively. The point utility-possibility frontiers for these two aggregates are shown by $d'd''$ and $w'w''$ in Figure 2. Suppose the actual distribution of utilities is given by point d in autarky and point w in free trade. The curve $d'd''$ runs southwest of point w, revealing that the autarky commodity totals shown by D could not be reallocated to yield the utility combination shown by w (corresponding to free trade). But as drawn in Figure 2, the $w'w$ locus runs southwest of point d. This implies that the consumption basket after trade (point W in Figure 1) could not be used to attain the utility bundle (d) corresponding to autarky. But this does not matter. The relevant comparison is between the autarky and free-trade situation utility-possibility frontiers. If the autarky distribution of income is shown by d in Figure 2, free trade would allow both individuals' utilities to rise, say, to point v. The existence of points such as V in Figure 1 northeast of autarky choices such as D implies that the free-trade utility-possibility curve is superior to that available in autarky. Lump-sum redistributions of income can make everyone better off with trade than under autarky.[4]

The argument for the potential superiority of free trade in the large-country case follows similar lines. Samuelson adapted a graphical device due to Baldwin [1] whereby the origin of the foreign country's offer curve can be placed at successive

---

[4]As Samuelson points out, the autarky and free-trade loci may (or may not) be tangent as shown at u in Figure 2. Note that the $v'v''$ contour in Figure 2 dominates the $d'd''$ locus. This seems appropriate if V lies northeast of D in Figure 1, but it was contradicted in Samuelson's Figure 4 in the 1962 article [97, p. 824].

points on the home country's transformation schedule. The outer envelope of points on the foreign offer curve as it slides along the transformation curve—the Baldwin envelope—shows the consumption possibilities frontier with trade. It would not be linear as is the *EUF* locus of Figure 1. Since the large country exerts influence on world prices, the Baldwin envelope will be tangent to the transformation schedule at a point such as *U* (Figure 1) and bend in towards the axes to hit between *E* and *P* on the vertical axis (and between *Q* and *F* on the horizontal axis). To achieve a point on this frontier, the home country would have to impose an optimal tariff; the free-trade locus of consumption possibilities (not drawn by Samuelson) would lie between the Baldwin envelope and the transformation schedule. In any event, the kind of argument used in the small-country case applies either to optimally restricted trade or free trade in the large-country case. The situation utility-possibility frontier for optimally restricted trade or free trade lies outside the situation utility-possibility frontier in autarky. (There may or may not be a point of tangency.) Therefore there exists some lump-sum redistributions that could make everyone better off with trade.

In a companion piece to Samuelson's 1962 article, Murray Kemp [41] extended the argument to compare any distorted trade situation with autarky, as long as the distortions did not involve trade *subsidies*. This latter proviso seems important, for by means of a subsidy a country might export a commodity in which it has a comparative *dis*advantage. In such a case it might be possible for trade to lead to a situation inferior to autarky. In a classic treatment of this subject, Michihiro Ohyama [70] has established that even in a trade situation involving both taxes and subsidies, a sufficient condition for restricted trade to be preferable to autarky is that *net* tariff revenue be positive. This is an attractive result, for it confirms that an aggregate question ("With appropriate compensation, is restricted trade superior to autarky?") can be handled by means of an aggregate criterion (total tax revenues net of subsidies). The composition of duties and subsidies may be quite intricate, but for an aggregate question such compositional details do not matter.[5]

In discussing the gains from trade Samuelson restricted himself to comparing free trade with autarky or, in the large-country case, optimal trade restriction to autarky. An exception to this remark is suggested in a brief passage in his 1939 article:

> Is it possible to state that the more prices "deviate" . . . from those of the isolated state, the better off all individuals will be? The answer is in the affirmative. . . . I withhold the rigorous proof of this proposition until a future occasion [82, p. 203].

Samuelson does not seem to have followed up with this proof (although the future is yet young). In his 1962 article, Kemp provides a criterion for prices diverging more from autarky. Let p^o be the autarky price vector, and p' and p'', two alternative sets of prices. If there exists positive numbers, μ^o and μ', such that p' equals $\mu^o p^o$ plus

---

[5]Ohyama has an extensive analysis of general consumption and production taxes and comparisons of one trading situation with another. A simplified account is provided in Caves and Jones [4, Supplement to Chap. 12]. A more recent treatment, making explicit use of duality theory, is provided by Dixit and Norman [11, especially Chap. 3].

$\mu'p''$, p'' is said to deviate from autarky p^o by more than does p'. Kemp was aware that not all p' and p'' can be ordered in this way, but the objection is, I think, more serious. With more than two commodities, given a p^o and a p', the set of all p'' that could satisfy this relationship is of measure zero.[6]

Since the time of Samuelson's basic contributions, there has emerged a voluminous literature dealing with gains from trade in a context slightly different from his. In particular, there has been much concern with distortions of various kinds. Is free trade superior to a state of autarky in which taxes or monopoly power or wage distortions have caused relative prices to differ from opportunity costs? If a country insists upon maintaining certain levels of production in its import-competing sector, what restrictions (for example, subsidies or tariffs) do least damage to welfare? A variety of questions and answers can be given. Space limitations allow only passing mention of the important work of Meade, Corden, Bhagwati, Johnson, Kemp, and numerous others. A related question more closely connected to Samuelson's work concerns the instruments that might be used to redistribute incomes so that a potential superiority of free trade over autarky might be translated into an actual improvement for every individual. Samuelson relies on lump-sum taxes and transfers. In recent work, Dixit and Norman [12] show that indirect consumer taxes can also accomplish this end if the country is small. The techniques of proof again closely parallel the original 1939 proof provided by Samuelson.

The Samuelson articles cited here focus on normative issues in the theory of trade. However, his concern with gains from trade spills over into his researches into positive models. In particular, his views on these matters in the context of time-phased Ricardian models will be described in a subsequent section.

2 THE TRANSFER PROBLEM

"In the century and a half that has gone by since the science of economics began, few topics have been so vigorously and inconclusively debated as the Transfer Problem." So John Chipman begins his extensive 1974 reappraisal of this issue [8, p. 19]. And probably the most celebrated of the articles in this long literature are the companion 1952 and 1954 pieces by Samuelson in the *Economic Journal*, [89] and [92]. As important as these articles are, they represent neither the first nor the last word that Samuelson has written on the subject.

The *transfer* under discussion represents a payment, gift, reparation, or loan from one country to another. The principal question that runs through the Samuelson articles and the related literature is: Which way do the terms of trade change when one country makes a transfer payment to another? Typically the answer suggested is that the terms of trade can move in either direction. Samuelson has dubbed as *orthodox* the case in which the paying country suffers a *secondary* burden represented by a decline in its terms of trade as well as the *primary* burden of

---

[6]The question of price diversion, with partial reliance on the Kemp definition, is taken up in Krueger and Sonnenschein [46].

the payment itself. Into the orthodox camp he classifies such giants as Keynes, Pigou, and Taussig.[7] Keynes, indeed, had a special case in mind. He believed that the German reparation payments required by the Allies in the Versailles Treaty would cause substantial lowering of German export prices.[8] Arrayed against this view was not an *antiorthodox* presumption so much as a neutral, agnostic view most strongly put by Ohlin.[9]

As Ohlin points out, previous arguments had tended to neglect important income effects associated with the transfer. Indeed, as Samuelson was to stress, the price elasticities of demand for imports, the presumed low value of which encouraged Keynes' orthodox stance, have *no* role to play in simple models in determining which way the terms of trade will change. Instead, a transfer disturbs world markets for tradeables at initial prices in a manner that depends upon the relative marginal propensities to consume individual tradeables in the two countries. In the two-country (Europe and America), two-commodity (food and clothing) case investigated in his 1952 article, Samuelson shows that if Europe (the presumed clothing exporter) makes a payment to America, its terms of trade will deteriorate (in orthodox fashion) if and only if

$$\frac{m_C^A}{m_F^A} < \frac{m_C^E}{m_F^E} \tag{5}$$

where m_j^i denotes country i's marginal propensity to consume commodity j.[10]

Samuelson's first published pronouncements on the transfer problem seem to be contained in his 1945 review [83] of Jacob Mosak's *General Equilibrium Theory in International Trade* [64]. Almost half the review is devoted to Mosak's treatment of the transfer problem, especially the issue of presumption as to which way the terms of trade change. For the simple two-commodity case with zero transport costs or tariffs, Samuelson states Mosak's conclusions with obvious approval: "*Absolutely no presumption in either direction seems indicated*" [83, p. 944, Samuelson's italics].[11]

---

[7]Numerous citations to the literature are provided in the previously mentioned articles by Samuelson and Chipman, as well as in Samuelson's 1971 piece for the Kindleberger *Festschrift* [104].

[8]Samuelson also seems, in his 1952 piece [89], to have a historical experience in mind—the end of the Marshall Plan.

[9]See the interchange between Keynes and Ohlin in the *Economic Journal* for 1929. Two of these, [45] and [68], have been reprinted in the A.E.A. *Readings in the Theory of International Trade* (1950).

[10]Alternatively phrased, if food and clothing represent the only commodities consumed and are freely traded with zero transport costs, condition (5) is equivalent to: $m_C^A + m_F^E < 1$. That is, the orthodox presumption that the paying country's terms of trade deteriorate rests upon a presumption that the sum of the marginal propensities to import for the two countries is less than unity. This inequality states that America's marginal propensity to consume Europe's export good, clothing, falls short of Europe's marginal propensity to consume clothing. Hence a transfer from Europe to America would lower world demand for clothing at initial prices.

[11]There follows the key observation that when Mosak takes other factors into account, "Mosak indicates how the answer depends upon relative substitutability and complementarity of domestic products and factors with the import and export goods of each country" [83, p. 944]. This is a theme that Samuelson repeats, but without much emphasis, in his 1952 and 1954 *Economic Journal* articles, and comes back to more strongly in his 1971 article.

The major point of the 1952 and 1954 *Economic Journal* articles is that without introducing impediments to trade there is no presumption as to the movement in the terms of trade with transfer,[12] and that support for orthodoxy can be argued if trade is impeded by tariffs (and possibly as well for the case of real transport costs). But even in the tariff case, presumption depends upon the kind of demand behavior exhibited by consumers. In particular, he takes pains to distinguish between the "basic convention" of Viner, which is the assumption of homothetic indifference curves with their implied equality between marginal and average propensities to consume, and the Pigou assumption about demand. With Pigou marginal utility curves are linear and independent, with income-consumption curves pointing towards some "satiation point" in the positive quadrant.[13]

The conclusion that no presumption could be established in the simple no-impediments-to-trade case was challenged in my 1970 *Economica* article [33]. Adopting the Viner convention of homothetic indifference curves, I argued for an antiorthodox presumption. My basic point was that the trade pattern is not independent of tastes. Consider a model with fixed commodity endowments.[14] If tastes differ, the contract curve will (assuming homotheticity) lie on one side of the diagonal or the other. If the endowment allocation between countries is now picked independently of tastes, in more cases than not it will lie in the larger of the two areas in the box separated by the contract curve. If it does lie in the larger area, an antiorthodox result is readily established. That is, a taste bias for food in Europe might account for Europe's importing food even if, in some cases, its endowment may be food abundant. Both in his diagrams and in words Samuelson assumes that the endowment allocation is highly skewed.[15] Therefore in the case that he sets out he is immune to the arguments I put forth.

"On the Trail of Conventional Beliefs About the Transfer Problem" is the descriptively accurate title of Samuelson's 1971 Kindleberger *Festschrift* piece in which the 1954 impediments argument, which only weakly supported orthodoxy, is replaced by a more vigorous defense in which the key role of nontraded goods (previously mentioned by Viner) is explicitly incorporated into the model. The trail leads to a model in which supply response to a transfer is crucial. The supply of traded goods produced at the initial terms of trade systematically shifts—inwards in the receiving country and outwards in the paying country. In the Samuelson

---

[12]Exception must be noted for Samuelson's remarks at the end of both these articles concerning the Viner discussion of nontraded goods. Thus "To my knowledge the only logically air-tight successful defense of the orthodox view is that given by Viner" [89, p. 302]. In footnotes and in passing remarks Samuelson does indeed lay out the argument for orthodoxy which he puts center stage in his 1971 [104] article. But in the 1952 and 1954 articles he is turning elsewhere for partial support—to tariffs and transport costs.

[13]In my 1970 article on transfer [33], I argued that the Viner assumption, rather than that of Pigou, would support the antiorthodox case. But the nature of the argument does not contradict Samuelson's case.

[14]This allows the box-diagram approach which Samuelson favored in his 1952 and 1954 articles. As he quite rightly emphasizes, in this simple model the assumption that outputs do not respond to prices in no way affects the direction of movement in the terms of trade.

[15]Thus: "If we like, we can think of Europe as producing little (or no) food and much clothing; of America as producing little (or no) clothing and much food" [89, p. 281].

argument the demand for leisure exhibits constant marginal utility. Thus in the receiving country at constant prices all extra income is devoted to leisure so that labor is released from the traded goods sectors.[16] Output of tradeables falls, while in the paying country the transfer cuts back on leisure and outputs of tradeables rise. A strong case for the orthodox presumption can be made if it is assumed that each country produces only one (tradeable) commodity—its export good. By previous reasoning exports of the receiving country are reduced (as more leisure is demanded), while the paying country's exports rise. These supply shifts at the initial terms of trade support a consequent improvement in the receiving country's terms of trade.

In this extreme case, with each country specialized in its export commodity, *must* the terms of trade deteriorate for the paying country? No, there is still only a presumption. Note that in Samuelson's model there are no direct income effects on either tradeable in either country, so that the antiorthodox presumption [33] based on the difference between countries' propensities to consume the paying country's export commodity disappears; both such propensities are zero. But demand and supply responses for tradeables are nonetheless triggered by the transfer at *initial terms of trade*. Return to the Europe-America, food-clothing example in which Europe, the transferor, exports clothing. In America the cost of leisure has risen, and substitution effects deflect demand toward tradeables. Suppose this is biased towards Europe's clothing. As well, small elasticities of substitution in food production might call for only a small reduction in production as the wage rate rises. An opposite scenario in Europe (the paying country) might call for a relatively small reduction in demand for Europe's clothing (and a large reduction in food demand) coupled with only a small increase in clothing production. The result—a subsequent antiorthodox improvement in paying Europe's terms of trade.

Samuelson's 1971 model serves as the prototype for the slightly more general treatment of Chipman [8] and Jones [35], in which the role played by leisure is taken over by a general nontraded commodity, with no constancy in the marginal utility of any good.[17] In this more general context several conclusions concerning presumption emerge. Assume the production structure supports a strictly bowed-out transformation surface.[18] The direct income effects of the transfer on demand for tradeables at initial terms of trade can go in either direction. (These are ruled out in Samuelson's case whereas they are presumed to work in an antiorthodox direction in mine.) Indirect effects, both on demand and supply of nontradeables, are triggered by the change in the price of nontradeables in both countries (at initial terms of trade). If in each country production (*and* demand) of nontradeables is especially substitutable with exportables (the Viner case mentioned by Samuelson), an orthodox presumption emerges. Or, barring this, if elasticities of substitution in

---

[16]Samuelson on occasion relies on the Ricardo-Viner model that I take up in Section 5. Here it ensures that with two (or more) traded goods, the wage rate rises in the receiving country as labor is released from all industries at the initial prices for traded commodities. By contrast, Chipman [8] relies heavily on a Heckscher-Ohlin model with (usually) two mobile factors and three commodities.

[17]Prior to Samuelson's 1971 *Festschrift* article appeared the important article of Ian McDougall [51].

[18]Much of Chipman's analysis in [8] concerns ruled surfaces, with two factors producing three commodities. Samuelson's 1971 article concludes with such an example.

production are generally higher than in demand, orthodoxy is again presumed to hold. The latter, in a special case, reduces to Joan Robinson's condition for a devaluation (associated with an outward transfer) to lead to a deterioration in the terms of trade.[19]

Years ago, Leontief [47] suggested that the terms of trade of the payer might move so strongly in the antiorthodox direction that the payer's real income rises. In the two-country case this result was ruled out by Samuelson in his 1952 *Economic Journal* article as involving an unstable equilibrium. However, the existence of more than two countries seems to reinstate this possibility. *A* can make a transfer to *B*. If *C* is also linked by trade (but not directly by transfer) to *A* and/or *B*, *A*'s terms of trade might improve so much that it is made better off without violating market stability.[20] And if the transfer takes place not in purchasing power but in the form of resources or technology, the paying country might well be made better off.[21] In general, if the world supply schedule for tradeables shifts at initial terms of trade, stability requirements may not suffice to bound real income changes.[22]

In 1977 Samuelson returned to the question of presumption with transfer in the context of a Ricardian model with a continuum of goods [14]. I turn now to his earlier work on Ricardo as a prelude to that model and to his reiterated support of orthodoxy.

3 RICARDIAN MODELS

The development of linear programming and activity analysis represents one of the major postwar breakthroughs in economic theory. Typically, Samuelson's contributions were made early. Of particular importance for trade theory were his research memoranda, "Market Mechanisms and Maximization," prepared for the RAND Corporation in 1949 [85].[23] In Part I of this report he illustrates the applicability of the new techniques to the classical problem of assigning commodities to countries according to the Ricardian theory of comparative advantage. The Ricardian model lends itself well to this treatment because of its simple assumptions as to constant labor input coefficients, leading to linear constraints on possible output combinations in any country.[24] Linear programming, with its

---

[19]Cf. Robinson [75]. In his 1971 piece Samuelson refers to the relevance of the Robinson result. These and other conclusions are spelled out in more detail in Jones [35].

[20]Details are provided by Makoto Yano [121], whose work is based on the interesting 1974 article of David Gale [21].

[21]In [4] I argue that a shift of resources might lead to an antiorthodox presumption precisely in the case in which, with a shift in purchasing power, Samuelson would argue for orthodoxy.

[22]Once the world supply curves shift, phenomena akin to immiserizing growth may appear. See, for example, Bhagwati [2].

[23]Of related relevance to the development of linear programming is Samuelson's 1952 paper [90] on spatial price equilibrium.

[24]It is perhaps clear from the context that I am speaking of the simple labor-only model of Ricardo used in trade theory. Samuelson, in [95] and [96], provides a thorough analysis of the role of land and capital in Ricardian theory. I discuss below the nature of his contributions to the area of time-phased Ricardian models. His 1949 RAND memoranda resurfaced as part of the general analysis of linear programming in 1958 in the Dorfman, Samuelson, Solow volume [13]. In Section 5 I discuss Samuelson's contributions to what he has termed the Ricardo-Viner model.

concern for distinguishing productive processes that will operate at positive levels from those that will shut down, is ideally suited to the problem faced by an individual country in a free-trade world as to what commodities it produces.

Samuelson's 1949 treatment of the problem illustrates the potential use of shadow prices that allow each country separately to maximize the value of its national output. As prices vary parametrically, remaining common to all countries, Samuelson shows how a world production-possibilities frontier is traced out. This concept, developed for the case of smoothly bowed-out transformation curves by Lerner in 1932 [49], leads in a Ricardian world to a transformation surface made up of linear segments. Figure 3 illustrates the two-country, two-commodity case. Country A has a comparative advantage in producing commodity 1. Should world prices be represented by the slope of the λ line, each country would be completely specialized in producing the commodity in which it possesses a comparative advantage, and world production would be shown by vertex point M.

The concept of a world transformation surface, and the tools of linear programming and activity analysis, were applied early in the 1950s by two students of Frank Graham to show how his previous trial-and-error attempts to establish positions of efficient production in a world of many countries and many commodities [23] could be improved upon by the new techniques. Whitin in 1953 [119] surveyed Graham's conclusions with the new tools and provided a three-commodity, three-country illustration. In a series of classic articles, Lionel McKenzie [52], [53], and [55], discussed the problem of existence in Graham's

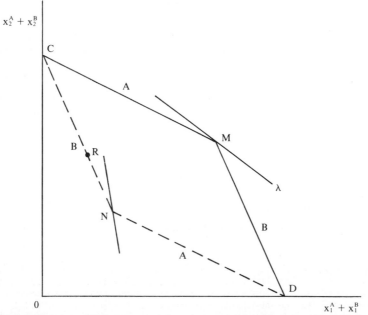

Figure 3
World production possibilities frontier.

model and addressed himself explicitly to the task of tracing out the correct, efficient, assignment of countries to commodities in the Ricardo-Graham model. Figure 3 illustrates a simple example of the general McKenzie proposition that the world transformation surface can be traced out with knowledge of only a finite number of points—the vertices (such as *C, M,* and *D*) in which each country specializes completely to a single commodity. Of course, finding which pattern of specializations is efficient (for example, choosing between *N* and *M* in Figure 3) is not so simple in higher dimensional cases. But Samuelson's insight that efficient patterns of world specialization will evolve when each country separately responds in maximizing fashion to world prices can be used to develop criteria for comparative advantage in a multicountry, multicommodity Ricardian world.[25]

Samuelson has shown special interest in a version of the two-country, many-commodity Ricardian model. In an article on purchasing power parity and the dollar problem [98], which Samuelson published in 1964, the germ of the *continuum* concept for handling the many-commodity case was introduced. More recently [14], Samuelson joined forces with Rudiger Dornbusch and Stanley Fischer to flesh out this idea and apply it to a number of problems in real and monetary trade theory. Think of two countries, each capable of producing any of an infinite number of commodities. Suppose these commodities are indexed along the unit interval from zero to one in such a manner that the ratio of foreign (fixed) labor costs for commodity z, $a^*(z)$, to home labor costs, $a(z)$, falls as z goes from zero to one. Furthermore, assume there are no gaps—the ratio of labor costs falls smoothly and continuously. Then the ratio of wage rates in the two countries (corrected for the exchange rate) must equal the ratio of labor costs for the borderline commodity (only one) which can be produced in both countries. All commodities with a lower index are produced at home, those with a higher index, abroad.

Of course which commodity proves to be on the border depends endogenously on taste patterns throughout the world and upon country size and technology. Changes in any of these underlying factors will affect the location of the borderline commodity and relative wages and thus the terms of trade. Artificial (tariffs, quotas) or real (transport costs) impediments also affect the solution. Indeed, the model is applied precisely to these and other issues. In order to facilitate their analysis, Dornbusch, Fischer, and Samuelson make a strong assumption about demands: Both countries share common Graham-type demand functions exhibiting unit income elasticities for all goods. That is, underlying utility functions are Cobb-Douglas, and in each country the share of income spent on any range of commodities remains constant even if relative prices change. This assumption allows a unique, monotonic ranking between relative wages in the two countries (w/w^*) and the position of the borderline commodity (for given sizes of the two

---

[25]McKenzie [53] established the equivalence between efficient patterns of production and potential competitive equilibria in a fashion that led to the formal criterion I put forth in [29]: For efficient specializations the product of labor input coefficients is minimized compared with any other alternative specialization that involves no change in the number of countries assigned to each commodity. Much of this literature, traced back to Ricardo and Torrens, is reviewed in Part I of Chipman's 1965–66 scholarly survey [6].

labor forces, L and $L*$). Let $\tilde{z}$ represent the borderline commodity. If the fraction of world income spent on goods indexed from zero to $\tilde{z}$ is $\theta(\tilde{z})$, the ratio of $\theta(\tilde{z})$ to $[1 - \theta(\tilde{z})]$ must correspond to the ratio of home and foreign (labor) incomes. This is equation (6):

$$\frac{w}{w*} = \frac{\theta(\tilde{z})}{1 - \theta(\tilde{z})} \frac{L*}{L} \tag{6}$$

For given country size this allows a neat diagram in which the position of the borderline commodity is determined by the previously mentioned technological relationship between cost ratios and a curve showing the relationship between relative wages and $\tilde{z}$ shown in equation (6).

In evaluating the usefulness of the continuum assumption, it is important to be clear that it is not the Ricardian model itself that is being judged. Indeed, I would argue that for trade issues involving many commodities but only two countries, the Ricardian model represents an ideal vehicle for analysis because it strips production relationships down to a simple expression revealing the invariant resource (labor) cost of producing a unit of a commodity in each country. But how difficult is the discrete model? The problem with the latter is that any equilibrium involves two countries producing a commodity in common (there can be only one if cost ratios are not equal for any pair of goods)—a situation Frank Graham argued was more "likely" [23]—or two countries producing completely separate bundles of goods. By contrast, both countries in the continuum model produce (negligible) amounts of a borderline commodity. For comparative statics in the discrete case, the analysis reveals either how adjustments take place via quantity changes, with wage rates in the two countries locked together via the commonly produced good, or how relative wages change as a consequence of price changes required to clear markets. But the Hicksian composite commodity theorem converts the many-commodity case to a two-commodity case. In each country constant labor coefficients bind together the relative prices of all goods produced. That is, the discrete model with many commodities is simple to analyze.

To take an example, suppose the foreign country grows (by a small amount). In the discrete model if countries produce commodity 5 in common and no demands are inferior, adjustment requires the foreign country to increase production of commodity 5 by more than the increase in world demand to allow home labor to be released to produce more of each of its commodities. No price changes occur. If no commodity is produced in common, growth abroad implies increased production of at least some of its commodities over and above foreign demand (at initial prices), and therefore a reduction in prices of *all* foreign goods (via a fall in $w*$) relative to home goods. The continuum version of the model allows a blend of these conclusions—a fall in $w*$ relative to w, coupled with a release of home labor from the borderline commodity *and* others indexed near it. In this description there was no need to tie demand to identical Cobb-Douglas utility functions in the two countries.

It is clear that the continuum versus discrete issue will be debated in the literature.[26] My own view is that the choice of model depends on the question being asked, as well as the assumptions one wishes to make about demand in order to avail oneself of the neat diagrams in [14].[27] In recent work [37] and [38], I analyze the impact of technical progress in one country on real incomes (or relative wages) in both countries. I choose a discrete version of the multicommodity Ricardian model, because it more readily handles asymmetries in demand that could account for the home country's welfare being reduced despite an improvement in foreign technology in some commodity imported at home. Generally speaking, if interest centers on the changing location of the borderline commodity, a continuum model may be appropriate. On the other hand, a discrete model may be easier to handle if, say, the major question concerns the terms of trade or real wages.[28]

Recently Samuelson has become embroiled in a debate concerning time-phased systems.[29] Some of this literature concerns a Ricardian model in which labor is used to produce commodities, but in which time enters in an essential way. Labor today is required as input into a process that yields output only tomorrow (or some other future date). If commodities differ in the time required in the production process and/or if rates of profit (interest) differ among countries, Samuelson shows how trade patterns might reverse compared with a zero-profit world, and that such reversals might lead to a steady state in which less of *all* goods are forever consumed by every person.[30]

Figure 3 can be used to illustrate the argument. The outer locus shows the world outputs attainable when countries' production patterns correspond to comparative advantage. The inner locus shows the worst combination of outputs (assuming labor is always fully employed), involving country B specializing in good 1 before country A (the country with the comparative advantage in the first commodity) produces any. Now suppose it takes time to produce the first commodity and that interest rates are positive. If the rate of profit (interest) in country A is higher than in

---

[26]Indeed, Samuelson has indicated he has a piece on this topic forthcoming in the *Journal of International Economics.*

[27]In a recent article [120], Charles Wilson extends the continuum assumption to a model with more general demand structure. Not surprisingly, integrals abound.

[28]Both the discrete and continuum versions of Ricardian models point toward an orthodox result for the transfer problem with nontraded goods present. For the discrete case, let each country be specialized to one group of traded goods. Both countries also produce a nontradeable. The kind of secondary reactions I described in Section 2, whereby the orthodox presumption could be overturned, depend upon a change in the relative price of nontradeables and tradeables. In a Ricardian world this price ratio is locked in each country (for the tradeables produced by that country). Therefore the increased production of tradeables as the demand for nontradeables falls (at initial prices) in the paying country, and the reduced supply of tradeables (as demand for nontradeables increases) in the receiving country *must* be met by an orthodox deterioration in the terms of trade for the paying foreign country. The continuum analysis would reveal as well that the receiving country reduces the range of traded goods produced.

[29]See, for example, the comments by Mainwaring [57] on the 1975 article by Samuelson [107]. The Mainwaring article is followed by a reply by Samuelson [109]. This latter exchange concerns itself with the factor-price equalization possibilities with trade. This issue would not arise if, as is standard in Ricardian models, countries are assumed to possess different technologies.

[30]The relevant Samuelson articles are the 1973 Halm *Festschrift* article [106], the 1975 Bourneuf *Festschrift* article [108], and the previously mentioned lengthly contribution to the *Journal of International Economics* in 1975 [107]. The Bourneuf article is devoted to challenging the Emmanuel thesis of unequal exchange [16]. See also the comments by Emmanuel [17] and Samuelson [110] in 1978.

country B, the relative cost of good 1 in A could be driven above its cost in B. Trade might lead to a pattern of production in which B is specialized to good 1 and A to good 2, leading to world steady-state production flows shown by point N. The existence of positive profit rates also serves to tilt the world price line (through N) steeper than the relative (undiscounted) labor costs of production of good 1 in producing country B.

Having set up this possibility of trade reversals, Samuelson then demonstrates that the solution (at N) cannot be considered Pareto-inferior.[31] The path from one steady-state solution (say with zero interest) to another (say at N) involves a transition phase, so that steady-state solutions alone cannot be directly compared. The example does not violate the assertion that countries gain from trade.

Samuelson's contributions both to the continuum literature and the time-phased literature are not restricted to the Ricardian model. Instead, in each he makes applications to a Heckscher-Ohlin world where countries share a similar technology.

4 HECKSCHER-OHLIN THEORY

The contributions that Paul Samuelson has made in developing Heckscher-Ohlin theory have been so basic that he is often awarded a hyphen: The Heckscher-Ohlin-Samuelson model of trade, which incorporates the most popular model of production relationships for open economies. Together with Wolfgang Stolper he provided a simple diagrammatic and algebraic analysis of Ohlin's [69] and Heckscher's [25] general theories, an analysis that paved the way for countless explicit results in small-scale general equilibrium models of trade. In his classic 1953 *Review of Economic Studies* article [91], Samuelson imbedded the simple theory into a context of more general production structures with many factors and many commodities, as well as venturing suggestions as to conditions for factor-price equalization that led to developments in mathematics and economics that still continue. And, in 1980, he joined with Rudiger Dornbusch and Stanley Fischer to consider the applicability of the continuum concept to the two-country, many-commodity version of Heckscher-Ohlin theory [15].

In discussing these contributions I shall consider first Samuelson's 1941 article on protection with Stolper [115], together with his two *Economic Journal* articles on factor-price equalization and the relationship of this work both to the earlier student paper of Abba Lerner's [50], and the new wave of interest in Heckscher-Ohlin theory triggered by Leontief's paradoxical findings concerning American trade patterns in 1953 [48]. Basically these papers fill out the modern view of Heckscher-Ohlin theory for two countries, two commodities, and two productive factors. Subsequently I shall discuss Samuelson's contributions to the case of many goods and factors, with particular reference to the issue of factor-price equalization.

Although the 1941 Stolper-Samuelson contribution would serve to introduce the

---

[31] Samuelson [107] describes situations such as point R in which some country (B) is *in*completely specialized, as a *limbo* equilibrium. This is a curious choice of words, as it directly contradicts the frequent use by Frank Graham in [23] of limbo to refer to positions of complete specialization. (The terms of trade are left in limbo, untied to any country's cost ratio.)

core ingredients of Heckscher-Ohlin theory for small-scale models of trade, its motivation seems based on an applied issue: Can a tariff effectively raise the real return to a broad-based factor such as labor? It was their view that a careful piecing together of the ingredients available in the contributions of Heckscher and Ohlin could lead to an argument demonstrating not only the possibility, but also the unambiguous necessity of protection serving to increase the *real* wage of labor, if labor is the scarce factor of production.[32] In the course of the argument they assumed that the tariff would raise the relative domestic price of importables, the necessity for which was later challenged by Lloyd Metzler [63]. However, modern interpretations of the Stolper-Samuelson theorem tend to disconnect it from the analysis of tariffs alone. Instead, the central result links a change in the domestic price ratio to the real returns to the factor used intensively in the industry favored by the price rise. However interesting the Metzler result, it does not contradict the essence of what has become known as the Stolper-Samuelson theorem.

The Stolper-Samuelson article introduced to the profession the production box-diagram, as an analog to the consumption box earlier developed by Edgeworth and Bowley.[33] In discussing some of the main features of their argument, as well as the succeeding issues raised by Samuelson in his factor-price equalization articles [84] and [86], I shall refer not to the production box-diagram but to another diagram which has come to be known as the Harrod-Johnson diagram (Figure 4). It received this name from the use to which it was put by Harry Johnson in his famous *Manchester School* article in 1957 [27], in which he acknowledges the previous application (of the top half of the diagram) by Harrod [24]. The diagram is, with a 90° turn, essentially that used by Samuelson in his second *Economic Journal* article [86, p. 188, n. 1] in 1949. Figure 4's top half shows how actual techniques for producing food and clothing would adapt in competitive markets to changes in the ratio of wages to rents, w/r (assuming labor and land are the only two factors of production, mobile between industries). The vertical axis measures land/labor ratios in each sector and can as well show the land/labor overall endowment ratio for an economy. Thus suppose an economy's factor endowment ratio is shown by ρ. This limits the possible range for that economy's factor price ratio to AB, which

---

[32] In a recent article [112], Samuelson discusses the relationship of the Stolper-Samuelson argument to the findings of the Brigden report on the Australian tariff [3] and the insightful arguments put forth in the 1939 article by Marion Crawford Samuelson [79]. Quite aside from the question of what, or who, influenced whom, is the point that the model Marion Samuelson used is literally at the juncture of the Heckscher-Ohlin two-by-two model and the Ricardo-Viner model I discuss in Section 5. In her work Australia produces food with two factors, labor and land, and manufacturers with one, labor alone— both industries operating competitively under constant returns to scale. If a tariff raises the price of manufactures, wages rise by an equivalent proportional amount, and therefore (as long as any food is consumed by labor) real wages must rise. This model is a form of a Heckscher-Ohlin model with two mobile factors (labor and land), in which factor proportions in one industry (manufactures) happen to be extreme. It is also a specific-factors model (land only used to produce food) in which in the other sector the use of *another* specific factor (say, capital) is assumed to be negligible. One wonders how trade theory might have developed if Marion Crawford Samuelson's model had first been extended in the Ricardo-Viner direction instead of the Heckscher-Ohlin direction.

[33] An exception must be made for the earlier use of the production box by Lerner [50] in his 1933 seminar paper prepared at the London School of Economics. This article, however, was not published until almost twenty years after it was written.

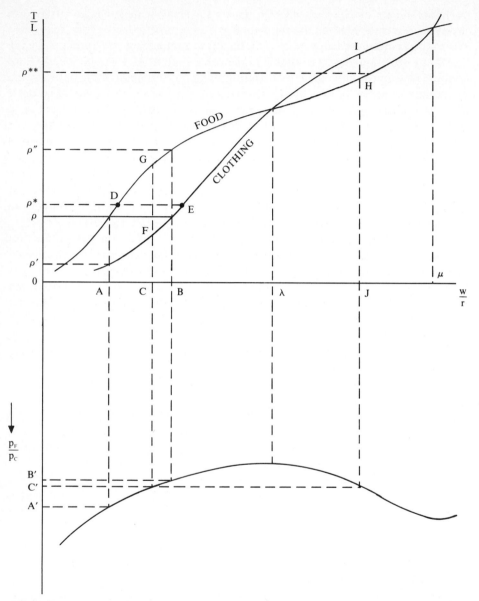

Figure 4
Factor proporation and factor prices.

corresponds to the range of slopes of isoquants along the contract curve of a production box for such an economy.

One point that Stolper and Samuelson took pains to explain, because of the potential paradoxical tone of the statement, was that if a country protects an industry (say clothing), factor proportions in both sectors respond in the *same* direction despite the fixity of overall factor endowments. From an initial equilibrium at C, expansion of the protected clothing sector must give it a heavier weight.[34] Since clothing is labor-intensive, the wage/rental ratio must rise, causing both sectors to economize on their use of labor. It is this rise in the land/labor ratio employed in each sector that causes labor's marginal product to rise in both. The real wage must unambiguously rise. This is the Stolper-Samuelson theorem.

The curve drawn in the bottom half of the diagram reveals how the factor-price ratio and commodity-price ratio would be related *if* a country's factor endowments allowed it to be incompletely specialized at those prices. For an economy whose endowment ratio is ρ, only the section of this lower curve cut off by the AB range of factor prices is relevant. It is important to note that the lower curve must be drawn such that a given percentage change in the commodity-price ratio results in a greater percentage change in the factor-price ratio (the "magnification effect" [31]).[35] The rationale lies in the underlying assumed absence of joint production, so that competitive commodity-price changes must each be trapped between (and be distributive-share weighted averages of) factor-price changes. This is what allows unambiguous conclusions to be reached about the real wage.

Nothing in the Stolper-Samuelson tariff argument requires that technological knowledge or the degree of specialization abroad match that at home. This is worth stressing, for much of what is left of Heckscher-Ohlin theory requires one or both of these assumptions to some degree. Indeed, the incredulity with which Samuelson's factor-price equalization results were first received in 1948, leading him to follow up a year later with a more complete account [86], perhaps revealed that the key role of the assumption that both countries shared identical technologies was not suffi-ciently appreciated.

If two countries do share the same technology, both parts of Figure 4 apply to each in the range appropriate to their factor endowments. Thus suppose the foreign country exhibits a slightly higher land/labor endowment ratio, ρ^*, and that world free-trade commodity prices are shown by ratio OC'. OC would then reflect the common factor price ratio in each country. Not only relative, but also absolute factor prices would get equilibrated by trade. Endowment differences do count for something; as the upper half of Figure 4 reveals, the land-abundant foreign country must weight land-intensive food more heavily in its production pattern at the common set of prices.

For countries sharing the same technology will free trade in commodities be sufficient to equalize factor prices even if factors are internationally immobile? The position Samuelson has consistently taken is that factor prices will be completely equalized as long as factor endowments are sufficiently close together. If productive factors were available in identical proportions in all countries and only free trade in commodities allowed, factor prices would be equalized.[36] With reference to Figure

---

[34]The ρ-line averages out the vertical distances to the food and clothing land/labor ratio curves, with the weights showing the labor allocations.

[35]There are many instances in the journal literature (and the textbooks) in which diagrams flout this requirement. I did so myself in my 1956 article on the Heckscher-Ohlin model [28], (corrected in the reprinted version). And so did Samuelson in his 1949 *Economic Journal* article [86, p. 188].

[36]Trade could take place if demand conditions are dissimilar. Free trade in commodities makes the national *source* of demand inconsequential as a force determining factor prices.

4, suppose the average land/labor endowment ratio in the world is ρ. Furthermore, assume the weak conditions sufficient to ensure that *given* world demand conditions determine a unique equilibrium, with the commodity-price ratio shown by OC' and factor-price ratio by OC. If factors were now to move between countries, the equilibrium pattern of world production (*not* the national totals) would remain unchanged *if* factor prices remain the same in all countries.[37] Thus as long as demand conditions are unaltered, any free-trade equilibrium with some arbitrary distribution of factor endowments nationally can lead to factor-price equalization only if commodity prices are shown by OC' and common factor-price ratios by OC. How far apart can endowments in the two countries stray and still allow this same *world* pattern of production and common OC factor-price ratio? The *cone of diversification*, FG, appropriate to the OC factor-price ratio provides the answer.[38] Factor prices are equalized with free trade if and only if (given the demand conditions) both countries' endowment ratios lie in this cone of diversification.[39]

All this assumed a given set of demand conditions. If tastes can be altered, what can be said? Suppose the home country's endowment proportions are given by ρ in Figure 4. If the foreign factor endowment proportions lie in the range $\rho'\rho''$, there exist *some* patterns of demand that could lead to factor-price equalization. That is, if $\rho*$ is in this range, the set of factor prices possible for the foreign country overlaps the home range, AB, and thus some demand could lead to a commodity price ratio in the appropriate section of $A'B'$.[40] Alternatively, given ρ, if foreign $\rho*$ lies outside the $\rho'\rho''$ range, free trade cannot equalize factor prices, no matter what the demand conditions. Finally, how must ρ and $\rho*$ be related if factor-price equalization is to become necessary *regardless* of demand conditions? They must be identical. Suppose ρ and $\rho*$ are as shown in Figure 4. If world demand is heavily biased toward clothing, a free trade *and* internationally mobile factor equilibrium could have food's relative price slightly lower than OB'. In such a case, free trade in commodities alone could not equalize factor prices.

Figure 4 also shows a range of wage/rent ratios between λ and μ for which the factor intensities of the two commodities have been reversed. Samuelson illustrates this case in his 1949 *Economic Journal* article [86, p. 188] and shows that once factor intensities are reversed, so is the direction of the relationship between factor prices and commodity prices. Furthermore, two countries could be facing the same free-trade commodity prices, for example, the ratio OC', but if one country's endowment ratio is ρ and the other country is much more land-abundant (in the

---

[37]In 1959, Uzawa [117] compared free-trade equilibria that lead to factor-price equalization with a world of completely free factor mobility. If factor prices are equalized without mobility, no further world production gains accrue to freeing factors from their national boundaries. See also Mundell [65].

[38]This apt phrase was introduced by Chipman [6, Part 3], who provides an extensive discussion of the literature up to 1965, including the classic activity analysis approach adopted by McKenzie [54], who uses the concept of countries' endowments lying within the same cone of diversification.

[39]Samuelson provides an explicit statement of this condition in a footnote on p. 180 of his 1948 article. This line of argument, whereby reference is made to the factor prices ruling in a world of factor mobility, has been made in a masterly discussion by Dixit and Norman [11, Chap. 4]. Especially suggestive is their use of production box-diagrams for the world to show how the possibility of factor-price equalization is altered when more commodities are produced.

[40]Factor-price ranges can be interpreted as *cones* in the dual space of factor-price frontiers.

range *IH*), both countries could be incompletely specialized without their factor prices being driven to equality.

The phenomenon of factor-intensity reversal, and its consequences in preventing factor-price equalization with trade, was given considerable attention by Abba Lerner in his rightfully acclaimed 1933 paper, subsequently published in *Economica* in 1952 [50].[41] Lerner also provides the case for equalization when intensities do not reverse, and in his 1949 *Economic Journal* paper, Samuelson gives full credit to Lerner's earlier "definitive treatment" (which had been rescued by Lionel Robbins after Samuelson's 1948 paper appeared). But Lerner did not view the solution in which both countries produced both goods with factor prices not equalized as anything but "an unlikely coincidence."[42] This is incorrect. In Figure 4 if countries with endowments ρ and ρ^{**} both face free-trade prices *OC′*, the two countries *must* be incompletely specialized with wage/rent ratios at *OC* and *OJ* respectively. Samuelson thought that reversals might not be prevalent empirically, but the issue was interesting theoretically. Indeed, much of the subsequent more technical literature is involved with this point.

Heckscher-Ohlin theory is only in part concerned with the relationship between commodity prices and factor prices, which formed the focus for Samuelson's articles in this area through 1953. Ironically, Leontief's empirical findings [48], suggesting that America's trade patterns seem not to have corresponded with the view of America as capital-abundant, were published in that same year. Samuelson was not a direct contributor to the subsequent outpouring of theoretical work aimed at examining just what the model he had developed had to say on the issue of patterns of trade. Did Heckscher-Ohlin theory predict that a nation relatively heavily endowed with capital would export the capital-intensive commodity? The basis for such a prediction, in the sense of the bias in the shape of the transformation schedule imparted by relative factor endowments, was almost casually (but correctly) stated by Samuelson in his 1948 article [84, p. 171]. Indeed, on the same page he points out the possibility of trade reversals stemming from systematic differences in tastes. But it was left to the next generation to explore this 2×2 model in more detail for the effect of differences in factor endowments and growth in endowments on trade and production patterns.[43] For example, Samuelson, Lerner, and Pearce, in their analyses of factor intensity reversals, focused on the significance for the factor-price equalization result rather than on the Heckscher-Ohlin view that capital-abundant countries export capital-intensive goods.[44] Reversals aside, subsequent literature pointed out that the conditions under which

[41]Ivor Pearce uses the reversal phenomenon to challenge the relevance of Samuelson's "myth" of factor-price equalization [71]. See also Samuelson's response [88].

[42]In a note on Lerner's paper [72], Pearce comments on Lerner's fear that a solution with unequal factor prices and incomplete specialization might be unstable. Pearce shows that it is not. I think Lerner was making a different point—that it would be sheer coincidence to have such a solution.

[43]The literature of this period is vast. See, for example, R. Robinson [76], Jones [28], Johnson [27], Rybczynski [78], Corden [9], Mundell [65], Bhagwati [2], and Findlay and Grubert [20].

[44]Reversals imply that both countries either export their capital-intensive good or their labor-intensive good, making predictions as to factor endowments from observed trade patterns impossible. See Jones [28].

Heckscher-Ohlin theory would most likely result in factor-price equalization with free trade, namely countries diverging but little in their factor endowments, were precisely the conditions under which the Heckscher-Ohlin view of the link between trade patterns and underlying factor proportions would be most in danger of being falsified.

To many trade theorists, Samuelson's 1953 article on prices of factors and goods in general equilibrium [91] represents the pinnacle of his work in the field. He presents a Walrasian model in modern garb—complete with the activities-analysis set of inequalities to allow for the shutting-down of some productive activities. If he had merely discussed the conditions for full Walrasian equilibrium, this article would be of less interest to trade theory. Instead (or additionally), Samuelson considers the kinds of equilibrium possible for a *trading* community facing a *given* set of commodity prices. It is in this context that the question of comparing the number of factors and number of (tradeable) produced commodities becomes important.

Samuelson's main points concerning this issue of dimensionality can ᴅe summarized as follows:

(1) In the case in which the number of productive factors equals the number of produced and freely traded commodities, the natural extension to higher dimensions of the standard 2×2 model, there is a presumption that free trade will equalize factor prices for countries sharing the same technology. Letting the $n \times n$ matrix, A, denote the set of input-output coefficients, a_{ij}, themselves cost-minimizing functions of factor prices, pure competition ensures that in equilibrium if all n commodities are produced,

$$Aw = p \tag{7}$$

where (w,p) are the factor-price and commodity-price vectors. This set of n equations can, in certain circumstances, be solved uniquely for the set of n factor prices given the commonly shared world commodity prices. However, conditions must be imposed on the technology matrix before uniqueness can be assured. These conditions would certainly include the nonsingularity of A, a statement that commodities are produced with genuinely independent factor proportions.

(2) If more commodities than factors are freely traded, either a country will be forced to specialize to a subset of commodities (generally no larger than the number of factors) or, perhaps due to the country's size, world commodity prices adjust to local cost conditions, allowing production of more commodities with exactly zero profits. If two or more countries have more than r commodities produced in common (where r equals the number of factors), a basic indeterminacy as to the national location of productive activity appears, but no indeterminacy in world totals. Two countries may each produce as many commodities as they possess factors, but if these do not represent the same set of commodities, factor prices can well be different.

(3) The case in which r, the number of productive factors, exceeds n, the number of commodities, is one in which no factor-price equalization result is to be expected.

The equation set (7) contains more factor prices than given world free-trade commodity prices, and thus can in general not be solved for w. The implication is that other characteristics of the nation's economy—specifically its factor endowments—have an independent role to play in determining factor prices. A special case is the Ricardo-Viner model discussed in the next section.

This article of Samuelson's is famous also for its recurrent emphasis on duality features of the production sector.[45] In particular he briefly introduces the "reciprocity relationship" whereby

$$\frac{\partial X_j}{\partial V_i} = \frac{\partial w_i}{\partial p_j} \tag{8}$$

where X_j and V_i refer to output of commodity j and endowment of factor i. This relationship has been extremely useful in simplifying the theory of foreign investment.[46] A country that has invested abroad is naturally concerned with the impact of its tariff policy (which causes the price of its exports, p_j, to change) on the return to its capital located abroad, say w_i. By varying the quantity of its investment, V_i, it alters the quantity of its foreign output competing with its exports, X_j. The reciprocity relationship (8) reveals that the underlying technology connects the direct pricing relationship with the direct impact of foreign investment on outputs. Therefore only one feature of the technology, either side of (8), need appear in the formal analysis of foreign investment.[47]

Since 1953 much of Samuelson's work on Heckscher-Ohlin theory has been tied up with the question of factor-price equalization, either with the mathematical search for conditions sufficient to guarantee uniqueness of factor prices given a set of commodity prices or with the question of whether free trade serves to equalize interest rates among countries sharing the same technology. The uniqueness issue has had a long, if somewhat tortuous, history, with the Appendix to Samuelson's 1953 article [91] setting up a set of conditions that were challenged by Nikaido and led eventually to the Gale-Nikaido conditions [22]. A set of articles in the *International Economic Review* in 1967 gave an opportunity to McKenzie to publish his counterexample [56] to Pearce's conjecture [73] and [74] that the determinant of input-output coefficients remaining nonsingular over the domain of factor prices would suffice to guarantee univalence. Samuelson's contribution [100] agreed with McKenzie's counterexample. The latest word in this debate seems to belong to Andreu Mas-Colell [59], who has argued that conditions placed on the matrix of input distributive shares will suffice. If θ_{ij} is the share of factor i in

---

[45]See also the classic 1953 work of Shephard [114]. The advantages of a dual approach to trade theory are heavily emphasized in the recent book by Dixit and Norman [11]. In two pieces in 1965 [30] and [31], I stressed the dual relationship between the Stolper-Samuelson link between commodity and factor prices, on the one hand, and the Rybczynski theorem [78], dealing with output-factor endowment relations at given commodity prices, on the other hand.

[46]In particular, see the articles by Kemp [42] and Jones [32].

[47]A more leisurely proof of the reciprocity relationship is given in Jones and Scheinkman [39]. Kemp and Ethier [43] have extended the interpretation of the reciprocity relationship.

producing commodity j, the condition that the determinant of shares $|\theta|$ exceed some ϵ greater than zero will guarantee a unique set of factor prices corresponding to a given set of commodity prices. In a brief 1965 postscript to his 1953 paper [99], Samuelson had suggested switching from the input-output matrix to a matrix of distributive shares and had imposed minimal (positive) bounds on the size of the determinant $|\theta|$ and all principal minors. According to Mas-Colell, these further conditions on principal minors are not necessary.

It deserves to be emphasized, as Samuelson has done, that this technical question of univalence, when it is assumed that two countries produce the same set of commodities in free trade, is not equivalent to asking whether free trade will equalize factor prices. The latter depends on factor endowments being sufficiently similar, whereas the univalence question only concerns the technology (once the proper degree of incomplete specialization has been assumed). In the 2×2 case illustrated in Figure 4, suppose the home country's endowment is fixed at ρ, whereas the foreign endowment becomes progressively more land-abundant. Eventually one or both countries are forced to specialize, and factor prices are then no longer equalized. If the conditions for univalence are not satisfied, as they are not in Figure 4, eventually the two countries can be incompletely specialized again (for example, when foreign endowments reach ρ^{**}). But this makes factor-price equalization no more likely.

A parallel literature has developed focusing on possible generalizations of the Stolper-Samuelson (or dual-Rybczynski) result to countries with many factors and commodities. On the one hand, special restrictions on the technology have been imposed that assure that a rise in the price of some commodity will raise the real reward of one factor and lower that of all others. Of this vast literature the work of Chipman [7], Uekawa [116], Kemp and Wegge [44], and Inada [26] stand out. On the other hand, Ethier [18] has asked what general properties emerge when few restrictions are imposed (such as the lack of joint production). This 1974 piece of Ethier's has been complemented by the succeeding articles by Diewert and Woodland [10], Jones and Scheinkman [39], and Chang [5]. Although Samuelson has been much less involved in this literature, his 1953 article [91] explicitly set out the model.[48]

Samuelson's recent involvement in the time-phased literature is prompted in part by a variation on the factor-price equalization theme: Does trade equalize interest (or profit) rates among countries sharing the same technology? Twenty years ago Samuelson circulated privately his affirmative answer to this query in the context of a Heckscher-Ohlin model in which capital goods are locally produced but not traded.[49] The key to the argument is that both countries are assumed to be producing the same two traded consumption goods (as well as the capital good), which (barring intensity reversals) guarantees factor-price equalization for wages and *rentals* on capital equipment. But such equalization forces the unit costs of nontraded capital goods also to be brought into line. Hence interest rates, the ratio

---

[48] Mention should also be made of Samuelson's 1958 discussion of the fixed-coefficients case [94], an obvious stimulus to the Diewert-Woodland article.

[49] This article [100] was published five years after it was written.

of rentals to the cost of capital, must be equalized by trade. One difficulty with this argument is that the existence of nontraded productive activities opens the door to demand differences between countries forcing specialization to one of the traded commodities and thus subverting the tendency for rental equalization. Thus the two countries could have *identical endowments* as well as technology, but if one country wishes to produce relatively large quantities of (nontraded) capital, it may be forced to specialize away from one of the traded consumption goods.

In 1975 Samuelson presented a lengthy analysis of both trade patterns and factor-price behavior in time-phased systems. He made contact with the Metcalfe-Steedman branch of trade theory [61] and [62] that argued against the notion of capital as a homogeneous productive factor fixed in supply for a trading community. Since relative commodity prices need not be monotonically related to the rate of interest, interest rate equalization need not be implied by trade, unless factor endowments are very close together. As well, Samuelson discusses the impact of trade at *given* profit rates, both when these are equal between countries and when they are not. The connection between trade results in the time-phased literature and the standard Heckscher-Ohlin model is the subject of current dispute (see Ethier [19] and the forthcoming reply by Metcalfe and Steedman).

The continuum concept, which Samuelson, together with Dornbusch and Fischer, applied imaginatively to the Ricardian model [14], has recently been applied as well to a Heckscher-Ohlin model with two countries [15]. As in the Ricardian model (see Section 3), a judgmental question arises as to the usefulness of the continuum concept compared with the discrete form of the two-country, many-commodity case. The principal comparative statics problem that they address—the effect of endowment changes in one country on factor and commodity prices—could, I would argue, be more easily handled in a discrete two-country model with each country producing two commodities, perhaps one of them (but not both) in common, and with factor prices not equalized. One difficulty with having each country produce more commodities than factors is that a range of indeterminacy exists as to the composition of national production at any set of endowments and commodity prices. This difficulty, which makes the analysis more tedious if nonetheless determinate once demand conditions are introduced, is inescapably present in the continuum model, although it can be avoided in the discrete analog. As in the Ricardian case, a fair appraisal of the value of the continuum concept depends in large part on the question being raised.

5 THE SPECIFIC-FACTORS MODEL

The past decade has witnessed renewed interest in a model of production that, in historical perspective, precedes the Heckscher-Ohlin model. Factors of production are sharply distinguished by the degree to which they are able to respond to changes in market conditions. One factor—typically assumed to be labor—is quick to reallocate in the face of any lowering of its wage in one sector as compared with alternative employment. All other factors are specifically tied to one occupation and one commodity. Samuelson attributes aspects of this model to the Ricardian theory of rent and to Viner's classic 1931 article on cost and supply curves [118], and thus refers to the model as the Ricardo-Viner model.

Features of this model were discussed by Samuelson in two 1971 papers, namely, the previously discussed article reviewing the presumption argument in the transfer problem [104] and an article that combines a concern with partial equilibrium analysis and the Hume adjustment mechanism [103]. Each of these pieces essentially focused on different issues, and apparently it was a subsequent letter from Martin Bronfenbrenner that encouraged Samuelson to probe more directly into detailed features of the Ricardo-Viner model, with special reference to the possibility that free trade only in commodities would encourage an incomplete tendency toward factor-price equalization [105]. Indeed, both his choice of title ("Ohlin Was Right") and journal (*The Swedish Journal of Economics*) attest to his interest in showing that Ohlin's claim that free trade helped to bring factor prices closer together, but not to the point of equality, could find analytical support in a model somewhat different from the Heckscher-Ohlin model.

A principal feature of this specific factors model is that the number of primary factors exceeds the number of produced commodities, so that a world market-determined set of commodity prices would generally *not* determine factor prices uniquely, independent of factor endowments. Unlike the Heckscher-Ohlin model, the problem is not that trade might force countries to specialize in production to a subset of commodities they produce in autarky.[50] Rather, even without specialization the number of competitive profit equations in the set (7) falls short of the number of factor rewards to be determined.

Figure 5 can be used to illustrate some of Samuelson's main findings. Consider, first, a world equilibrium in which all *factors* are geographically mobile (although V_1 and V_2 are occupationally specific). Given a set of demand conditions, some equilibrium set of relative world factor (and commodity) prices will be determined, along with cost-minimizing techniques. These, together with the fixed world totals of labor and specific factors, support the constraints on outputs represented by the three solid lines. The common intersection point, A, reveals full employment and the unique set of world outputs. Now suppose national boundaries constrain factor mobility and that at these same factor prices country 1's endowments of the two specific factors support the vertical and horizontal dashed constraint lines intersecting at B in Figure 5. Full employment of all factors at these prices could only follow with the singularly unique labor endowment illustrated by the dashed L^1 line through B. Thus factor-price equalization with commodity trade is unlikely if labor endowments are arbitrary. But if labor alone were internationally mobile, factor prices would always be equalized. This property—factor prices being equalized with labor the *only* internationally mobile factor—is peculiar to the Ricardo-Viner model and is not shared by potential geographical mobility of a specific factor. Thus suppose at the factor prices that would prevail if the world were a single economy, country 1 had the fixed quantity of V_2^1 shown by the horizontal dashed line and a fixed quantity of labor that would support a downward-sloping

---

[50] Indeed, Samuelson points out that slopes along the transformation curve could span the entire range.

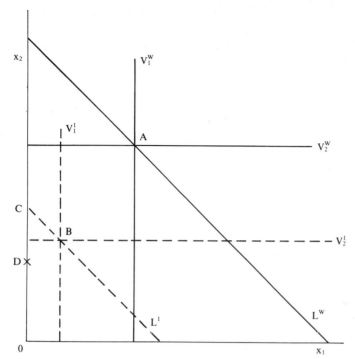

Figure 5
Factor-Price equalization with special factors.

constraint line hitting the vertical axis at D. Even if V_1 were internationally mobile, full employment of specific factor two at these factor prices would be impossible in country 1; factor prices would have to diverge between regions.[51] (In this case the scarcity of labor in country 1 would drive the wage rate above its level in the rest of the world and all the world's geographically mobile V_1 would reside abroad.)

The specific-factor model has many strong properties that are associated with partial equilibrium models, and this source of appeal was emphasized by Samuelson in [103]. In particular, given a nation's endowment pattern, the level of output in any one sector (sector j in the general n-sector, $n + 1$ factor version) depends only upon *one* relative price—the ratio between p_j and the wage rate. The mathematical appendix to Samuelson's "Ohlin was Right" article discusses this and other properties of the general multidimensional version of the Ricardo-Viner model.[52]

Two key articles in 1974, one by Wolfgang Mayer [60] and the other by Michael Mussa [66] went far in linking the Ricardo-Viner model to the standard Heckscher-Ohlin model. The key element was the interpretation of factor specificity as

---

[51]For a different graphical version of this argument see Dixit and Norman [11, pp. 122–125].
[52]Applications of the multidimensional version to the theory of effective protection are found in Jones [36]. This article is based on the two-sector, three-factor version of the Ricardo-Viner model analyzed in Jones [34], rather than on Samuelson's 1971 Swedish model.

temporal. Given enough time, perhaps with the aid of depreciation and replacement, specific factor V_1 could be transformed into the other specific factor, V_2. Thus the Heckscher-Ohlin model with intersectorally mobile labor and capital can be viewed as a long-run version of the Ricardo-Viner model with mobile labor but with capital in the short run tied in its use to single industries. The link between these two models was further developed by J. Peter Neary [67] with an ingenious blend of box-diagram geometry and the diagram showing marginal products of the mobile factor, familiar from partial equilibrium usage. In this connection it is interesting to recall what, in Samuelson's view, was one of the chief advantages of the Ricardo-Viner set of supply conditions:

> They provide what this intricate subject can use to advantage, an alternative *simple* model that can free the discussion from the straight-jacket of the box-diagram analysis which Stolper and I imposed on the trade literature decades ago [105, p. 366].

Geometry aside, this passage reveals an attitude about the potential advantage of a model that does not require factor prices to be locked into place by commodity prices.[53]

International trade can itself provide an alternative rationale for this kind of link between specific-factor and Heckscher-Ohlin models. Factors of production may be specifically used in one productive activity and not in others. But occupational specificity is not the same thing as geographical immobility. Specific factors that can enter into trade at given world prices can be amalgamated into a single Hicksian composite input.[54] Thus a country's autarkic Ricardo-Viner productive structure could be converted by trade into a Heckscher-Ohlin model.[55]

Samuelson not only showed how factor-price equalization was unlikely in the Ricardo-Viner model, but he also analyzed how factor returns respond to price changes that correspond to trade or tariffs. Suppose the price of food rises. Mobile labor now finds its wage rising in terms of clothing but falling in terms of food, thus being faced with the "neoclassical ambiguity" as to the impact on the real wage.[56] It was this ambiguity that is avoided in the Stolper-Samuelson tariff argument in the Heckscher-Ohlin context.

6   CONCLUDING REMARKS

Samuelson's contributions to the theory of international trade have been so pervasive that even this long article must of necessity treat many issues lightly if at

---

[53]In my 1971 Kindleberger *Festschrift* article [34], I described as an advantage of the specific-factor model that "This still allows the straight-jacket of the factor-price equalization theorem to be removed, while preserving most of the simple methods of analysis characteristic of the two-by-two model" (p. 4). In the literature on this subject mention should also be made of the sophisticated analysis of Jorge Marquez-Ruarte [58].

[54]This kind of connection between the two models is developed in detail in Sanyal and Jones [113].

[55]In [113] Sanyal and I credit Doug Purvis with the remark that in this context, "Heckscher-Ohlin does not explain trade, trade explains Heckscher-Ohlin." The distinction between occupational specificity and geographical immobility would be made sharp if only the specific factors (and commodities) are traded, while mobile labor remains trapped behind national boundaries.

[56]More details are provided in Ruffin and Jones [77].

all.[57] It is striking that although over forty-two years have passed since Samuelson's initial writings in the trade area, in the past decade he has made new contributions in each of the five areas discussed in this article. He does not give up.

I choose to close with a few words about style. Samuelson's style cuts across all the fields covered in this volume and, in true Renaissance fashion, goes way beyond the confines of economics. The ease and informality that characterize his teaching provide a positive invitation to think.[58] Throughout his writings one encounters such a rich reference to doctrine that at times our field seems more like a humanity than a social science. And the field of international trade has benefited by his treating it as hard-core economics:

> . . . even if one wanted to be an economist dealing purely with the problems of a closed economy, he would be well advised to study international economic analysis. . . . Our subject puts its best foot forward when it speaks out on international trade [102, p. 683].

To pursue the analogy—a technique most characteristic of his style—he displays a productive empathy for stripped-down models of economic interaction: a two-country model of commodity exchange to capture the essence of the transfer problem, a box-diagram in two dimensions to picture the interaction of six economic variables in explaining the Heckscher-Ohlin model. In trade theory Paul Samuelson has not only helped to lay the foundations, he has also set a good example.

REFERENCES

1 Baldwin, R. E. 1948: "Equilibrium in International Trade: A Diagrammatic Analysis," *Quarterly Journal of Economics* 52 (Nov.) pp. 748–62.
2 Bhagwati, Jagdish 1958: "Immiserizing Growth: A Geometrical Note," *Review of Economic Studies* 25 (June) pp. 201–5.
3 Brigden, J. B., et al., 1929: *The Australian Tariff: An Economic Inquiry*, Melbourne, University Press.

[57]For example, I have neglected Samuelson's work in balance of payments theory. In the recent Sohmen memorial volume [111], Samuelson is at pains to set the record straight on the price-specie-flow mechanism enunciated by David Hume over two centuries ago. He despairs at Hume's suggestion that a monetary disturbance is eventually self-correcting through a mechanism that causes prices to differ between countries for the same commodities. Instead, the key role of direct adjustments in spending out of extra or depleted monetary hoards *at given prices* is stressed. My own view is that Samuelson is a bit harsh, both here and in his previous 1971 article [103], in his interpretation of others' views on the Hume mechanism. In any case I think it useful to point out the potential analogy between the Humean error and the "mistake" that Ohlin and Samuelson attribute to Keynes in the transfer literature. In both cases a correct analysis must emphasize the direct impact at unchanged prices of changes in purchasing power (with transfer) or spending (with monetary changes) as well as subsequent changes triggered off by alterations in prices.

[58]I here indulge myself in a peculiarly Samuelsonian characteristic—the reminiscence. I first saw Samuelson in the spring of 1952 when, as a college senior, I travelled to Cambridge to see M.I.T. as a prospective graduate student (filled with curiosity about Samuelson, the first edition of whose Principles Text was the Bible used by my first economics professor, Wolfgang Stolper). I was invited by some graduate students to attend his second-semester theory class. I joined the congregation for the lecture on value theory. I forget the question, but I remember how he wanted the students to answer—all who thought "yes" were instructed to grab their right ear lobes. It teaches one to think before grabbing.

4 Caves, Richard E. and R. W. Jones 1981: *World Trade and Payments*, 3d ed., New York, Little, Brown.

5 Chang, Winston 1979: "Some Theorems of Trade and General Equilibrium with Many Goods and Factors," *Econometrica* 47 (May) pp. 709–26.

6 Chipman, John S. (1965, 1966): "A Survey of the Theory of International Trade: Parts I–III," *Econometrica* 33 and 34, (July, October, January) pp. 477–519, 685–760, 18–76.

7 ———. 1969: "Factor Price Equalization and the Stolper-Samuelson Theorem," *International Economic Review* 10 (October) pp. 399–406.

8 ———. 1974: "The Transfer Problem Once Again," in G. Horwich and P. A. Samuelson, eds., *Trade, Stability and Macroeconomics* (Essays in Honor of Lloyd A. Metzler), New York, Academic Press.

9 Corden, W. Max 1956: "Economic Expansion and International Trade: A Geometric Approach," *Oxford Economic Papers* 8 (June) pp. 223–28.

10 Diewert, W. E. and A. D. Woodland 1977: "Frank Knight's Theorem in Linear Programming Revisited," *Econometrica* 45 (March) pp. 375–98.

11 Dixit, Avinash and Victor Norman 1980: *Theory of International Trade*, Cambridge, Cambridge University Press.

12 ———.: "The Gains from Free Trade," unpublished paper.

13 Dorfman, Robert, P. A. Samuelson, and R. M. Solow 1958: *Linear Programming and Economic Analysis*, New York, McGraw-Hill.

14 Dornbusch, Rudiger, S. Fischer, and P. A. Samuelson 1977: "Comparative Advantage, Trade, and Payments in a Ricardian Model with a Continuum of Goods," *American Economic Review* 67 (Dec.) pp. 823–839.

15 ———. 1980: "Heckscher-Ohlin Trade Theory with a Continuum of Goods," *Quarterly Journal of Economics* 95 (Sept.) pp. 203–224.

16 Emmanuel, A. 1972: *Unequal Exchange: A Study of the Imperialism of Trade,* New York, Monthly Review Press.

17 ———. 1978: "A Note on 'Trade Pattern Reversals'," *Journal of International Economics* 8 (Feb.) pp. 143–145.

18 Ethier, Wilfred 1974: "Some of the Theorems of International Trade with Many Goods and Factors," *Journal of International Economics* 4 (May) pp. 199–206.

19 ———. 1979: "The Theorems of International Trade in Time-Phased Economies," *Journal of International Economics* 9 (May) pp. 225–238.

20 Findlay, Ronald and H. Grubert 1959: "Factor Intensities, Technological Progress and the Terms of Trade," *Oxford Economic Papers* 11 (Feb.) pp. 111–21.

21 Gale, David 1974: "Exchange Equilibrium and Coalitions," *Journal of Mathematical Economics* 1 (March) pp. 63–66.

22 ——— and H. Nikaido 1965: "The Jacobian Matrix and the Global Univalence of Mappings," *Mathematische Annalen* 159 pp. 81–93.

23 Graham, Frank 1948: *The Theory of International Values*, Princeton, Princeton University Press.

24 Harrod, Roy F. 1958: "Factor Price Relations Under Free Trade," *Economic Journal* 68 (June) pp. 245–255.

25 Heckscher, Eli 1919: "The Effect of Foreign Trade on the Distribution of Income," *Ekonomisk Tidskrift* pp. 497–512, translated in the A.E.A., *Readings in the Theory of International Trade*, Philadelphia, Blakiston, 1949.

26 Inada, Ken-ichi 1971: "The Production Coefficient Matrix and the Stolper-Samuelson Condition," *Econometrica* 39 (March) pp. 219–240.

27 Johnson, Harry G. 1957: "Factor Endowments, International Trade, and Factor Prices," *The Manchester School of Economic and Social Studies* 25 (Sept.)

28 Jones, Ronald W. 1956: "Factor Proportions and the Heckscher-Ohlin Theorem," *Review of Economic Studies* 24 (Oct.) pp. 1–10, reprinted as Chap. 1 in R. W. Jones, *International Trade: Essays in Theory,* Amsterdam, North-Holland, 1979.

29 ———. 1961: "Comparative Advantage and the Theory of Tariffs: A Multi-Country, Multi-Commodity Model," *Review of Economic Studies* 28 (June) pp. 161–175, reprinted as Chap. 3 in R. W. Jones, *International Trade: Essays in Theory,* Amsterdam, North-Holland, 1979.

30 ———. 1965: "Duality in International Trade: A Geometrical Note," *Canadian Journal of Economics and Political Science* 31 (Aug.) pp. 390–393, reprinted as Chap. 5 in R. W. Jones, *International Trade: Essays in Theory,* Amsterdam, North-Holland, 1979.

31 ———. 1965: "The Structure of Simple General Equilibrium Models," *Journal of Political Economy* 73 (Dec.) pp. 557–572, reprinted as Chap. 4 in R. W. Jones, *International Trade: Essays in Theory,* Amsterdam, North-Holland, 1979.

32 ———. 1967: "International Capital Movements and the Theory of Tariffs and Trade," *Quarterly Journal of Economics* 81 (Feb.) pp. 1–38, appearing in slightly revised form as Chap. 12 in R. W. Jones, *International Trade: Essays in Theory,* Amsterdam, North-Holland, 1979.

33 ———. 1970: "The Transfer Problem Revisited," *Economica* 37 (May) pp. 178–184, reprinted as Chap. 9 in R. W. Jones, *International Trade: Essays in Theory,* Amsterdam, North-Holland, 1979.

34 ———. 1971: "A Three-Factor Model in Theory, Trade, and History," in J. Bhagwati, et al., eds., *Trade, Balance of Payments, and Growth*, Amsterdam, North-Holland, and reprinted as Chap. 6 in R. W. Jones, *International Trade: Essays in Theory*, Amsterdam, North-Holland, 1979.

35 ———. 1975: "Presumption and the Transfer Problem," *Journal of International Economics* 5 (Aug.) 1975, pp. 263–274, reprinted as Chap. 10 in R. W. Jones, *International Trade: Essays in Theory,* Amsterdam, North-Holland, 1979.

36 ———. 1975: "Income Distribution and Effective Protection in a Multi-Commodity Trade Model," *Journal of Economic Theory* 11 (Aug.) pp. 1–15.

37 ———. 1979: "Technical Progress and Real Incomes in a Ricardian Trade Model," Chap. 17 in R. W. Jones, *International Trade: Essays in Theory,* Amsterdam, North-Holland.

38 ———. 1980: "Demand Behavior and the Theory of International Trade," Chap. 17 in J. S. Chipman and C. P. Kindleberger, eds., *Flexible Exchange Rates and the Balance of Payments*, Amsterdam, North-Holland.

39 ———. and José A. Scheinkman 1977: "The Relevance of the Two-Sector Production Model in Trade Theory," *Journal of Political Economy* 85 (Oct.) pp. 909–35.

40 Kaldor, Nicholas 1940: "A Note on Tariffs and the Terms of Trade," *Economica* 7 (Nov.) pp. 377–80.

41 Kemp, Murray C. 1962: "The Gain from International Trade," *Economic Journal* 72, (Dec.) pp. 803–819.

42 ———. 1966: "The Gain from International Trade and Investment: A Neo-Heckscher-Ohlin Approach," *American Economic Review* 56 (Sept.) pp. 788–809.

43 ——— and Wilfred Ethier 1976: "A Note on Joint Production and the Theory of International Trade," Chap. 7 in M. C. Kemp, ed., *Three Topics in the Theory of International Trade,* Amsterdam, North-Holland.

44 ——— and L. Wegge 1969: "On the Relation Between Commodity Prices and Factor Rewards," *International Economic Review* 10 (Oct.) pp. 407–413.

45 Keynes, J. M. 1929: "The German Transfer Problem," *Economic Journal* 39 (March) pp. 1–7.

46 Krueger, Anne and H. Sonnenschein 1967: "The Terms of Trade, the Gains from Trade and Price Divergence," *International Economic Review* 8 (Feb.) pp. 121–127.

47 Leontief, Wassily 1937: "Note on the Pure Theory of Capital Transfer," Chap. 8 in *Explorations in Economics: Notes and Essay Contributed in Honor of F. W. Taussig*, New York, McGraw-Hill.

48 ———. 1953: "Domestic Production and Foreign Trade; the American Capital Position Re-examined," *Proceedings of the American Philosophical Society*, 97 (Sept.), reprinted as Chap. 30 in R. Caves and H. Johnson, eds., *Readings in International Economics*, Homewood, Ill., Irwin, 1968.

49 Lerner, Abba P. 1932: "The Diagrammatical Representation of Cost Conditions in International Trade," *Economica* 12 (Aug.) pp. 346–56.

50 ———. 1952: "Factor Prices and International Trade." *Economica* 19 (Feb.) pp. 1–15, originally appearing in mimeo form in December 1933, London School of Economics.

51 McDougall, Ian 1965: "Non-Traded Goods and the Transfer Problem," *Review of Economic Studies* 32 (Jan.) pp. 67–84.

52 McKenzie, Lionel W. 1954: "On Equilibrium in Graham's Model of World Trade and Other Competitive Systems," *Econometrica* 22 (April) pp. 147–161.

53 ———. 1954: "Specialization and Efficiency in World Production," *Review of Economic Studies* 21 (June) pp. 165–180.

54 ———. 1955: "Equality of Factor Prices in World Trade," *Econometrica* 23 (July) pp. 239–257.

55 ———. 1955: "Specialization in Production and the Production Possibility Locus," *Review of Economic Studies* 23 (No. 1) pp. 56–64.

56 ———. 1967: "The Inversion of Cost Functions: A Counter-Example," *International Economic Review* 8 (Oct.) pp. 271–278.

57 Mainwaring, L. 1978: "The Interest Rate Equalisation Theorem with Nontraded Goods," *Journal of International Economics* 8 (Feb.) pp. 11–19.

58 Marquez-Ruarte, Jorge 1975: *The Two-Sector Model of Production*, Ph.D. dissertation, University of Chicago.

59 Mas-Colell, Andreu 1979: "Two Propositions on the Global Univalence of Systems of Cost Functions," in J. Green and J. Scheinkman, eds., *General Equilibrium, Growth, and Trade: Essays in Honor of Lionel McKenzie*, New York, Academic Press.

60 Mayer, Wolfgang 1974: "Short-Run Equilibrium for a Small Open Economy," *Journal of Political Economy* 82 (Sept./Oct.) pp. 955–968.

61 Metcalfe, J. S. and Ian Steedman 1972: "Reswitching and Primary Input Use," *Economic Journal* 82 (March) pp. 140–57.

62 ———. 1973: "Heterogeneous Capital and the Heckscher-Ohlin-Samuelson Theory of Trade," in J. M. Parkin, ed., *Essays in Modern Economics*, New York, Barnes and Noble.

63 Metzler, Lloyd 1949: "Tariffs, the Terms of Trade, and the Distribution of National Income," *Journal of Political Economy* 57 (Feb.)

64 Mosak, Jacob L. 1944: *General Equilibrium Theory in International Trade,* Cowles Commission Monograph no. 7, Bloomington, Ind., Principia Press.

65 Mundell, Robert A. 1957: "International Trade and Factor Mobility," *American Economic Review* 47 (June) pp. 321–335.

66 Mussa, Michael 1974: "Tariffs and the Distribution of Income: The Importance of Factor Specificity, Substitutability, and Intensity in the Short and Long Run," *Journal of Political Economy* 82 (Nov./Dec.) pp. 1191–1204.

67 Neary, J. Peter 1978: "Short-Run Capital Specificity and the Pure Theory of International Trade," *Economic Journal* 88 (Sept.) pp. 488–510.

68 Ohlin, Bertil 1929: "Transfer Difficulties, Real and Imagined," *Economic Journal* 39 (June) pp. 172–78.

69 ———. 1933: *Interregional and International Trade*, Cambridge, Harvard University Press.

70 Ohyama, Michihiro 1972: "Trade and Welfare in General Equilibrium," *Keio Economic Studies* 9, pp. 37–73.

71 Pearce, Ivor F. 1952: "The Factor Price Equalization Myth," *Review of Economic Studies* 19 (No. 2) pp. 111–119.

72 ———. 1952: "A Note on Mr. Lerner's Paper," *Economica* 19 (Feb.) pp. 16–18.

73 ———. 1959: "A Further Note on Factor-Commodity Price Relationships," *Economic Journal* 69 (Dec.) pp. 725–732.

74 ———. 1967: "More About Factor Price Equalization," *International Economic Review* 8 (Oct.) pp. 255–270.

75 Robinson, Joan 1937: "Beggar-My-Neighbor Remedies for Unemployment" in J. Robinson, *Essays in the Theory of Employment*, New York, Macmillan.

76 Robinson, Romney 1956: "Factor Proportions and Comparative Advantage," *Quarterly Journal of Economics* 70 (May and Aug.) pp. 169–92, 346–63.

77 Ruffin, Roy and R. W. Jones 1977: "Protection and Real Wages, The Neo-Classical Ambiguity," *Journal of Economic Theory* 14 (April) pp. 337–348.

78 Rybczynski, T. M. 1955: "Factor Endowment and Relative Commodity Prices," *Economica* 22 (Nov.) pp. 336–41.

79 Samuelson, Marion C. 1939: "The Australian Case for Protection Re-examined," *Quarterly Journal of Economics* 54 (Nov.) pp. 143–149.

80 Samuelson, Paul A. 1938: "A Note on the Pure Theory of Consumer's Behaviour," *Economica* 5 (Feb.) pp. 61–71; *Collected Scientific Papers*, I, Chap. 1.

81 ———. 1938: "Welfare Economics and International Trade," *American Economic Review* 28 (June) pp. 261–266; *Collected Scientific Papers*, II, Chap. 60.

82 ———. 1939: "The Gains from International Trade," *Canadian Journal of Economics and Political Science* 5 (May) pp. 195–205; *Collected Scientific Papers*, II, Chap. 61.

83 ———. 1945: Book review of Jacob L. Mosak, *General Equilibrium Theory in International Trade* in *American Economic Review* 35 (Dec.) pp. 943–945; *Collected Scientific Papers*, II, Chap. 63.

84 ———. 1948: "International Trade and Equalisation of Factor Prices," *Economic Journal* 63 (June) pp. 163–184; *Collected Scientific Papers*, II, Chap. 67.

85 ———. 1949: *Market Mechanisms and Maximization*, Part I: "The Theory of Comparative Advantage"; Part II: "The Cheapest-Adequate-Diet Problem"; and Part III: "Dynamics and Linear Programming", RAND Corporation, Parts I and II, March 28, Part III, June 29; *Collected Scientific Papers*, I, Chap. 33.

86 ———. 1949: "International Factor-Price Equalisation Once Again," *Economic Journal* 59 (June) pp. 181–197; *Collected Scientific Papers*, II, Chap. 68.

87 ———. 1950: "Evaluation of Real National Income," *Oxford Economic Papers* (new series) 2 (Jan.) pp. 1–29; *Collected Scientific Papers*, II, Chap. 77.

88 ———. 1952: "A Comment on Factor Price Equalisation," *Review of Economic Studies* 20 (Feb.) pp. 121–122; *Collected Scientific Papers*, II, Chap. 69.

89 ———. 1952: "The Transfer Problem and Transport Costs: The Terms of Trade When Impediments Are Absent," *Economic Journal* 62 (June) pp. 278–304; *Collected Scientific Papers*, II, Chap. 74.

90 ———. 1952: "Spatial Price Equilibrium and Linear Programming," *American Economic Review* 42 (June) pp. 283–303; *Collected Scientific Papers*, II, Chap. 72.

91 ———. 1954: "Prices of Factors and Goods in General Equilibrium," *Review of Economic Studies* 21 1953–1954, pp. 1–20; *Collected Scientific Papers*, II, Chap. 70.

92 ———. 1954: "The Transfer Problem and Transport Costs, II: Analysis of Effects of Trade Impediments," *Economic Journal* 64 (June) pp. 264–289; *Collected Scientific Papers*, II, Chap. 75.

93 ———. 1956: "Social Indifference Curves," *Quarterly Journal of Economics* 70 (Feb.) pp. 1–22; *Collected Scientific Papers*, II, Chap. 78.

94 ———. 1958: "Frank Knight's Theorem in Linear Programming," *Zeitschrift Für Nationalökonomie*, Band 18, Heft 3, pp. 310–317; *Collected Scientific Papers*, I, Chap. 35.

95 ———. 1959: "A Modern Treatment of the Ricardian Economy: I. The Pricing of Goods and of Labor and Land Services," *Quarterly Journal of Economics* 73 (Feb.) pp. 1–35; *Collected Scientific Papers*, I, Chap. 31.

96 ———. 1959: "A Modern Treatment of the Ricardian Economy: II. Capital and Interest Aspects of the Pricing Process," *Quarterly Journal of Economics* 73 (May) pp. 217–231; *Collected Scientific Papers*, I, Chap. 32.

97 ———. 1962: "The Gains from International Trade Once Again," *Economic Journal* 72 (Dec.) pp. 820–829; *Collected Scientific Papers*, II, Chap. 62.

98 ———. 1964: "Theoretical Notes on Trade Problems," *Review of Economics and Statistics* 4 (May) pp. 145–154; *Collected Scientific Papers*, II, Chap. 65.

99 ———. 1965: "1965 Postscript," in *Collected Scientific Papers*, II, p. 908.

100 ———. 1965: "Equalization by Trade of the Interest Rate Along with the Real Wage," in *Trade, Growth and the Balance of Payments*, essays in honor of Gottfried Haberler, Chicago, Rand McNally; *Collected Scientific Papers*, II, Chap. 71.

101 ———. 1967: "Summary on Factor-Price Equalization," *International Economic Review* 8 (Oct.) pp. 286–295; *Collected Scientific Papers*, III, Chap. 161.

102 ———. 1969: "The Way of an Economist," in P. A. Samuelson, ed., *International Economic Relations: Proceedings of the Third Congress of the International Economic Association,* London: Macmillan, pp. 1–11; *Collected Scientific Papers*, III, Chap. 186.

103 ———. 1971: "An Exact Hume-Ricardo-Marshall Model of International Trade," *Journal of International Economics* 1 (Feb.) pp. 1–18; *Collected Scientific Papers*, III, Chap. 162.

104 ———. 1971: "On the Trail of Conventional Beliefs about the Transfer Problem," in J. Bhagwati, et al., eds., *Trade, Balance of Payments, and Growth: Papers in International Economics in Honor of Charles P. Kindleberger*, Amsterdam, North-Holland; *Collected Scientific Papers*, III, Chap. 163.

105 ———. 1971: "Ohlin Was Right," *Swedish Journal of Economics* 73 (Dec.) pp. 365–384; *Collected Scientific Papers*, IV, Chap. 254.

106 ———. 1973: "Deadweight Loss in International Trade from the Profit Motive?" in C. F. Bergsten and W. G. Tyler, eds., *Leading Issues in International Economic Policy, Essays in Honor of George N. Halm*, Lexington, Lexington Books, D.C. Heath; *Collected Scientific Papers*, IV, Chap. 253.

107 ———. 1975: "Trade Pattern Reversals in Time-Phased Ricardian Systems and Intertemporal Efficiency," *Journal of International Economics* 5 (Nov.) pp. 309–363; *Collected Scientific Papers*, IV, Chap. 251.

108 ———. 1976: "Illogic of Neo-Marxian Doctrine of Unequal Exchange," in D. A. Belsley, et al., eds., *Inflation, Trade, and Taxes*, Columbus, Ohio State University Press; *Collected Scientific Papers*, IV, Chap. 252.

109 ———. 1978: "Interest Rate Equalization and Non-Equalization by Trade in Leontief-Sraffa Models," *Journal of International Economics* 8 (Feb.) pp. 21–27.

110 ———. 1978: "Free Trade's Intertemporal Pareto-Optimality," *Journal of International Economics* 8 (Feb.) pp. 147–149.

111 ———. 1980: "A Corrected Version of Hume's Equilibrating Mechanisms for International Trade," Chap. 9 in J. S. Chipman and C. P. Kindleberger, eds., *Flexible Exchange Rates and the Balance of Payments*, Amsterdam, North-Holland.

112 ———. 1981: "Summing Up on the Australian Case for Protection," *Quarterly Journal of Economics* 96 (Feb.) pp. 147–60.

113 Sanyal, Kalyan and R. W. Jones (1979): "The Theory of Trade in Middle Products," Seminar Paper no. 128, Institute for International Economic Studies, University of Stockholm.

114 Shephard, Ronald W. 1953: *Cost and Production Functions*, Princeton, Princeton University Press.

115 Stolper, W. F. and P. A. Samuelson 1941: "Protection and Real Wages," *Review of Economic Studies* 9 (Nov.) pp. 58–73.

116 Uekawa, Yasuo 1971: "Generalization of the Stolper-Samuelson Theorem," *Econometrica* 39 (March) pp. 197–213.

117 Uzawa, Hirofumi 1959: "Prices of the Factors of Production in International Trade," *Econometrica* 27 (July) pp. 448–468.

118 Viner, Jacob 1931: "Cost Curves and Supply Curves," *Zeitschrift für National-ökonomie*, pp. 23–46.

119 Whitin, T. M. 1953: "Classical Theory, Graham's Theory, and Linear Programming in International Trade," *Quarterly Journal of Economics* 67 (Nov.) pp. 520–544.

120 Wilson, Charles 1980: "On the General Structure of Ricardian Models with a Continuum of Goods: Applications to Growth, Tariff Theory, and Technical Change," *Econometrica* 48 (Nov.) pp. 1675–1702.

121 Yano, Makoto: "Welfare Aspects in the Transfer Problem: On the Validity of the 'Neo-orthodox' Presumptions," unpublished working paper.

FINANCIAL ECONOMICS

Robert C. Merton

PREFACE

In this collective tribute to Paul Samuelson, the editors wisely chose a path differing somewhat from the usual route of a Festschrift. Rather than asking the contributors to report some research of their own that derives from Samuelson's work, they have asked us to try our hands at synthesizing his chief contributions to our respective spheres of economic theory. And since Paul Samuelson would probably confess that his discoveries in economic theory constitute the core of his multiform writings, there could scarcely be a better format for honoring this universal man of economics. His theoretical contributions have been ecumenical and his ramified influence on the whole of economics has led economists in just about every branch of economics to claim him as one of their own. This volume provides a special opportunity to do so once again although presumably each contributor to it knows full well that the claims of all the rest are just as valid.

Paradoxically, this "best" format is in fact only second-best (or perhaps one should say, n^{th} best). For, as everyone knows, Paul Samuelson is his own best synthesizer and critic. It therefore follows with inexorable logic that he should be writing his own Festschrift (which would then be truly critical). This rational, if unorthodox, alternative would have been especially apt for this chapter on his contributions to financial economics, a subject in which Rational Man reigns supreme. Nevertheless, that alternative would have been dubiously optimal since the volume is designed to do him honor rather than delegate him to perform still another feat of critical synthesis for the benefit of his fellow economists. Just another instance, I suppose, of the complexity of rationality in action.

After this proper rationalization—in both the psychological and economic senses of the term—of our collectively undertaking the task of synthesis rather than

105

imposing it on Paul Samuelson himself, there remains the problem of establishing a synthesizing design adequate to encompass his contributions. We know that synthesis involves abstraction from the complex original. Here, we must be severely selective in our abstractions since the wide-ranging scope and unflagging volume of his researches allows only a few dimensions of the work to be examined. To make matters worse, the understandable focus on his contributions to economic science leads us to neglect the noneconomic latent themes that are so distinctive of the Samuelsonian corpus. One such thematic interest pervading practically all his writings consists of observations in the history and sociology of science. The law of comparative disadvantage rules out my examining this matter in fitting detail. Besides, the effort would consume too much of the scarce space available for filing the financial economists' claim on Samuelson, and they, no less than the economists from the nine other branches of economic theory represented here, would not wish to receive anything less than their 10 percent pro rata share. Still, I cannot wholly resist the temptation to call attention to this theme in the hope that it will lead others, better qualified, to explore this matter elsewhere.

And so this preface to a miniaturized Samuelson Sampler will only touch upon some characteristic Samuelsonian observations in the history and sociology of science before turning to a more detailed, annotated Contents of his fundamental work in financial economic theory, this to be followed by a brief Afterword.

As is readily apparent from even a quick perusal of the four volumes of his collected scientific papers, Samuelson's writings on Smith, Ricardo, and Marx and his many essays on the evolution of more contemporary economic thought provide much grist for the mill of the historian of science. But, bountiful as they are, to focus exclusively upon these explicit undertakings in the history of economics is to miss much. Part of the unmistakable stamp of a Paul Samuelson article is his interjection of anecdotes and stories around and between his substantive derivations, which are nuggets to be mined by even the most mathematically timid historian of science who, by necessity, must bypass the bristling equations. These stories, of course, also serve as way stations of entertainment and enlightenment for those who are riding the locomotive of his substantive analysis.

One happy example in financial economics is Samuelson's brief description in the "Mathematics of Speculative Price" [1972a, IV, Chap. 240, p. 428] of the rediscovery of Bachelier's pioneering work on the pricing of options. In the text, he wrote:

> In 1900 a French mathematician, Louis Bachelier, wrote a Sorbonne thesis on the *Theory of Speculation*. This was largely lost in the literature, even though Bachelier does receive occasional citation in standard works on probability. Twenty years ago a circular letter by L. J. Savage (now, sadly, lost to us), asking whether economists had any knowledge or interest in a 1914 popular exposition by Bachelier, led to his being rediscovered. Since the 1900 work deserves an honored place in the physics of Brownian motion as well as in the pioneering of stochastic processes, let me say a few words about the Bachelier Theory.*

The footnote elaborates

*Since illustrious French geometers almost never die, it is possible that Bachelier still survives in Paris supplementing his professional retirement pension by judicious arbitrage in puts and calls. But my widespread lecturing on him over the last 20 years has not elicited any information on the subject. How much Pioncaré, to whom he dedicates the thesis, contributed to it, I have no knowledge. Finally, as Bachelier's cited life works suggest, he seems to have had something of a one-track mind. But what a track! The rather supercilious references to him, as an unrigorous pioneer in stochastic processes and stimulator of work in that area by more rigorous mathematicians such as Kolmogorov, hardly does Bachelier justice. His methods can hold their own in rigor with the best scientific work of his time, and his fertility was outstanding. Einstein is properly revered for his basic, and independent, discovery of the theory of Brownian motion 5 years after Bachelier. But years ago when I compared the two texts, I formed the judgment (which I have not checked back on) that Bachelier's methods dominated Einstein's in every element of the vector. Thus, the Einstein-Fokker-Planck Fourier equation for diffusion of probabilities is already in Bachelier, along with subtle uses of the now-standard method of reflected images.

In addition to providing the facts on how Bachelier's seminal work found its way into the mainstream of financial economics after more than a half century of obscurity, Samuelson's compact description provides a prime example of multiple and independent discoveries across the fields of physics, mathematics, and economics. On the issue of allocating the credit due innovative scholars, he also provides an evaluation of the timing and relative quality of the independent discoveries. His mention of Poincaré provides a hint that there may be still more to the complete story. And, of course, what economist wouldn't relish this revelation of the great debt owed to this early financial economist by the mathematical physicists and probabilists to be added to the well-known debt owed to Malthus by the Darwinian biologists?

Along with the anecdotes and stories, there are the eponyms that would surely appear in everyone's benevolent parody of a typical Samuelson paper. These highly synoptic histories of the subject[1] serve to remind us all—from the economist well-practiced in the history of economic thought to the novice theorist, unencumbered by such knowledge, who benefits from such cram courses—that we owe credit to a sequence of scientists (as we have just seen in his preceding footnote with its allusion to the "Einstein-Fokker-Planck Fourier equation"). While such penchant for hyphenation is, of course, not unique, no one uses it more profitably and with greater skill than Paul Samuelson.

One example of such skillful use is his treatment of Benoit Mandelbrot and the stable distributions. As we all know, Mandelbrot is responsible for some of the most

---

[1]As the sociologist R. K. Merton notes (1976, p. 130, footnote 53): "Every scientific discipline has some practitioners who take pleasure in keeping green the memory of developers of ideas though none, to my limited knowledge, more so than Paul Samuelson, master constructor of those freight trains of eponyms that instantly catch up main lines in a genealogy of ideas ('an exact Hume-Ricardo-Marshall model of international trade' can serve as the example of the hyphenated variety although a longer search would surely uncover as long a freight train as the adjacency type exemplified in 'the economic theory of index numbers associated with the names Pigou, Könus, Keynes, Staehle, Leontief, Frisch, Lerner, R. G. D. Allen, Wald, and my own theories of revealed preference')."

fundamental research on infinite-variance stable distributions and was the first to introduce them into financial economics. However, as we all also know, the practice among economists (including Samuelson) is to refer to these distributions as "Pareto-Lévy distributions." On the occasion of his paper "Limited Liability, Short-Selling, Bounded Utility, and Infinite-Variance Stable Distributions" [1976c, IV, Chap. 247], it appears that Samuelson chose to correct this "injustice." In the opening footnote (p. 534), he acknowledges Mandelbrot's contributions with "Every economist working with stochastic processes has room to be grateful to Dr. Benoit Mandelbrot of IBM, for his pioneering work in extending finite-variance models to the infinite domain of Lévy and beyond; and the author feels a particular debt to his works of the last 15 years." However, the key acknowledgement occurs three pages later in the section subtitle where he substitutes "Mandelbrot-Lévy Stable Distributions" for the standard "Pareto-Lévy." To justify and to underscore the significance of this substitution, he adds in a footnote:

> Mandelbrot uses "Pareto-Lévy distributions" to describe the stable-additive functions with finite mean but infinite variance. However, as he points out, Pareto only knew their tail's asymptotic property; so my label is more fitting than that which Mandelbrot too modestly originally suggested; moreover, it can also be used for the stable case where the mean is not defined, an area to which Mandelbrot has also made great contributions.

Although he is not a card-carrying sociologist of science, Paul Samuelson's work is pervasive as we know from the testimony of the veteran sociologist of science, Robert K. Merton (1973). This sociological subtheme in Samuelson's writings can perhaps be traced to his early, soon-abandoned thought of possibly taking up life as a sociologist.[2] From his papers devoted exclusively to the history of ideas to the cryptic-but-critical asides that pepper all his writings, Samuelson consistently demonstrates a deep insight into the social structure for the allocation of rewards in science. His papers also provide a wealth of examples and analyses of multiple discoveries and rediscoveries; waxing and waning fame in science; precocity in science; allocation of credit as a zero-sum game; oral publication; loss of credit from publication in obscure places and from obliteration of source by incorporation in canonical knowledge; and "near misses" in scientific discovery. As is evident from even this short inventory (drawn exclusively from Merton's catalog of sociology of science problems), Samuelson's excursions into the history and sociology of science cover much of the terrain in these fields.

As demonstrated, for example, in his "The Balanced-Budget Multiplier: A Case Study in the Sociology and Psychology of Scientific Discovery" [1975, IV, Chap. 274], Samuelson has the cognitive distance needed to evaluate his own work as well as that of others. His substantive contributions to financial economics provide a rich source for another such case study, and were Samuelson writing this chapter, he

---

[2] In his autobiographical piece, "Economics in a Golden Age: A Personal Memoir" [1972b, IV, Chap. 278, p. 885 and infra], Samuelson reveals that "there was a minute in my sophomore year when I toyed with the notion of becoming a sociologist. . . ." Citations of Samuelson's *Collected Scientific Papers* give year of original publication, volume in roman numerals, chapter, and sometimes specific pages.

would surely discuss his work as exemplifying these varied sociological concepts. Just one more reason why this volume's best format is really only second-best.

Designed to whet the appetite for further exploration of the latent themes in his writings, this teaser on his observations in the history and sociology of science also underscores the losses that inevitably occur when one tries to synthesize Samuelson originals. There is the further difficulty in finding a synthesizing design that can capture the distinctive flow of his developing problem formulations and solutions. If, however, abstraction is a necessity (as it is here), then it is surely better to abstract by selecting and reproducing in their entirety a small subset of his articles rather than attempting to summarize them all. Hence the notion of a Samuelson Sampler. The choice of an anthology also neatly provides the opportunity for some tradeoff between the best synthesis (which requires that he undertake the task) and doing Paul Samuelson honor (which certainly requires that he not). And so the constrained solution is to ask Paul to select the subset of financial economic articles for inclusion and then to have me write the introduction to them. (Note that by having Samuelson himself choose the articles, this format quite fittingly has the additional feature of providing some interesting data to the historian of science.)

In asking Paul to make his selections, I presented him with a list of his thirty articles in financial economics and left the criteria for choice purposely vague. By the not-so-tacit demanding criterion that was evidently applied, he was drastically selective, choosing only six. These are now listed in the Contents, followed by that promised Introduction of mine. Four of the six articles appear in journals not on the beaten path of most economists, and at one time their reprinting would have made them far more accessible to a wider audience. They all now appear in Samuelson's collected scientific papers, and so it is happily unnecessary to reproduce them here.

CONTENTS

INTRODUCTION

Although most would agree that finance, microinvestment theory and much of the economics of uncertainty are within the sphere of modern financial economics, the boundaries of this sphere, like those of other specialties, are both permeable and flexible. It is enough to say here that the core of the subject is the study of the individual behavior of households in the intertemporal allocation of their resources in an environment of uncertainty and of the role of economic organizations in facilitating these allocations. It is the complexity of the interaction of time and uncertainty that provides intrinsic excitement to study of the subject, and, indeed, the mathematics of financial economics contains some of the most interesting applications of probability and optimization theory. Yet, for all its seemingly obtrusive mathematical complexity, the research has had a direct and significant influence on practice. The impact of efficient market theory, portfolio selection, risk analysis, and option pricing theory on money management and capital budgeting procedures is evident from even a casual comparison of current practices with, for example, those of the early 1960s. The effects of financial research have even been observed in legal proceedings such as appraisal cases, rate of return hearings for regulated industries, and revisions of the "prudent person" laws governing behavior for fiduciaries. Evidence that this influence on practice will continue can be found in the curricula of the best-known schools of management where the fundamental financial research papers (with their mathematics included) are routinely assigned to MBA students. Although not unique, this conjoining of intrinsic intellectual interest with extrinsic application is a prevailing theme of research in financial economics. Samuelson, once again, did much to establish this theme as a commonplace and to exemplify it in his substantive writings.

It was not always thus. Thirty years ago, before the birth of the economics of uncertainty and before the rediscovery of Bachelier, finance was essentially a collection of anecdotes, rules of thumb, and manipulations of accounting data with an almost exclusive focus on corporate financial management. The most sophisticated technique was discounted value and the central intellectual controversy centered on whether to use present value or internal rate of return to rank corporate investment projects. The subsequent evolution from this conceptual potpourri to a rigorous economic theory subjected to systematic empirical examination was the work of many and, of course, the many included Paul Samuelson.

In economic theory, it is traditional to take the existence of households and their tastes as exogenous to the theory. However, this tradition does not extend to economic organizations that are regarded as existing primarily because of the functions they serve and are, therefore, endogenous to the theory. Hence, to derive the functions of these economic organizations, the behavior of individuals must first be derived. It is, therefore, not surprising that the evolution of modern financial economics began with the study of individual choice under uncertainty and that Samuelson's early contributions to this evolution were in this area.

In financial economics, the basic problem of choice for an individual is to determine the optimal allocation of his or her wealth among the available investment opportunities. The solution to the general problem of choosing the best mix is called portfolio selection theory. Of course, for this problem to be well posed, it must be assumed that the individual has a preference ordering for ranking alternative choices. While it has long been the accepted standard to assume that preference orderings satisfy the axioms of the von Neumann-Morgenstern expected utility maxim, this was not the general view among economists in the early 1950s, when Samuelson published a sequence of papers investigating the legitimacy of these axioms.

The essence of the expected utility maxim is that for each individual, there exists a unique (up to a positive affine transformation) nondecreasing function $U(\ )$ whose expected value can be used to determine the preference orderings of that individual among stochastic alternatives. That is, if x_i denotes the random variable payoff to choosing the ith alternative where the individual's assessment of the distribution for x_i is $x_i = x_{ik}$ with probability $p_{ik}, k = 1, \ldots, m_i$, then that individual will strictly prefer the ith alternative to the jth alternative if and only if $E[U(x_i)] > E[U(x_j)]$ where "E" denotes the expectation operator [that is, $E[U(x_i)] \equiv \sum_{k=1}^{m_i} p_{ik} U(x_{ik})$]. It follows that in selecting among n mutually exclusive alternatives, the individual will choose the one that has the largest value for $E[U(x)]$.

As is readily apparent, the orderings generated by this maxim are not invariant to a positive monotonic transformation of U and they are hence represented by a unique additive cardinal utility function. However, by the late 1940s, economic theorists were in general agreement that the nonstochastic theory of consumer choice required only that preference orderings be ordinal and that nothing of operational significance would be added by a cardinal ordering. (Another important commonplace that, as we all know, Samuelson did more than just help to establish.)

Thus, since von Neumann and Morgenstern claimed that their axioms imply a cardinal utility representation for preferences, the validity of the axioms would seem to create a fundamental discontinuity between the nonstochastic and stochastic theories of consumer choice. That is, when events are known with certainty, then only ordinal preferences matter, but when events are uncertain, (even a "little bit") cardinality becomes essential. This perhaps explains why the early reaction to these axioms by many economists including Samuelson [1950, I, Chap. 12] was a composite of puzzlement and criticism.

The essence of the puzzlement was that, on the one hand, the von Neumann-Morgenstern axioms were quite "sensible" and on the other hand, their apparent implication of additive cardinal utility was not. There existed at that time many examples of nonstochastic preference orderings that could not be represented in an additive cardinal form, and those that did admit a unique additive cardinal representation required such special assumptions about the marginal rates of substitution among goods that they were regarded as empirically irrelevant. This puzzle was at least in part resolved by Samuelson and others when they recognized the failure of von Neumann and Morgenstern to make explicit the independence axiom (or as Samuelson also called it, their zeroth axiom), which is essential to their system. As Samuelson later described the situation:

> Around 1950, Marschak, Dalkey, Nash, and others independently recognized the crucial importance of the independence axiom. Prior to this the Neumann-Morgenstern axioms had puzzled many economists, including myself. A number of interpretations of those

axioms, much like the Manne octane example, has seemed to fulfill the spirit of those axioms and yet to *not* lead to additive cardinal utility. Marschak, I, and no doubt others had come to suspect that the independence axiom had been implicitly assumed in the pre-axiom concepts of the *Games* discussion. At the Paris conference, M. Malinvaud presented me with a confirmation of this suspicion. [1952, I, Chap. 14, p. 140, fn. 3]

It was undoubtedly the recognition of this "missing" axiom together with some critical correspondence with L. J. Savage that led to Samuelson's reconciliation of the expected utility maxim with the nonstochastic theory of consumer choice in his seminal paper,[3] "Probability, Utility, and the Independence Axiom." As Samuelson summarized it in the second paragraph of that paper (p. 137),

> When we come to a theory of consumers' preference in stochastic situations, the basic methodology is the same [as in nonstochastic situations]. We are alone interested in the "more or less" ordinal relations that determine how the consumer will choose between one uncertain prospect with its "probable prizes" and any other specified uncertain prospect. . . . Recently, Ramsey, de Finetti, and Savage have worked out an interesting theory of what I term "consistent ordinal reactions to uncertainty situations." . . . If a person is to be "consistent" in dealing with "mutually exclusive" outcomes, we find ourselves postulating for him "strong independence conditions" in the uncertainty realm of the type that we regard as empirically absurd in the nonstochastic realm. It is these strong independence conditions that create the existence of certain special or canonical indices of utility and probability that are "additive."

In his elaboration of this summary, Samuelson indicates that "mutually exclusive" were the "magic words" that convinced him of a legitimacy of the "strong independence axiom" in the stochastic realm that it does not have in the nonstochastic realm.

Having reconciled the expected utility maxim with the nonstochastic theory of consumer choice, Samuelson endorsed the theory ("Having blown cold concerning the theory, I should like to conclude by again blowing hot" [p. 144]). However, he did so only after expressing his legitimate concerns over being "caught between the Scylla and Charybdis of theoretical formulation and operational empirical hypothesis formation" with respect to the appropriate dimensional space in which the axioms are presumed to be operating. Pushing his point to the extreme, Samuelson noted "If every time you find my axiom falsified, I tell you to go to a space of still higher dimensions, you can legitimately regard my theories as irrefutable and meaningless." Upon rereading this section of the paper, I was struck by the prophetic nature of the discussion (especially the part that focuses on the use of the axioms in a dynamic framework) because of its connection with the intertemporal consumption choice and portfolio selection problem, a problem that did not even begin to be analyzed until a decade later.

The early development of this problem by Phelps, Hakansson, Leland, Mossin, and, of course, Samuelson, used the method of stochastic dynamic programming

---

[3] As Samuelson notes in the paper, he was not the only economist to reconcile the axioms with the nonstochastic theory of consumer preferences. True to form as his own most historical critic, in almost the same breath that he used to select this paper for the sampler, he remarked, "I think that Marschak's formulation was the best."

together with the assumption that the expected utility maxim applied to preferences for lifetime consumption. Because they all made some rather specialized additional assumptions (for example, intertemporally additive utility, with a single consumption good and serially independent and identically distributed random variables for the returns on investments), the only stochastic argument of the "derived" or indirect utility function was wealth. Therefore, at each point in time, the derived behavior of the intertemporal maximizers in these formulations is operationally indistinguishable from a "static" maximizer whose preferences with respect to "end-of-period" wealth satisfy the von Neumann-Morgenstern axioms. However, as these early analyses were generalized to include the empirically more realistic possibilities of multiple consumption goods with stochastic relative prices and distributions of investment returns that are neither serially independent nor identical, the resulting indirect utility functions have other stochastic arguments in addition to wealth. And, for these more general cases, it is, of course, possible to derive behavior that is consistent with the axioms of the expected utility maxim in the higher dimensional space of lifetime consumption but which is inconsistent with these axioms when applied to the single dimension of "end-of-period" wealth.[4]

Samuelson's premonitory remarks are thus as pertinent to current research in financial economics as they were in 1952. Indeed, they will undoubtedly become even more pertinent as research on this fundamental problem of choice progresses. Future refinements in the theoretical analysis of the consumption and portfolio selection problem will almost certainly require increasing the dimensional space in which the axioms are assumed to apply. Such progress will therefore, by necessity, make ever finer the distinction between increasing the dimensionality in an attempt to capture more empirically realistic detail and increasing it in an endless attempt to save the theory.

As exemplified by the advice in that ancient and familiar adage, "Don't put all your eggs in one basket," diversification is regarded as sound and prudent behavior by investment practitioner and lawmaker alike and was so regarded long before the advent of the modern theory of portfolio selection. One need hardly do more than contemplate the images associated with the words "gambler," "plunger," "risklover," "speculator" (all used to describe those who behave in an antipodal fashion) to note that diversification as normal behavior in investment matters is a widely shared belief. As a reflection of this belief, it is now almost the universal practice for analyses of the portfolio selection problem to exclude as "empirically irrelevant" those preference orderings that do not exhibit this normal behavior but that otherwise satisfy the axioms of the expected utility maxim.

As indicated by its title, Samuelson's "General Proof That Diversification Pays" [1967a, III, Chap. 201] derives the important general conditions under which individual optimal portfolio selection behavior is to diversify. When Samuelson's paper was published in 1967, the Markowitz-Tobin mean-variance theory of portfolio selection was already well developed. This theory does provide specific content to the rule of diversification. From earlier classic insurance examples, it was

---

[4]See Merton, (1982, pp. 654–655) for a discussion of such inconsistencies.

well known that for independently and identically distributed investments, the expected return on the portfolio is the same for all "mixes," and that an equal investment in each will minimize the variance of the return on the portfolio. By restricting investor preferences to "risk averters" (for whom variance in the portfolio's return is a "bad"), the mean-variance theory demonstrates that such "equal" diversification behavior is indeed optimal.

However, as was well known to Samuelson and the others before 1967, choosing a portfolio on the basis of its mean and variance alone will be consistent with the axioms of the expected utility maxim only under some rather restrictive and unsatisfactory assumptions about both preference orderings and the joint probability distribution of available investments. Despite the intuitive appeal and analytical tractability of the mean-variance theory, many economists were, therefore, understandably skeptical of results derived in this special framework. It is this valid skepticism that makes Samuelson's general proof of diversification behavior so important to the field even though such behavior had been clearly demonstrated in the mean-variance context. That Samuelson saw this as the central purpose of his general analysis is clear from his statement of intent: "The whole point of this paper is to free the analysis from dependence on means, variances, and covariances" (p. 854).

As we know, it is often difficult to define an intuitive concept such as diversification behavior; to give it meaningful content is not always easy. A seemingly sensible general definition, for example, might be that the investor chooses to take some position in (almost) all available investments. In the absence of restrictions on borrowing and shortselling, a contradiction of such behavior would require that the investor's optimal demand for at least some investments be exactly zero. However, because the conditions under which the investor's demand for an investment will equal zero are so singular, this proposed definition imposes virtually no restrictions on either preferences or the distribution of investment returns. Were such a general definition of diversification behavior adopted, therefore, it would have practically no operational meaning.

In the general proof, Samuelson characteristically deals simply and effectively with this problem of definition. Rather than becoming bogged down in an explicit and necessarily tedious discussion of an appropriate general definition of diversification behavior, he does so implicitly by proceeding through a sequence of assumptions and theorems in an almost inductive manner. Throughout the analysis, moreover, the reader never has cause to lose sight of the central theme of the paper: namely, that the essential behavioral characteristics of portfolio selection can be derived without using the mean-variance model.

Samuelson begins his analysis in the general proof with the limited but agreeable concept of equal diversification and derives the restrictions on preferences and investment distributions required for such behavior. In Theorem I, he proves that if preferences satisfy the axioms of the expected utility maxim with the associated utility function U strictly concave, and if the available investments are independently and identically distributed, then the investor's optimal behavior will be to invest an equal fraction of his wealth in each investment. This "almost obvious" theorem (as Samuelson describes it—p. 848) demonstrates the identical "equal" diversification behavior derived in the corresponding mean-variance framework while still avoiding the objectionable assumptions of that framework.

The theorem is almost obvious in the sense that if diversification behavior (as intuitively understood) is ever to be realized, then it surely would be realized for this posited distribution of investment returns. Yet, without the assumption of strict concavity for U, the conclusions of the theorem are, of course, false. Thus, by making the natural but very specific assumption of independently and identically distributed investment returns, in his first case Samuelson establishes concavity (or equivalently, global positive-risk-aversion in the Arrow-Pratt sense) as the essential watershed for preference orderings if diversification behavior is posited to be the norm. Because this concavity restriction permits preference orderings that are not permissible under the risk-aversion restriction required in the comparable mean-variance analysis, Samuelson also establishes that this stronger requirement of the mean-variance model is not essential for diversification behavior.

Having established the watershed restrictions on preferences, Samuelson focuses the analysis on determining conditions for the distribution of investment returns that will ensure diversification behavior. In Theorem II, he shows that equal diversification will still be the optimal rule if the assumption of independence used in Theorem I is replaced by the less restrictive assumption of a symmetric joint distribution that is defined by the cumulative joint density function, $P(x_1, x_2, \ldots, x_n)$, being a symmetric function of its arguments. However, as Samuelson quickly verifies, "if equal diversification is to be mandatory, symmetry or some assumption like it is of course needed" (p. 851).

Having shown the severe restrictions imposed on the distribution of investment returns by this narrow definition of diversification behavior, Samuelson broadens the definition to positive diversification where investments need only be held in positive (but not necessarily equal) amounts. (As my earlier comments indicate, I believe this to be about as general a meaningful definition of diversification behavior as one is likely to find.) In Theorem III, he shows that if all investments have a common mean and one investment is distributed independently of the rest, then the optimal investor behavior will be to put some, but not all, his wealth in this investment. He also points out two corollaries (p. 853):

Corollary I. If any investment has a mean at least as good as any other investment and is independently distributed from all other investments, it must enter positively in the optimal portfolio.

Corollary II. If all investments have a common mean and are independently distributed, all must enter positively in the optimum portfolio.

Noting the role of independence in the theorem and its corollaries, Samuelson explores the conditions under which positive diversification becomes mandatory when the strict independence assumption is dropped. By a simple counterexample drawn from mean-variance analysis, he demonstrates that in general, every investment in a group with identical means need not enter with positive weight in the optimum portfolio. Specifically, Samuelson shows that a necessary condition for positive diversification in his two-investment example is that $\text{Var}[x_1] \geqslant \text{Cov}[x_1, x_2]$ and $\text{Var}[x_2] \geqslant \text{Cov}[x_1, x_2]$ where (x_1, x_2) are the respective returns on the two investments posited to have the same means. For sufficiently large positive correlation, this condition will be violated unless the variances of both returns are the same.

Having shown that positive diversification is not mandatory when returns are positively correlated, Samuelson examines the suggestion (which he assigns to Robert Solow) that "abandoning independence in favor of negative correlation ought to improve the case for diversification" (p. 854). As Samuelson points out, it is easy to prove positive diversification in the mean-variance framework for any number of investments with common mean among which all the pair-wise linear correlations are negative. But, to do so in his framework requires a more general and stronger concept of negative interdependence. As an appropriate generalization of pair-wise negative correlation, Samuelson chose the requirement that the conditional cumulative density function of the returns for each of the n available investments satisfy

$$\frac{\partial P(x_i | \underline{x}_i)}{\partial x_j} > 0, i, j = 1, \ldots, n$$

where $P(x_i | \underline{x}_i)$ is the conditional probability that the return on investment i is less than or equal to x_i when the returns on all other investments are given by the vector of values, $\underline{x}_i \equiv (x_1, \ldots, x_{i-1}, x_{i+1}, \ldots, x_n)$. This definition of negative interdependence leads to Theorem IV, which states that positive diversification is mandatory if all available investments have the same expected return and have this property of negative interdependence. Thus, Samuelson closes his analysis of diversification: "Having now shown that quite general conclusions can be rigorously proved for models that are free of the restrictive assumption that only two moments count, I ought to say a few words about how objectionably special the 2-moment theories are (except for textbook illustration and simple proofs)" (p. 855). Before discussing these few words of Samuelson's and their significance for the theory of portfolio selection, I digress to point out a characteristic of his style of thought that is handsomely illustrated by the preceding analysis.

That Samuelson closed his study of diversification as he did is typical of a pattern found in many of his most important contributions to financial economics as well as other fields. He opens the gate to a new area of (demonstrated) fruitful research and then leaves it sufficiently open so that others can enter, to build upon his work and determine the detailed outer boundaries of the insight he has provided. In this case of the general proof, he provides the fundamental insight (that the interesting behavioral results derived in the mean-variance context can, in essence, be replicated in the general context of the expected utility maxim) and then presents sufficient analysis to demonstrate its validity using the most straightforward model or example.

That this opening of gates is no idle claim can be exemplified by the following case study. Upon rereading the general proof (this time as carefully as I should have done in the past) and upon some reflection, I found myself able to make the following extensions to Samuelson's Corollary I and Corollary II (which, to my knowledge, have not been written down elsewhere).

Define the conditional expected return on investment i by $E(x_i| \underline{x}_i) \equiv \int^\infty x_i\ \partial P(x_i| \underline{x}_i)/\partial x_i dx_i$ where $P(x_i| \underline{x}_i)$ is the conditional probability function defined by Samuelson. The extensions to Corollary I and Corollary II respectively can be written as

Corollary I′: If investment i has a mean at least as good as any other investment, and satisfies

$$\frac{\partial E[x_i| \underline{x}_i]}{\partial x_j} < 1, \qquad \text{for all } j \neq i,$$

then investment i must enter positively in the optimal portfolio.

Corollary II′: If all investments have a common mean and if, for each i, $i = 1, \ldots, n$,

$$\frac{\partial E[x_i| \underline{x}_i]}{\partial x_j} < 1, \qquad \text{for all } j \neq i,$$

then all investments must enter positively in the optimal portfolio.

These corollaries include the cases explicitly analyzed by Samuelson in the general proof. That is, if investment i is independently distributed from all other investments, then $\partial E[x_i| \underline{x}_i]/\partial x_j = 0$ for all $j \neq i$, and if investment i has negative interdependence (that is, $\partial P(x_i| \underline{x}_i)/\partial x_j > 0$) with all other investments, then $\partial E[x_i| \underline{x}_i]/\partial x_j < 0$ for all $j \neq i$. Moreover, Corollary II′ shows that, provided that $\partial E[x_i| \underline{x}_i]/\partial x_j < 1$, positive diversification is mandatory among a group of investments with identical mean, even though there may be generalized positive interdependence among all investments. As Samuelson demonstrated in his mean-variance counterexample, too much positive interdependence will, of course, negate positive diversification. In particular, if $\partial E[x_i| \underline{x}_i]/\partial x_j > 1$ for all $j \neq i$, then among a group of investments with identical mean, investment i will not be held in a positive amount in the optimal portfolio.

These two corollaries are merely extensions of the analysis in the general proof. They are proved by using the identical procedure used by Samuelson to prove Theorem III. Moreover, in his discussion of why positive diversification need not be mandatory once the independence assumption is dropped, Samuelson pointed out that "Only if, so to speak, the component of an investment that is orthogonal to the rest has an attractive mean can we be sure of wanting it." (p. 853). It was this explanation, along with his definition of negative interdependence, that led me to posit the restriction on the joint probability distribution of returns in terms of the derivatives of the conditional mean.

To see the connection between Samuelson's orthogonality statement and the conditional mean function most readily, consider the special ($n = 2$) example of two investments where the mean return to investment i is denoted by μ_i and where it is assumed that $\partial E[x_i | x_j]/\partial x_j = b_{ij}$, a constant. Define the random variable $\epsilon_i \equiv x_i - b_{ij} x_j$. Then, by construction, $x_i = b_{ij} x_j + \epsilon_i$ where $E(\epsilon_i | x_j) = E(\epsilon_i) = \mu_i - b_{ij}\mu_j$. Because $\partial E[\epsilon_i | x_j]/\partial x_j = 0$, ϵ_i represents the component of investment i that is orthogonal to investment j. Under the posited conditions of Corollary I', $\mu_i \geqslant \mu_j$ and $b_{ij} < 1$, and therefore, $E(\epsilon_i) > 0$. Hence, a sufficient condition for the orthogonal component to have an attractive mean is that this mean be positive. Thus, Corollary I' simply confirms Samuelson's discerning statement that it is the mean of the *orthogonal* component of an investment's return that determines whether or not that investment enters positively in the optimal portfolio.

It is indeed illustrative of the Samuelson style of thought that fourteen years after its first publication, one can still be led by his paper to further extensions of the theory. I need hardly say that the two corollaries presented here by no means exhaust the possibilities for fruitful research along the lines of the analysis laid out in the general proof. And although this is not the occasion to pursue such a development further, I end this digression with the following theorem as an indication of just one direction that such further research might take.

Theorem: Let x^* denote the return on any optimal portfolio with mean μ^* and positive variance. Let μ_i denote the mean return on investment i and R denote the mean return on an investment whose return is orthogonal to x^*.

(i) If $\dfrac{\partial E[x_i | x^*]}{\partial x^*} > 1$, then $\mu_i > \mu^*$

(ii) If $0 < \dfrac{\partial E[x_i | x^*]}{\partial x^*} < 1$, then $R < \mu_i < \mu^*$

(iii) If $\dfrac{\partial E[x_i | x^*]}{\partial x^*} < 0$, then $\mu_i < R$

(iv) If $\dfrac{\partial E[x_i | x^*]}{\partial x^*} = b_i$, a constant, then $\mu_i - R = b_i(\mu^* - R)$

Obviously, this theorem provides essentially the same type of restrictions on the expected returns of investments as the classic Sharpe-Lintner-Mossin Capital Asset Pricing Model, but does so without that model's dependence on the mean-variance theory of portfolio selection. It is thus just one more example of Samuelson's fundamental insight that all the interesting restrictions implied by the mean-variance model can be derived in the general context of the expected utility maxim.

As noted just before that digression, Samuelson ends the general proof with a critical review of the conditions under which the mean-variance theory of portfolio selection is consistent with the expected utility maxim. He shows that if the mean-variance criterion is to be consistent with (virtually) any joint distribution of investment returns, then preferences must be represented by a strictly concave, quadratic utility function (that is, $U(x) = x - bx^2$, $b > 0$). However, as Samuelson goes on to note, even this restriction on preferences is not sufficient if the range of possible values of x can exceed $1/2b$. He also shows that consistency with (virtually) any concave utility function requires that the joint distribution of investment returns be Gaussian. Here, too, Samuelson observes that this restriction on investment returns is not sufficient if preferences are permitted that exhibit infinite marginal utility at $x = 0$ or at some other subsistence level. Moreover, using the rectangular distribution as a counterexample, Samuelson also dispels the mistaken belief of some that the mean-variance theory is consistent with the expected utility maxim if each investment's return simply belongs to the same 2-parameter (but not necessarily Gaussian) family of probability distributions.

Having demonstrated just how specialized and empirically objectionable the conditions are for the mean-variance theory to be rigorously applicable, Samuelson explores the possibilities of mean-variance as an approximation theory for investor behavior. He casts doubt on the assumption that the Gaussian distribution will, in general, be a reasonable approximation for investment returns by noting that this distribution is wholly inconsistent with limited liability, an important characteristic shared by most financial investments. This doubt is extended even to the asymptotic case of large numbers of investments by Samuelson's demonstration of the treachery involved in the improper interchange of limits that can easily occur in naive applications of the central limit theorem. However, he does point out that the quadratic approximation to $U(x)$ and its associated mean-variance solution provides asymptotic approximation to optimal investor behavior as the amount of dispersion around each investment's expected return becomes smaller and smaller. Indeed, as we now know from a later Samuelson paper and from the analyses by others of the continuous-time portfolio selection model, this valid asymptotic approximation result provides the primary justification for the use of the mean-variance theory in situations other than textbook examples and illustrations.

That the points made in Samuelson's critical review of the mean-variance theory were important to the field is evident from a collection of three papers on the same topic which appeared in the January 1969 issue of the *Review of Economic Studies*. Two of these papers, one by Karl Borch and the other by Martin Feldstein, criticize the use of the mean-variance analysis, and the third is a reply to these criticisms by James Tobin. This collection of papers also provides for the historian of science an unfortunate, but dramatic, example of the costs in the velocity of circulation of ideas and in the lost recognition accruing to their author associated with publishing a paper like the general proof in a narrowly circulated journal (which the *Journal of Financial and Quantitative Analysis* was in 1967). Although all the essential issues raised in the three *Review of Economic Studies* papers are covered in the general proof, none of these papers cite the coverage. Apparently, even a Samuelson paper can encounter difficulties in making its way into the mainstream when published in a thoroughly obscure journal.

There is little doubt that the Borch-Feldstein-Tobin interchange as well as the development of the continuous-time model with its "mean-variance-like" simplicities provided the stimulus for Samuelson's "The Fundamental Approximation Theorem of Portfolio Analysis in Terms of Means, Variances, and Higher

Moments." [1970a, III, Chap. 203]. In this expansion on his discussion in the general proof, the focus is on the usefulness of the quadratic approximation when the dispersion of investment returns is small. As Samuelson put it, "In a sense, therefore, it provides a defence of mean-variance analysis—in my judgment the most weighty defence yet given" (p. 877). Indeed, this paper remains the definitive statement on the valid use of mean-variance analysis, and for that matter, higher-moment analyses, as approximation theories for optimal investor behavior.

The essential requirement of Samuelson's "Fundamental Approximation Theorem" is that the distribution of investment returns has (what he calls) "compact" probabilities. As a reasonably general example, suppose that the random variable return per dollar on investment i, x_i, can be written in terms of a parameter σ as

$$x_i = \mu + \sigma^2 a_i + \sigma \epsilon_i$$

where μ and a_i are nonstochastic and as a function of σ, are $O(1)$; and where the random variable ϵ_i has the properties that (i) $E(\epsilon_i) = 0$; (ii) $E(\epsilon_i^2) = \sigma_i^2 > 0$; (iii) $E|\epsilon_i|^{k+1} < \infty$, for $k = 1, 2, \ldots, r$. Then, in the asymptotic sense as $\sigma \to 0$, x_i will have a compact distribution.

Let $\omega_i(\sigma)$ denote the optimal fraction of an investor's portfolio allocated to investment i, which is derived as the solution to

$$\underset{\{\omega_i\}}{\text{Max}} \left\{ E\left[U\left(\sum_1^n \omega_i(\sigma) x_i \right) \right] \right\}$$

subject, of course, to the constraint that

$$\sum_1^n \omega_i(\sigma) = 1.$$

Let $\omega_i^{**}(\sigma)$ denote the optimal solution to the "r-moment problem"

$$\underset{\{\omega_i^{**}\}}{\text{Max}} \left\{ \sum_1^r \left[\frac{U^{(j)}(\mu)}{j! \, U'(\mu)} \right] E\left[\sum_1^n \omega_i^{**}(\sigma) (x_i - \mu) \right]^j \right\}$$

Then, for $\{x_i\}$ with compact distributions, Samuelson's fundamental theorem (p. 880) states that:

> The solution to the general problem [$\omega_i(\sigma)$] is related asymptotically to that of the r-moment problem [$\omega_i^{**}(\sigma)$] by the high-contact equivalences $\omega_i(0) = \omega_i^{**}(0)$, $\omega_i'(0) = \omega_i^{**}{}'(0), \ldots, \omega_i^{[r-2]}(0) = \omega_i^{**[r-2]}(0)$.

Not only does this theorem show that the true optimal solution and the solution to the associated r-moment problem converge in the limit, but it also provides bounds for the errors in using this approximating solution for small, but finite, values of σ. That is, $|\omega_i^{**}(\sigma) - \omega_i(\sigma)| = o(\sigma^{r-2})$ where "$o(\ \ )$" is the usual asymptotic order symbol.[5]

The special case of the fundamental theorem when $r = 2$ is, of course, the quadratic approximation associated with the mean-variance solution. This special case (highlighted by Samuelson as a separate theorem) shows that, indeed, the mean-variance solution and the true optimal solution will converge and the error in using the mean-variance solution will be $o(1)$.

As noted by Samuelson, a prototype example of his compact distributions is a Wiener process or Brownian motion with a drift where the parameter σ is identified as the square root of time. Thus, his analysis "does throw light on the reasons why enormous 'quadratic' simplicities occur in continuous-time models" (p. 879) where the processes are posited to be continuous sample-path diffusions and the length of time between transactions is the infinitesimal $dt\,(= \sigma^2)$.

I need hardly do more than mention the "Sharpe-Lintner-Mossin Capital Asset Pricing Model" to underscore the significance of Samuelson's approximation theorem to financial economic theory. Moreover, it is, if anything, even more important to empirical financial research and financial practice, both of which have focused almost exclusively on the mean-variance type of analyses. Of course, Samuelson is not alone in having pointed out the perils associated with this mode of analysis. However, unlike the blanket condemnation implicit in the simple counterexamples used by purists to make their point, the error bounds of Samuelson's theorem provide selective condemnation and thereby permit the empirical economist and practitioner alike to judge the merits of their analyses in each individual case. If, for example, the time between observations and the time interval between (potential) revisions of a portfolio are "sufficiently short," then the Samuelson theorem provides a justification for using the mean-variance specification as a reasonable approximation. As Samuelson summarizes it in the closing sentences of his paper, "But it also needs emphasizing that near to $\sigma = 0$ when 'risk is quite limited,' the mean-variance result is a very good approximation. When the heat of the controversy dissipates, that I think will be generally agreed on" (p. 882).

A question repeatedly arises in both financial economic theory and practice: When are the market prices of securities traded in capital markets equal to the best estimate of their values? I need hardly point out that if value is defined as "that price at which one can either buy or sell in the market," then the answer is trivially "always." But, of course, the question is rarely, if ever, asked in this tautological sense, although the distinction between value and price is often subtle. Moreover, as the following examples suggest, the answer to this question has important implications for a wide range of financial economic behavior.

In the fundamentalist approach of Graham and Dodd to security analysis, the distinction between value and price is made in terms of the (somewhat vague) notion

---

[5] That is, if $g(\sigma) = o[h(\sigma)]$, then $\lim[g(\sigma)/h(\sigma)] = 0$ as $\sigma \to 0$. If $g(\sigma) = 0[h(\sigma)]$, then $\lim[g(\sigma)/h(\sigma)]$ is bounded.

of intrinsic value. Indeed, the belief that the market price of a security need not always equal its intrinsic value is essential to this approach because it is disparities such as these that provide meaningful content to the classic prescription for successful portfolio management: buy low (when intrinsic value is larger than market price) and sell high (when intrinsic value is smaller than market price).

In appraisal law, the question is phrased in terms of how much weight to give to market price in relation to other nonmarket measures of value in arriving at a fair value assessment to compensate those whose property has been involuntarily expropriated. In corporation finance, the answer to that question determines the extent to which corporate managers should rely upon capital market prices as the correct signals for the firm's production and financing decisions.

Characteristically, Samuelson's version provides both a clear distinction between value and price and a focus on the broadest and most important issue raised by this question: When are prices in a decentralized capital market system the best estimate of the corresponding shadow values of an idealized central planner who efficiently allocates society's resources? Thus, in "Mathematics of Speculative Price" [1972a, IV, Chap. 240, p. 425], he wrote

> A question, for theoretical and empirical research and not ideological polemics, is whether real life markets—the Chicago Board of Trade with its grain futures, the London Cocoa market, the New York Stock Exchange, and the less-formally organized markets (as for staple cotton goods), to say nothing of the large Galbraithian corporations possessed of some measure of unilateral economic power—do or do not achieve some degree of dynamic approximation to the idealized "scarcity" or shadow prices. In a well-known passage, Keynes has regarded speculative markets as mere casinos for transferring wealth between the lucky and unlucky. On the other hand, Holbrook Working has produced evidence over a lifetime that futures prices do vibrate randomly around paths that a technocrat might prescribe as optimal. (Thus, years of good crop were followed by heavier carryover than were years of bad, and this before government intervened in agricultural pricing.)

As we know, such theoretical shadow prices are "prices never seen on land or sea outside of economics libraries." However, testable hypotheses can be derived about the properties that real-life market prices must have if they are to be the best estimate of these idealized values. Because it is intertemporally different rather than spatially different prices that are of central interest in financial economics, most of Samuelson's analyses in this area are developed within the context of a futures market. In his 1957 "Intertemporal Price Equilibrium: A Prologue to the Theory of Speculation" [1957, II, Chap. 73], however, he does use spatial conditions of competitive pricing as tools to deduce the corresponding conditions on intertemporal prices in a certainty environment. From these local "no-arbitrage conditions," he proves that the current futures price must be equal to the future spot price for that date. In completing his analysis of the price behavior over time, he shows that the dynamics of "allocation-efficient" spot prices can be determined as the formal solution to a particular optimal control problem.[6]

---

[6] As Samuelson notes, without the tranversality or other terminal boundary condition, these local arbitrage conditions are necessary but not sufficient to ensure an optimal path.

Samuelson underscores his use of the word *Prologue* in the title by pointing out that "A theory of speculative markets under ideal conditions of certainty is Hamlet without the Prince," (p. 970). Indeed, his later papers, "Stochastic Speculative Price" [1971a, III, Chap. 206], "Proof That Properly Anticipated Prices Fluctuate Randomly" [1965a, III, Chap. 198], and "Rational Theory of Warrant Pricing" [1965b, III, Chap. 199], have in common their deriving the stochastic dynamic behavior of prices in properly functioning speculative markets. They also share the distinction of being important papers published in obscure places, which nevertheless found their way into the mainstream. Such occurrences suggest that high visibility of scientific authors may tend to offset low visibility of publication outlets.

As these papers illustrate, the analysis of such price dynamics in an uncertain environment is considerably more difficult, both conceptually and analytically, than in the certainty case. And given the substantive importance of such analyses to the field, it is not surprising that Samuelson chose the mathematics of speculative price as his subject for the twelfth John von Neumann Lecture at the 1971 fall meeting of the Society for Industrial and Applied Mathematics. As part of this lecture (published as "Mathematics of Speculative Price") he presents a molecular model of the firm that he uses to connect optimal portfolio behavior in the financial markets with "real" investment characteristics of firms. With this model (that has the same characteristic simplicity of, for example, his exact consumption-loan model), Samuelson once again opens a gate to a new research area. However, on this occasion, his central purpose is the closing of gates to earlier research through a critical synthesis of a wide range of topics in capital market theory. As it happens, Samuelson's synthesis reviews the three papers that remain in our miniaturized Samuelson Sampler, thus making it happily unnecessary for this celebrative essay to do more than make a few passing observations on these seminal pieces.

In defending his Prologue model of speculative price against his own criticism of excluding uncertainty, Samuelson expressed the belief "that conquering the easier problem, in which future conditions are for simplicity's sake assumed to be foreseeable and foreseen, will provide a useful springbroad from which to attack the realistic speculative market problems" (p. 947). Fourteen years later in "Stochastic Speculative Price," he returned to that analysis and demonstrated the validity of this defense. In this elegant paper requiring little more than two pages in print, Samuelson shows that under the axiom that the *expected* rather than the known-for-certain prices can be substituted in the local arbitrage conditions, the stochastic dynamic behavior of the spot price is determined as the solution to a stochastic dynamic-programming problem. That is, if the spot price p_t for each t satisfies $q_t[E(p_{t+1})/p_t - (1 + r)/a] = 0$ where the carryover quantity q_t is positive only if the expected return from such storage is adequate to cover both capital and shrinkage costs, $1 + r$ and $1 - a$, then the dynamic path for p_t is given by the solution to

$$\max E\left\{ \sum_1^T (1+r)^{-t} U[H_t + aq_{t+1} - q_t] \right\}$$

where H_t is the uncertain harvest at time t and the function U is defined by

$U'[c] \equiv P[c]$ where $P[c_t]$ is the function relating consumption demand at time t, c_t, to price.

This relation reduces to exactly the one derived in Samuelson's prologue model when the harvests are nonstochastic and the expectation operator, E, becomes vacuous. Moreover, even if demand functions are stationary and harvests are independent and identically distributed over time, the resulting changes in the spot price will be neither independently nor identically distributed because of the intertemporal linkages caused by the optimal carryover decisions. However, the general properties of this optimal carryover rule are consistent with those that a technocratic planner would prescribe. The derived time series characteristics of spot prices are also broadly consistent with those observed for real life organized commodity markets and as $T \to \infty$, the spot price does have an ergodic distribution.

Published in the same issue of the *Industrial Management Review*, "Proof That Properly Anticipated Prices Fluctuate Randomly" and "Rational Theory of Warrant Pricing" are perhaps the two most important Samuelson papers for the field. During the decade before their printed publication in 1965, Samuelson had set down, in an unpublished manuscript, many of the results in these papers and had communicated them in lectures at MIT, Yale, Carnegie, the American Philosophical Society, and elsewhere. The sociologist or historian of science would undoubtedly be able to develop a rich case study of alternative paths for circulating scientific ideas by exploring the impact of this oral publication on research in rational expectations, efficient markets, geometric Brownian motion, and warrant pricing in the period between 1956 and 1965.

In "Proof That Properly Anticipated Prices Fluctuate Randomly," Samuelson provides the foundation of the efficient market theory that Fama and others have further developed into one of the most important concepts in modern financial economics. As indicated by its title, the principal conclusion of the paper is that in well-informed and competitive speculative markets, the intertemporal changes in prices will be essentially random. In a recent conversation with Samuelson, he described the reaction (presumably his own as well as that of others) to this conclusion as one of "initial shock—and then, upon reflection, that it is obvious." The time series of changes in most economic variables (GNP, inflation, unemployment, earnings, and even the weather) exhibit cyclical or serial dependencies. Further, in a rational and well-informed capital market, it is reasonable to presume that the prices of common stocks, bonds, and commodity futures depend upon such economic variables. Thus, the shock comes from the seemingly inconsistent conclusion that in such well-functioning markets, the changes in speculative prices should exhibit no serial dependencies. However, once the problem is viewed from the perspective offered in the paper, this seeming inconsistency disappears and all becomes obvious.

Starting from the consideration that in a competitive market, if everyone *knew* that a speculative security was expected to rise in price by more (less) than the required or fair expected rate of return, it would *already* be bid up (down) to negate that possibility, Samuelson postulates that securities will be priced at each point in time so as to yield this fair expected rate of return. Using a backwards-in-time induction argument, he proves that the changes in speculative prices around that fair return will form a martingale. And this follows no matter how much serial dependency there is in the underlying economic variables upon which such speculative prices are formed. Thus,

> We would expect people in the market place, in pursuit of avid and intelligent self-interest, to take account of those elements of future events that in a probability sense may be discerned to be casting their shadows before them. (Because past events cast "their" shadows after them, future events can be said to cast their shadows before them.) (p. 785).

In an informed market, therefore, current speculative prices will already reflect anticipated or forecastable future changes in the underlying economic variables that are relevant to the formation of prices, and this leaves only the unanticipated or unforecastable changes in these variables as the sole source of fluctuations in speculative prices.

Samuelson is careful to warn the reader against interpreting his conclusions about markets as empirical statements:

> You never get something for nothing. From a nonempirical base of axioms, you never get empirical results. Deductive analysis cannot determine whether the empirical properties of the stochastic model I posit come close to resembling the empirical determinants of today's real-world markets. (p. 783).

Nevertheless, his model is important to the understanding and interpretation of the empirical results observed in real-world markets.

Suppose that one observes that successive price changes are random (as empirically seems to be the case for many speculative markets). Without the benefit of Samuelson's theoretical analysis, one could easily interpret the fact that these prices wander like a drunken sailor as strong evidence in favor of the previously noted Keynes view of speculative markets. Whereas had it been observed that speculative markets were orderly with smooth and systematic intertemporal changes in prices, the corresponding interpretation (again, without Samuelson's analysis) could easily be that such sensible price behavior is (at least) consistent with that of the shadow prices of the idealized rational technocratic planner.

In the light of Samuelson's analysis, we all know that the correct interpretations of these cases are quite the reverse. For speculative market prices to correspond to their theoretical shadow values, they must reflect anticipated future changes in relevant economic variables. Thus, it is at least consistent with equality between these two sets of prices that changes in market prices be random. On the other hand, if changes in speculative prices are smooth and forecastable, then speculators who are quick to react to this known serial dependency and investors who are lucky to be transacting in the right direction will receive wealth transfers from those who are slow to react or who are unlucky enough to be transacting in the wrong direction. More important, under these conditions, current market prices are not the best estimate of values for the purposes of signalling the optimal intertemporal allocation of resources.

In studying the corpus of his contributions to the efficient market theory, one can only conclude that Paul Samuelson takes great care in what he writes. As is evident throughout his proof paper and in his later discussion of the topic in "Mathematics of Speculative Price," [1972a, IV, Chapt. 240] he is keenly aware of the everpresent danger of banalization by those who fail to see the subtle character of the theory. Thus, having proved the general martingale theorem for speculative prices, he concludes

> The Theorem is so general that I must confess to having oscillated over the years in my own mind between regarding it as trivially obvious (and almost trivially vacuous) and regarding it as remarkably sweeping. Such perhaps is characteristic of basic results. [1965a, III, Chap. 198, p. 786].

Without Samuelson's careful exposition, the martingale property could easily be seen as either a simple deduction (whose truth follows from the very definition of competitive markets) or as a mere tautology. That is, subtract from any random variable, Y_t, its conditional expectation as of $t - 1$, $E_{t-1}[Y_t]$, and as a truism, the sum of the $\{Y_t - E_{t-1}[Y_t]\}$ will form a martingale. Indeed, in discussing the fair expected returns $\{\lambda_t\}$ around which speculative prices should exhibit the martingale property, Samuelson points out that

> Unless something useful can be said in advance about the $[\lambda_{T-i}]$—as for example, $\lambda_t - 1$ small, or λ_t a diminishing sequence in function of the diminishing variance to be expected of a futures contract as its horizon shrinks, subject to perhaps a terminal jump in λ_1 as closing-date becomes crucial—the whole exercise becomes an empty tautology. [1972a, IV, Chap. 240, p. 443].

But, of course, such restrictions can be reasonably imposed (using the example, the capital asset pricing model and the term structure of interest rates), and it is these restrictions that form the basis for testing the theory.

Many less precise discussions of the efficient market theory equate the theory with the property that speculative price changes exhibit a random walk around the fair expected return. However, Samuelson clearly distinguishes his derived martingale property from this much stronger one by showing that such changes need not be either independently or identically distributed for the theory to obtain. He is also careful to make the distinction between *speculative* prices that will satisfy the martingale property and *nonspeculative* prices (as well as other economic variables) that need not exhibit this property in a well-functioning market economy. In his "Stochastic Speculative Price" analysis, for example, the optimal stochastic path for the spot price of a commodity is shown not to satisfy the martingale condition for a speculative price. Indeed, only in periods of positive storage when the spot price also serves the function of a speculative price will the expected changes in the spot price provide a fair expected rate of return (including storage costs). "Thus," Samuelson remarks, "Maurice Kendall almost proves too much when he finds negligible serial correlation in spot grain prices" [1965a, III, Chap. 198, p. 783]. I only allude to the import of this message for those in other areas of economics who posit and test models of rational expectations.

Samuelson not only exercises great theoretical care himself, but he also tries to induce such care in his readers. He warns, for example, against reading "too much into the established theorem":

It does not prove that actual competitive markets work well. It does not say that speculation is a good thing or that randomness of price changes would be a good thing. It does not prove that anyone who makes money in speculation is *ipso facto* deserving of the gain or even that he has accomplished something good for society or for anyone but himself. All or none of these may be true, but that would require a different investigation [1965a, III, Chap. 198, p. 789].

In the last paragraph of "Proof," Samuelson concludes by raising a number of questions, all of which focus on an issue central to making operational his concept of properly anticipated prices. Namely, where are the basic probability distributions (for which the martingale property of speculative prices applies) to come from? Although he makes no pronouncements on this issue, by identifying it he opened gates to its resolution in the important later work by Fama (1970). Fama defines market efficiency in terms of a hierarchy of information sets that are the basis for forming the probability distributions. He shows that if changes in speculative prices (around their fair expected returns) form a martingale based upon the probability distribution generated by information set Φ, then these price changes will also satisfy the martingale property for the distribution generated by any information set Φ' that is a subset of Φ. It therefore follows that if these prices do not satisfy the martingale property for information set Φ', they will not satisfy this property for any information set Φ that contains Φ' as a subset. Thus, Fama makes operational Samuelson's martingale requirement for properly anticipated prices by showing that it is possible to reject the martingale property (and hence, market efficiency) by using only a subset of the information available to any (or for that matter, all) investors. As Fama makes clear in his development of the strong, semi-strong, and weak versions of the efficient market theory, it is also possible for speculative prices to satisfy the martingale conditions for one information set but not to satisfy it for another.

The martingale property of speculative prices is the key element in Fama's development of procedures for testing market efficiency. Moreover, as he points out, virtually all empirical studies of speculative price returns (both pre- and post-"Proof") can be viewed as tests of this property that serve to underscore further the significance of Samuelson's having established it as the crucial one for price behavior in an efficient market.

The early empirical studies focused on tests for serial correlation and comparisons of return performance between buy-and-hold and various simple filter-type trading strategies. While their results were on the whole consistent with market efficiency, these studies were, by necessity, limited to investigations of small numbers of securities and relatively short observation periods. This perhaps explains why the practicing financial community paid little attention to the results of these studies. However, with the development in the late 1960s of large-scale stock return data bases (principally at the University of Chicago Center for Research in Security Prices) and the availability of high-speed computers, there came an avalanche of tests of the efficient market theory, which were neither limited to a few securities nor to short observation periods.

Using return data on thousands of securities over more than forty years of history, some of the studies extended the earlier work comparing buy-and-hold with various mechanical trading strategies. Others, such as the Jensen (1968) study of mutual fund performance, broke new ground and analyzed the performance of real-life portfolio managers. In collectively echoing the findings of the earlier limited examinations, these large-scale studies put to final rest the myth that professional money managers can beat the market by miles, and indeed, cast doubt on whether they could even beat it by inches.

As the evidence in support of the efficient market theory mounted, the results and their implications for optimal strategy were widely disseminated to both the investing professional and the investing public in popular and semipopular articles written by a number of academics. Included in this number is Paul Samuelson. With the widespread dissemination of this mountain of accumulated evidence, the practicing financial community could no longer ignore the efficient market theory although, as is perhaps not surprising, few (at least among the money managers in that community) accepted it. Here again, Samuelson exercises great care in his writings on this controversial issue by always keeping clear the distinction between "not rejecting" and "accepting" the efficient market theory. In discussing the controversy between practicing investment managers and academics in "Challenge to Judgment" [1974d, IV, Chap. 243, pp. 479–480], for example, he writes:

> Indeed, to reveal my bias, the ball is in the court of the practical men: it is the turn of the Mountain to take a first step toward the theoretical Mohammed. . . . If you oversimplify the debate, it can be put in the form of the question,
>
> > Resolved, that the best of money managers cannot be demonstrated to be able to deliver the goods of superior portfolio-selection performance.
>
> Any jury that reviews the evidence, and there is a great deal of relevant evidence, must at least come out with the Scottish verdict:
>
> > Superior investment performance is unproved.

With characteristic clarity, Samuelson provides a constructive perspective on the controversy by pointing out that while the existing evidence does not prove the validity of the efficient market theory, the burden of proof belongs to those who believe it to be invalid. In his final paragraph of "Challenge to Judgment," (p. 485), he summarizes the point:

> What is interesting is the empirical fact that it is virtually impossible for academic researchers with access to the published records to identify any members of the subset with flair. This fact, although not an inevitable law, is a brute fact. The ball, as I have already noted, is in the court of those who doubt the random walk hypothesis. They can dispose of the uncomfortable brute fact in the only way that any fact is disposed of—by producing brute evidence to the contrary.

If one were to describe the important research gains in financial economics during the 1960s as "the decade of capital asset pricing and market efficiency," then surely one would describe the corresponding research gains in the 1970s as "the decade of intertemporal analysis and option pricing." Once again, Samuelson was ahead of the field in recognizing option pricing as a rich area for problem choice and solution. His research interest in options can be traced back at least to the early

1950s when he directed Richard Kruizenga's thesis on puts and calls (1956). As is evident from that thesis, Samuelson had already shown that the assumption of an absolute random walk for stock prices leads to absurd prices for long-lived options, and this before the rediscovery of Bachelier's work in which this very assumption is made. Although Samuelson lectured on option pricing at M.I.T. and elsewhere throughout the 1950s and early 1960s, his first published paper on the subject, "Rational Theory of Warrant Pricing," appeared in 1965 [III, Chap. 199]. In this paper, he resolves a number of apparent paradoxes that had plagued the existing theory of option pricing from the time of Bachelier. In the process (with the aid of a mathematical appendix provided by H. P. McKean, Jr.), Samuelson also derives much of what has become the basic mathematical structure of option pricing theory today.

Bachelier postulates that stock prices follow a random walk so that the expected change in the stock price over any interval of time is zero. The limit of this stochastic process in continuous time in modern terms is called a Wiener process or a Brownian motion. Bachelier also postulated that the price of a call option (or warrant) that gives its owner the right to buy the stock at time T in the future for an exercise price of a must be such that the expected change in the option price is also zero. From these postulates, Bachelier deduced that the option price, $W(X; T, a)$ must satisfy the partial differential equation

$$1/2\sigma^2 W_{XX}(X;T,a) - W_T(X;T,a) = 0$$

subject to the boundary condition $W(X;0,a) = \text{Max}[0, X - a]$ where X is the price of the stock and σ^2 is the variance rate on the stock. The solution of this equation is given by

$$W(X; T, a) = (X - a)\, \Phi\left(\frac{X - a}{\sigma\sqrt{T}}\right) + \frac{1}{\sqrt{2\pi}} \exp\left[\frac{-a^2}{2\sigma^2 T}\right] \sigma\sqrt{T}$$

where $\Phi(\ )$ is the standard normal cumulative density function. For an at-the-money option (that is, $X = a$) and relatively short times to expiration T, the Bachelier rule that the value of option grows as $\sqrt{T}$ is a reasonable approximation to observed option prices. However, as Samuelson points out, for long-lived options the formula implies that the option will sell for more than the stock itself, and indeed, for perpetual warrants ($T = \infty$), the value of the option is unbounded.

Samuelson traces this result to the absolute Brownian motion assumption which for T large implies the possibility of large negative values for the stock prices with nontrivial probability. Noting that most financial instruments have limited liability and, therefore, cannot have a negative price, Samuelson introduces the idea of "geometric Brownian motion" to describe stock price returns. By postulating that the logarithmic price changes, $\log[X_{t+T}/X_t]$, follow a Brownian motion (with possibly a drift), he shows that prices themselves will have a lognormal distribution and, therefore, this ensures that they will always be nonnegative. Moreover, because lognormal distributions preserve themselves under multiplication, stock returns will have a lognormal distribution over any time interval. Indeed, this geometric Brownian motion has become the prototype stochastic process for stock returns in virtually all parts of financial economics.

Using much the same procedure of Bachelier, but modifying his postulates to include the geometric Brownian motion and the possibility of a nonzero expected rate of return on the stock, α, Samuelson derives a partial differential equation for the option price given by

$$1/2\sigma^2 X^2 W_{XX}(X; T, a) - \alpha X W_X(X; T, a) - \beta W(X; T, a) - W_T(X; T, a) = 0$$

subject to $W(X; 0, a) = \text{Max}[0, X - a]$ where β is the required expected return on the option. For the case corresponding to Bachelier's where the required expected return on the option is the same as on the stock (that is, $\beta = \alpha$), the solution can be written as

$$W(X; T, a) = X\Phi(h_1) - ae^{-\alpha T}\Phi(h_2)$$

where $h_1 \equiv [\log(X/a) + (\alpha + 1/2\sigma^2)T]/\sigma\sqrt{T}$ and $h_2 \equiv h_1 - \sigma^2 T$.

Even when $\alpha = 0$, Samuelson's solution satisfies $W(X; T, a) \leqslant X$ for all X and T. Hence, the substitution of the geometric Brownian motion for the arithmetic one eliminates the Bachelier paradox. However, as the reader can readily verify for $X = a$ and T small, $W(X; T, a) \sim \sigma\sqrt{T}$ as in the Bachelier case.

Bachelier considered options that could only be exercised on the expiration date. In modern times, the standard terms for options and warrants permit the option holder to exercise on *or before* the expiration date. Samuelson coined the terms "European" option to refer to the former and "American" option to refer to the latter. Although real-world options are almost always of the American type, published analyses of option pricing prior to his "Rational Theory" paper focused exclusively on the evaluation of European options and therefore did not include the extra value to the option from the right to exercise early.

Because he only requires that the option price be equal to $\text{Max}[0, X - a]$ at the expiration date, Samuelson's ("$\beta = \alpha$") analysis formally applies only to a European type of option. However, he also proves that his solution satisfies the strict inequality $W(X; T, a) > \text{Max}[0, X - a]$ for $T > 0$ and $\beta = \alpha \geqslant 0$. Thus, under the posited conditions, it would never pay to exercise a call option prior to expiration, and the value of an American call option is equal to its European counterpart. In consequence, he views the special "$\beta = \alpha$" case of this theory as incomplete and unsatisfactory. It is incomplete because it provides no explanation of early exercise of options or warrants. Although it resolves the Bachelier paradox, the theory is unsatisfactory because it creates a new one; namely, the value of a perpetual call or warrant, $W(X; \infty, a)$, is equal to the stock price, X, independently of the exercise price. That is, according to the theory, the right to buy the stock at any finite price a (where this right can never be exercised in finite time) is equal to the price of the stock (which in effect is an option to buy the stock at a zero exercise price where the right can be exercised at any time).

Although he rejects the special case of his theory when $\beta = \alpha$, Samuelson resolves both its incompleteness and its paradox within the context of his general theory by simply requiring that $\beta > \alpha$. He does so by first formally solving his differential equation for the value of a European warrant. He then shows that for $\beta > \alpha \geqslant 0$ and any $T > 0$, there exists a number $C_T < \infty$ such that $W(X; T, a) < X - a$ for all $X \geqslant C_T$. Thus, for $\beta > \alpha$, there is always a finite price for the stock where it pays to exercise prior to the expiration date, and hence, the American feature of an option has positive value. He also shows that for $\beta > \alpha$, $W(X; T, a) < X$ for $a > 0$ and the value of a European perpetual call option, $W(X; \infty, a)$, is zero.

Having established that the early exercise provision has value when $\beta > \alpha$, Samuelson then proves that the correct formula for an American call option or warrant will satisfy his partial differential equation subject to the boundary conditions: (i) $W(0; T, a) = 0$; (ii) $W(X; 0, a) = \text{Max}[0, X - a]$; (iii) $W(C_T; T, a) = C_T - a$; (iv) $W_X(C_T; T, a) = 1$. For those familiar with parabolic partial differential equations of this type, it may appear that the boundary conditions are overspecified. However, C_T, which is the time boundary of stock prices where the option should be exercised, is not known, and it is precisely the overspecification that permits the simultaneous determination of the option price and the time boundary. Of course, closed-form solutions to such boundary value problems are not easy to derive although Samuelson does solve the perpetual call option case. He also develops a recursive integral technique that is a precursor to the numerical approximation methods used to solve these equations today.

While Samuelson mentions the greater riskiness of a warrant over the stock and different tax treatment, his principal argument for the $\beta > \alpha$ case and possible early exercise is that the stock is paying or may pay dividends during the life of the warrant. As formulated in his differential equation, α is the expected rate of price appreciation in the stock and, therefore, will be equal to the expected rate of return on the stock only if there are no cash dividends. In the example he discusses at length, where the dividend rate is a constant fraction, δ, of the stock price, he shows that for the expected rate of return on the warrant to just equal that of the stock, $\beta = \alpha + \delta$, and therefore, $\beta > \alpha$. This analysis also makes it clear why a perpetual warrant on a currently nondividend-paying stock will not have a price equal to the stock price (as predicted by the $\beta = \alpha$ theory): namely, it could only do so if it were believed that the stock would never pay a dividend.

As Samuelson would be the first to say, his 1965 warrant pricing theory is incomplete in the sense that it simply postulates the first-moment relations between the warrant and stock. Yet, the basic intuitions provided by his theory have been sustained by later, more complete, analyses. For example, his focus on dividends as the principal reason for early exercise of call options and warrants was later justified in his 1969 "A Complete Model of Warrant Pricing That Maximizes Utility" [III, Chap. 200] (I was the junior coauthor), where it was shown that dividends are the only reason for such early exercise. Still later, an arbitrage argument presented in Merton (1973) proves that this result holds in general. Earlier warrant pricing theories uniformly neglected the possibility of early exercise in the development of their evaluation formulas. Samuelson, in addition to proving that early exercise was a possibility, shows that the effect of this possibility on value can be quite significant especially for longlived options and warrants. Further, his demonstration that the schedule of stock prices at which the warrant should be exercised can be endogenously determined as part of a simultaneous solution for the warrant price provides one of the cornerstones of modern option pricing theory and its application to the evaluation of more complex securities.

In a subsequent conversation, Samuelson contrasted the "Rational Theory" with its companion piece "Proof That Properly Anticipated Prices Fluctuate Randomly" by noting that "the results of the paper were not obvious," and that he "was not sure how they would come out until the work was done." Despite his obvious delight with the paper (I do not doubt that this is his favorite among his contributions to financial economics) and despite the many important contributions it contains, discussion of the paper led Paul to remark that "Too little is written about the 'near misses' in science." While far from unique in the history of science, Samuelson's "Rational Theory" is surely a prime example of such a near miss by an eminent scientist.

Virtually everyone would agree that the single paper most responsible for the explosion in option pricing research in the 1970s is the seminal Black-Scholes "The Pricing of Options and Corporate Liabilities" published in 1973. So much has been written about their theory and its extensions to the pricing of corporate liabilities, loan guarantees, deposit insurance, investment projects, and even tenure for professors, that there is no need to review the substantive importance of this contribution to both the theory and practice of financial economics. Instead I focus only upon the development of their basic option pricing formula and its relation to Samuelson's "Rational Theory."

The fundamental insight on the part of Black and Scholes was that, at least in principle, a dynamic hedging strategy could be derived to form a riskless portfolio of the option, the stock, and riskless bonds. Moreover, if such a portfolio could be created, then to avoid the opportunity for arbitrage, it must yield a return exactly equal to that earned on a riskless bond. From this condition, it follows that there must be a unique relationship among the option price, the stock price, and the riskless interest rate. Armed with this insight, Black and Scholes were able to derive this dynamic riskless hedge strategy and thus to solve for the unique option price that ensures no arbitrage opportunities.

Of course, hedge strategies using a warrant or other convertible securities and the stock were not uncommon undertakings by practitioners long before 1973. Thorp and Kasouff's *Beat the Market* (1967) is devoted entirely to such hedging strategies. In his "Rational Theory" paper, Samuelson discusses at length (including numerical examples) the use of hedge positions between the warrant and the stock as a means for deriving bounds on the discrepancies between β and α. These bounds translate through his warrant pricing equation into bounds on the range of rational warrant prices. In this discussion, he goes on to mention that the opportunity cost or carrying charges for the hedge should be included and therefore, the riskless rate of interest would enter into the bounds. Thus, Samuelson had in his paper the hedging idea for restricting prices and the possibility that the interest rate would enter into the evaluation, both of them key elements in the Black and Scholes analysis. Yet, neither he nor the others pushed their ideas in this area the extra distance required to arrive at what became the Black-Scholes formula. As Samuelson later wrote in "Mathematics of Speculative Price" [1972a, IV, Chap. 240, p. 438],[7]

> My 1965 paper had noted that the possibility of hedging, by buying the warrant and selling the common stock short, should give you low variance and high mean return in the $\beta > \alpha$ case. Hence, for dividendless stocks, I argued that the $\beta - \alpha$ divergence is unlikely to be great. I should have explored this further!

The most striking comparison to make between the Black-Scholes analysis and Samuelson's "Rational Theory" is the formula for the option price. In their derivation, Black and Scholes assume a nondividend-paying stock whose price dynamics are described by a geometric Brownian motion with a resulting lognormal distribution for stock returns. This is, of course, the identical assumption about stock returns that Samuelson made. Under these conditions, the Black-Scholes no arbitrage price for a European call option, $F(X; T, a)$, is shown to be the solution to the partial differential equation

$$1/2\sigma^2 X^2 F_{XX}(X; T, a) + rXF_X(X; T, a) - rF(X; T, a) - F_T(X; T, a) = 0$$

subject to the boundary condition $F(X; 0, a) = \text{Max}[0, X - a]$ and where r is the (instantaneous) riskless rate of interest that is assumed to be constant over the life of the option. By inspection, this equation is formally identical to the one derived in the "Rational Theory" for the special "$\beta = \alpha$" case if one substitutes for the value of "α" the interest rate "r". It follows, therefore, that the Black-Scholes option pricing formula, $F(X; T, a)$, is formally identical to the Samuelson option pricing formula, $W(X; T, a)$, if one sets $\beta = \alpha = r$ in the latter formula.

It should be underscored that the mathematical equivalence between the two formulas (with the redefinition of the parameter α) is purely a formal one. That is, the Black-Scholes analysis shows that the option price can be determined without specifying either the expected return on the stock, α, or the required expected return on the option, β. Therefore, the fact that the Black-Scholes option price satisfies the Samuelson formula with $\beta = \alpha = r$ implies neither that the expected returns on the stock and option are equal nor that they are equal to the riskless rate of interest. Indeed, Samuelson notes in his "Mathematics of Speculative Price" (1972a) that even if α is known and constant, β will not be for finite-level options priced according to the Black and Scholes methodology. It should also be noted that

---

[7] In a 1968 critique of the Thorp-Kasouff book, Samuelson quite correctly warns the reader that their reverse-hedge techniques in expiring warrants are no "sure-thing" arbitrage. Later [1972a, IV, Chap. 240, p. 438, n. 6], he reiterates a similar valid warning in his discussion of the Black-Scholes arbitrage argument. If, however, Samuelson had not discovered this overstatement in the Thorp-Kasouff analysis so quickly, then he might have used the occasion to pursue further his own earlier work in using hedge strategies to restrict the range of rational warrant prices. Perhaps this thought was in his mind when in a recent conversation with me, Paul commented on his 1968 review as one in which "I won farthings and lost pounds."

Black-Scholes pricing of options does not require knowledge of investors' preferences and endowments as is required, for example, in the Samuelson-Merton 1969 warrant pricing paper. The "Rational Theory" is clearly a miss with respect to the Black-Scholes analysis. However, as this analysis shows, it is just as clearly a near miss.

This said, it may seem somewhat paradoxical to suggest that the Black-Scholes breakthrough has actually added to the significance of Samuelson's "Rational Theory" for the field, yet I believe it has. Before Black-Scholes, there were a number of competing theories of warrant and convertible security pricing. Some, of course, were little more than rules of thumb based on empirical analyses with limited data. Others, however, like the "Rational Theory," were quite sophisticated. The Black-Scholes analysis provides a degree of closure for the field on this issue, and thus renders these earlier theories obsolete. However, as noted here and as shown in detail in the Appendix to "Mathematics of Speculative Price", virtually all the mathematical analysis in the "Rational Theory" (including its formidable McKean appendix) can be used (with little more than a redefinition of parameters) to determine the prices of many types of options within the Black-Scholes methodology. As one example, consider options where early exercise can occur. As is shown in Merton (1973), one can solve for the Black-Scholes price of either a European or an American call option on a proportional-dividend-paying stock simply by substituting $\beta = r$ and $\alpha = r - \delta$ into the "Rational Theory" analysis of the "$\beta > \alpha$" case. Similar results obtain for the evaluation of put options.

As a second example, there is the solution in the McKean appendix for the price of an option on a stock whose return is a Poisson-directed process that is discussed in Cox and Ross (1976) and Merton (1976). As still a third example, there is the Samuelson development in the "Rational Theory" of the partial differential equation for option pricing and its solution that uses a limiting process of discrete-time recursive difference equations and a local binomial process for stock price returns. This development is formally quite similar to the simplified procedure for Black-Scholes option pricing presented in Cox-Ross-Rubinstein (1979) as well as to the numerical evaluation procedure for options in Parkinson (1977). In light of these consequences, Samuelson's "Rational Theory of Warrant Pricing" is some near miss!

As is readily apparent from even the small subset of his writings selected for this sampler in financial economics, as in so many branches of economics, Paul Samuelson is a kind of gate-keeper. When he is not busy opening gates to new research problems for himself and an army of other economists to attack, he is busy closing gates with his definitive solutions. And in between, he somehow finds the time to convey to both the professional practitioner and the general public those important research findings that have survived the rigors of both careful analytical and empirical examination.

As noted at the outset of this Introduction, a prevailing theme of research in financial economics is the conjoining of intrinsic intellectual interest with extrinsic practical application. This research has significantly influenced the practice of finance whether it be on Wall Street, LaSalle Street, or in corporate headquarters throughout the world. In this regard, Paul Samuelson provides a sterling counterexample to the well-known dictum of Keynes that "practical men, who believe themselves to be quite exempt from intellectual influences, are usually the slaves of some defunct economist." Any attempt to trace *all* the paths of influence which Samuelson has had on finance practice is, of course, doomed to failure—we need only remember the eleven editions of his basic textbook on which so many practitioners were reared. Nevertheless, to emphasize the significance of just the one path explored here, I note only that in their widely adopted textbook for MBA students in financial management, *Principles of Corporate Finance*, Richard Brealey and Stewart Myers conclude with their list of the five most important ideas in finance. Three on the list are: the mean-variance capital asset pricing model, efficient market theory, and option theory.

As in all fields where the research is closely connected with practical application, in financial economics, conflicts in problem choice are not uncommon between those that have the most immediate consequences for practice and those that are more basic. As is evident from the following excerpt from his Foreword to *Investment Portfolio Decision-Making* [1974e, IV, Chap. 244, p. 488], there is surely no doubt how Paul Samuelson resolves such conflicts in his own research.

> My pitch in this Foreword is not exclusively or even primarily aimed at practical men. Let them take care of themselves. The less of them who become sophisticated the better for us happy few! It is to the economist, the statistician, the philosopher, and to the general reader that I commend the analysis contained herein. Not all of science is beautiful. Only a zoologist could enjoy some parts of that subject; only a mathematician could enjoy vast areas of that terrain. But mathematics as applied to classical thermodynamics is beautiful: if you can't see that, you were born color-blind and are to be pitied. Similarly, in all the branches of pure and applied mathematics, the subject of probability is undoubtedly one of the most fascinating. As my colleague Professor Robert Solow once put it when he was a young man just appointed to the MIT staff: "Either you think that probability is the most exciting subject in the world, or you don't. And if you don't, I feel sorry for you."
>
> Well, here in the mathematics of investment under uncertainty, some of the most interesting applications of probability occur. Elsewhere, in my 1971 von Neumann Lecture before the Society for Industrial and Applied Mathematics, I have referred to the 1900 work on the economic Brownian motion by an unknown French professor, Louis Bachelier. Five years before the similar work by Albert Einstein, we see growing out of economic observations all that Einstein was able to deduce and more. Here, we see the birth of the theory of stochastic processes. Here we see, if you can picture it, radiation of probabilities according to Fourier's partial differential equations. And finally, as an anticlimax, here we see a way of making money from warrants and options or, better still, a way of understanding how they must be priced so that no easy pickings remain.

In short, first things first.

AFTERWORD

Space, not source material, is the scarce resource in this chapter. While the six articles reviewed in this sampler are among Paul Samuelson's most important contributions to financial economics, they surely do not exhaust the set. Picking a cutoff under such conditions is no easy task. I am indeed indebted to Paul for having taken on this burden and for being so selective. Had the choices been mine, I would have violated the budget constraint by including at least half a dozen more. One of these is "Efficient Portfolio Selection for Pareto-Lévy Investments" [1967b, III, Chap. 202], where Samuelson was the first to solve the optimal portfolio choice problem when investments have stable distributions with infinite variances. Another is his important "Optimality of Sluggish Predictors under Ergodic Probabilities" [1976a, IV, Chap. 249], which could be claimed to be within the permeable and flexible boundaries of financial economics.

Although the quite proper focus here is on Samuelson's many new discoveries, his diligence in trying to subvert error is also deeply important to the field. Just as in investing where the most gold goes to those who show us how to make money, so the most academic gold (or credit) goes to new discoveries. But in investments, as Samuelson's work in efficient markets and portfolio theory amply demonstrates, there is also considerable value to being shown how not to lose money by avoiding financial errors. Just so, there is also considerable value to those who divert us away from the paths of error in research.

By defanging the St. Petersburg Paradox, Samuelson has taught us not to unduly fear unbounded utility and, thereby, he has left intact the important body of research into the economics of uncertainty that is based upon the HARA family of utility functions, most of whose members are unbounded functions. While defending the legitimacy of the HARA family, he has also kept us from becoming enthralled with the enticing geometric mean maximization hypothesis where log utility, a particular member of the family, is proclaimed to be the criterion function for "super" rational choice. Samuelson discriminates among brain children, and his success in saving the profession from being drawn further along these paths of error has been due in no small part to his willingness to reaffirm basic beliefs whenever, like the phoenix, some new version of an old error arises. Disposing of one version in his "The 'Fallacy' of Maximizing the Geometric Mean in Long Sequences of Investing or Gambling" [1971b, III, Chap. 207), Samuelson returned to battle a second one (this time taking me along as coauthor) in "Fallacy of the Lognormal Approximation to Optimal Portfolio Decision Making Over Many Periods" [1974b, IV, Chap. 245]. Still later in 1979, he countered a third with his paper of the monosyllabled title, "Why We Should Not Make Mean Log of Wealth Big Though Years to Act Are Long,"

This diligence and discrimination along with the strong opinions and decisive language so characteristic of Samuelson's writings might be mistaken by some as dogmatism and inflexibility. He has written much about occasional dogmatism among economists and Paul Samuelson practices what he preaches. It is indeed his willingness to change his own views and admit to errors that makes his steadfastness on some issues so credible. No better example of this willingness can be found than in his early work on the von Neumann-Morgenstern Expected Utility Theorem. Samuelson's first paper on their theorem, "Probability and the Attempts to Measure Utility" [1950, I, Chap. 12], is sharply critical of the required cardinality property of the preference orderings. In this paper, he sowed the seeds for what was to be called the "zeroth axiom" in his seminal 1952 paper included in this sampler, but his early criticism went too far. As he indicates in the later paper (and in a still later 1965 postscript in his collected scientific papers), he reversed his view and was converted. Samuelson's record here as elsewhere in his writings would provide a favorable data point for establishing the empirical validity of the astrophysicist John A. Wheeler's injunction for prime researchers: "Make yours mistakes fast, and you will more often than not be the first to find your errors."

Samuelson's attacks on error are not limited to engagements in the economics arena. He has upon occasion used the life works of other economists to discredit the widely held myth in the history of science that scientific productivity declines after a certain chronological age. The strongest debunking of this ill-founded belief would, of course, have been the self-exemplifying one. While my brief search of the literature produced neither an exact cutoff age where productivity is purported to decline nor whether this decline is to be measured by the flow of research output per unit time or by its rate of change, the data provided by Paul Samuelson's lifetime pattern of contributions are robust in rejecting this proposed result on all counts. Representing twenty-seven years of scientific writing from 1937 to the middle of 1964, the first two volumes of his Collected Scientific Papers contain 129 articles and 1772 pages. These were followed by the publication in 1972 of the 897-page third volume, which registers the succeeding seven years' product of seventy-eight articles published when he was between the ages of 49 and 56. A mere five years later, at the age of 61, Samuelson had published another eighty-six papers, which fill the fourth volume with 944 pages. Simple extrapolation (along with a glance at his list of publications since 1976) assures us the the fifth volume cannot be far away.

Perhaps a bit selfishly, we in financial economics are especially thankful that Paul paid no heed to the myth of debilitating age in science. Five of the six articles in this sampler and all but six of his thirty contributions to our branch of economics were published after he had reached the age of 50.

There is no need to dwell on the prolific and profound accomplishments of Paul Samuelson, which have become legend—especially when the legend is a brute fact. Rather I close this afterword with a few observations (drawn as his student, colleague, and coresearcher) on some of Paul's modes of thought that perhaps make such super achievement possible. First, there is his seemingly infinite capacity for problem finding and his supersaturated knowledge of just about every special sphere of economics. Second, there is his speed of problem solving together with the ability to put the solution quickly to paper with great skill, great verve, and lack of hesitation. Finally, although often masked by the apparent ease with which he produces, there is his diligence. Paul works hard.

On the matter of sustained hard work of this particular kind, Paul is fond of a story (and so, he repeated it in his presidential address to the I.E.A.) about the University of Chicago mathematician Leonard Dickson, who was to be found playing bridge all afternoon every afternoon. When a colleague asked how he could afford to spend so much of his time playing, Dickson is said to have replied: "If you worked as hard at mathematics as I do from 8 to 12, you too could play bridge in the afternoon." As Paul also notes in that address, much the same story holds for the mathematician G. H. Hardy, in his case watching cricket rather than playing bridge. I can improve on these yarns with one about Paul from the glorious days when as his research assistant I lived in his office. I was working (not very successfully) on the solution to an equation in warrant pricing that was needed for some research Paul was doing when he left for the tennis courts (as he often did and still often does). Sometime later, the phone rang. It was Paul calling from the courts (presumably between sets) to tell me exactly how that equation could be solved. Dickson and Hardy segregated creative work and well-earned play, and so it appears does Paul, but with a finite and significant difference. Even at play, he is at work.

REFERENCES

Bachelier, L. (1900): "Théorie de la Speculation," Paris, Gauthier-Villars, Cf. English translation in P. Cootner (ed.): *The Random Character of Stock Market Prices*, rev. ed. Cambridge, Massachusetts, M.I.T. Press, 1967.

Black, F. and M. Scholes (1973): "The Pricing of Options and Corporate Liabilities," *Journal of Political Economy* 81, pp. 637–659.

Borch, K. (1969): "A Note on Uncertainty and Indifference Curves," *Review of Economic Studies* 36, pp. 1–4.

Brealey, R. and S. Myers (1981): *Principles of Corporate Finance*, New York, McGraw-Hill.

Cox, J. and S. Ross (1976): "The Valuation of Options for Alternative Stochastic Processes," *Journal of Financial Economics* 3, pp. 145–166.

———, ———, and M. Rubinstein (1979): "Option Pricing: A Simplified Approach," *Journal of Financial Economics* 7, pp. 229–263.

Fama, E. (1970): "Efficient Capital Markets: A Review of Theory and Empirical Work," *Journal of Finance* 25, pp. 383–417.

Feldstein, M. (1969): "Mean-Variance Analysis in the Theory of Liquidity Preference and Portfolio Selection," *Review of Economic Studies* 36, pp. 5–12.

Jensen, M. (1968): "The Performance of Mutual Funds in the Period 1945–1964," *Journal of Finance* 23, pp. 389–416.

Kruizenga, R. (1956): "Put and Call Options: A Theoretical and Market Analysis," doctoral dissertation, M.I.T., Cambridge, Massachusetts.

Lintner, J. (1965): "The Valuation of Risk Assets and the Solution of Risky Investments in Stock Portfolio and Capital Budgets," *Review of Economics and Statistics* 47, pp. 13–37.

Markowitz, H. (1959): *Portfolio Selection: Efficient Diversification of Investments*, New York, John Wiley.

Merton, R. C. (1973): "Theory of Rational Option Pricing," *Bell Journal of Economics and Management Science* 4, pp. 141–183.

———. (1976): "Option Pricing when Underlying Stock Returns are Discontinuous," *Journal of Financial Economics* 3, 125–144.

———. (1982): "On the Microeconomic Theory of Investment under Uncertainty," in K. J. Arrow and M. D. Intriligator (eds.): *Handbook of Mathematical Economics*, vol. II, Amsterdam, North-Holland, pp. 601–669.

Merton, R. K. (1973): *The Sociology of Science*, Chicago, University of Chicago Press.

———. (1976): *Sociological Ambivalence and Other Essays*, New York, The Free Press.

Mossin, J. (1966): "Equilibrium in a Capital Asset Market," *Econometrica* 34, pp. 768–783.

Parkinson, M. (1977): " Option Pricing: The American Put," *Journal of Business* 50, pp. 21–36.

Samuelson, P. A. (1966): *The Collected Scientific Papers of Paul A. Samuelson*, vols. I and II, J. E. Stiglitz (ed.), Cambridge, M.I.T. Press.

———. (1972): *The Collected Scientific Papers of Paul A. Samuelson*, vol. III, R. C. Merton (ed.), Cambridge, M.I.T. Press.

———. (1977): *The Collected Scientific Papers of Paul A. Samuelson*, vol. IV, H. Nagatani and K. Crowley (eds.): Cambridge, M.I.T. Press.

———. (1950): "Probability and the Attempts to Measure Utility," *The Economic Review* 1, pp. 167–173; *Collected Scientific Papers*, I, Chap. 12.

———. (1952a): Utility, Preference and Probability," Conference on "Les fondements et applications de la théorie du risque en économétrie," Paris; *Collected Scientific Papers*, I, Chap. 13.

———. (1952b): "Probability, Utility, and the Independence Axiom," *Econometrica* 20, pp. 670–678; *Collected Scientific Papers*, I, Chap. 14.

———. (1957): "Intertemporal Price Equilibrium: A Prologue to the Theory of Speculation," *Weltwirtschaftliches Archiv* 79, pp. 181–219; *Collected Scientific Papers*, II, Chap. 73.

———. (1960): "The St. Petersburg Paradox as a Divergent Double Limit," *International Economic Review* 1, pp. 31–37; *Collected Scientific Papers*, I, Chap. 15.

———. (1963): "Risk and Uncertainty: A Fallacy of Large Numbers," *Scientia* 57, pp. 1–6; *Collected Scientific Papers*, I, Chap. 16.

———. (1965a): "Proof that Properly Anticipated Prices Fluctuate Randomly," *Industrial Management Review* 6, pp. 41–49; *Collected Scientific Papers*, III, Chap. 198.

———. (1965b): "Rational Theory of Warrant Pricing," *Industrial Management Review* 6, pp. 13–39; *Collected Scientific Papers*, III, Chap. 199.

———. (1967a): "General Proof that Diversification Pays," *Journal of Financial and Quantitative Analysis* 2, pp. 1–13; *Collected Scientific Papers*, III, Chap. 201.

———. (1967b): "Efficient Portfolio Selection for Pareto-Lévy Investments," *Journal of Financial and Quantitative Analysis* 2, pp. 107–122; *Collected Scientific Papers*, III, Chap. 202.

———. (1968): "Book Review of E. D. Thorp and S. T. Kasouff's *Beat the Market*," *Journal of American Statistical Assocation* 10, pp. 1049–1051.

———. (1969a): "Lifetime Portfolio Selection by Dynamic Stochastic Programming," *Review of Economics and Statistics* 51, pp. 239–246; *Collected Scientific Papers*, III, Chap. 204.

——— and R. C. Merton (1969b): "A Complete Model of Warrant Pricing that Maximizes Utility," *Industrial Management Review* 10, pp. 17–46; *Collected Scientific Papers*, III, Chap. 200.

———. (1970a): "The Fundamental Approximation Theorem of Portfolio Analysis in Terms of Means, Variances and Higher Moments," *Review of Economic Studies* 37, pp. 537–542; *Collected Scientific Papers*, III, Chap. 203.

———. (1970b): "Foreword" in R. Roll: *The Behavior of Interest Rates: An Application of the Efficient Market Model to U.S. Treasury Bills*, New York, Basic Books, Inc., pp. ix–xi; *Collected Scientific Papers*, III, Chap. 205.

———. (1971a): "Stochastic Speculative Price," *Proceedings of the National Academy of Sciences* 68, pp. 335–337; *Collected Scientific Papers*, III, Chap. 206.

———. (1971b): "The 'Fallacy' of Maximizing the Geometric Mean in Long Sequences of Investing or Gambling," *Proceedings of the National Academy of Sciences* 68, pp. 2493–2496; *Collected Scientific Papers*, III, Chap. 207.

———. (1972a): "Mathematics of Speculative Price" in R. H. Day and S. M. Robinson (eds.): *Mathematical Topics in Economic Theory and Computation*, Philadelphia; Society for

Industrial and Applied Mathematics, reprinted in *SIAM Review* 15, 1973, pp. 1–42; *Collected Scientific Papers*, IV, Chap. 240.

———. (1972b): "Economics in a Golden Age: A Personal Memoir" in G. Holton (ed.): *The Twentieth Century Sciences: Studies in the Biography of Ideas*, New York, W. W. Norton, pp. 155–170; *Collected Scientific Papers*, IV, Chap. 278.

———. (1972c): "Proof that Unsuccessful Speculators Confer Less Benefit to Society than Their Losses," *Proceedings of the National Academy of Sciences* 69, pp. 1230–1233; *Collected Scientific Papers*, IV, Chap. 260.

———. (1973): "Proof that Properly Discounted Present Values of Assets Vibrate Randomly," *Bell Journal of Economics and Management Science* 4, pp. 369–374; *Collected Scientific Papers*, IV, Chap. 241.

——— and R. C. Merton (1974a): "Generalized Mean-Variance Tradeoffs for Best Perturbation Corrections to Approximate Portfolio Decisions," *Journal of Finance* 29, pp. 27–30; *Collected Scientific Papers*, IV, Chap. 246.

——— and R. C. Merton (1974b): "Fallacy of the Log-Normal Approximation to Optimal Portfolio Decision Making over Many Periods," *Journal of Financial Economics* 1, pp. 67–94; *Collected Scientific Papers*, IV, Chap. 245.

———. (1974c): "Comments on the Favorable-Bet Theorem," *Economic Inquiry* 12, pp. 345–355; *Collected Scientific Papers*, IV, Chap. 248.

———. (1974d): "Challenge to Judgment," *Journal of Portfolio Management* 1, pp. 17–19; *Collected Scientific Papers*, IV, Chap. 243.

———. (1974e): "Foreword" in J. L. Bicksler and P. A. Samuelson (eds.): *Investment Portfolio Decision Making*, Lexington, D. C. Heath ; *Collected Scientific Papers*, IV, Chap. 244.

———. (1975): "The Balanced-Budget Multiplier: A Case Study in the Sociology and Psychology of Scientific Discovery," *History of Political Economy* 7, pp. 43–49; *Collected Scientific Papers*, IV, Chap. 274.

———. (1976a): "Optimality of Sluggish Predictors under Ergodic Probability," *International Economic Review* 17, pp. 1–7; *Collected Scientific Papers*, IV, Chap. 249.

———. (1976b): "Is Real-World Price a Tale Told by the Idiot of Chance?" *Review of Economics and Statistics* 58, pp. 120–123; *Collected Scientific Papers*, IV, Chap. 242.

———. (1976c): "Limited Liability, Short Selling, Bounded Utility, and Infinite-Variance Stable Distributions," *Journal of Financial and Quantitative Analysis* 11, pp. 485–503; *Collected Scientific Papers*, IV, Chap. 247.

———. (1977): "St Petersburg Paradoxes: Defanged, Dissected and Historically Described," *Journal of Economic Literature* 15, pp. 24–55.

———. (1979a): "Why We Should Not Make Mean Log of Wealth Big Though Years to Act Are Long, *Journal of Banking and Finance*, 3, pp. 305–307.

———. (1979b): "Myths and Realities about the Crash and Depression," *Journal of Portfolio Management* 6, pp. 7–10.

Sharpe, W. (1964): "Capital Asset Prices: A Theory of Market Equilibrium Under Conditions of Risk," *Journal of Finance* 19, pp. 425–442.

Thorp, E. O. and S. T. Kasouff (1967): *Beat the Market: A Scientific Stock Market System*, New York, Random House.

Tobin, J. (1958): "Liquidity Preference as Behavior Towards Risk," *Review of Economic Studies* 25, pp. 65–86.

Tobin, J. (1969): "Comment on Borch and Feldstein," *Review of Economic Studies* 36, pp. 13–14.

von Neumann, J. and O. Morgenstern (1947): *Theory of Games and Economic Behavior*, 2d ed. Princeton, Princeton University Press.

PUBLIC GOODS

Richard A. Musgrave*

The modern theory of public goods may be dated from June 1954, when Samuelson's "Pure Theory of Public Expenditures" appeared.[1] Never have three pages had so great an impact on the theory of public finance. They spawned a large body of literature with many variations on the theme, but the basic model had been set. The conditions of Pareto optimality had been expanded to include public goods and the optimum optimorum based on a social welfare function had been restated accordingly. At the same time—and Samuelson made this clear from the outset— his model was not designed to show how the optimum might be arrived at in practice. At the formal level of welfare theory all was resolved, but much remained and remains to be done to put the theoretical jewel to practical use. To place Samuelson's contribution in perspective, I begin with a sketch of fiscal theory up to 1954. I shall then summarize and examine his basic model, to be followed by a review of its major offshoots.

ANTECEDENTS

The history of doctrine, here as in other contexts, defies pedantic chronology. New ideas arise, overlap the old, and progress in discontinuous fashion. We may thus date the prehistory of public goods theory from 1776 (Adam Smith) to 1928 (A.C.

---

*Thanks are due to James Buchanan for helpful comments.

[1] [1954, II, Chap. 92]. Citations of Samuelson's *Collected Scientific Papers* give year of original publication, volume in roman numerals, chapter and sometimes specific pages. To permit focus, this paper is limited to Samuelson's contribution to the theory of public goods, thus omitting some other writings in public finance, especially his paper on the theory of capital income taxation [1964, III, Chap. 179]. His crucial early papers on the macroaspects of fiscal policy are dealt with elsewhere in this volume.

Pigou), with history overlapping from the 1880s (Sax and Mazzola) to 1954 (Samuelson), and posthistory thereafter.

Prehistory

Unlike most of his classical successors, Adam Smith did not view the economics of public finance as merely a matter of minimizing the evils of taxation. Book V of his *Wealth of Nations* gives more space to the expenditure than to the tax side of the budget. Public expenditures had a positive and important role to play. Maintenance of the courts, defense, justice, and free education for the poor were needed. Beyond this, the sovereign's duty

> is that of erecting and maintaining those public institutions and those public works, which, though they may be in the highest degree advantageous to a great society, are, however, of such a nature, that the profit could never repay the expence to any individual or small number of individuals, and which it therefore cannot be expected that any individual or small number of individuals should erect or maintain.[2]

Smith thus recognized the occurrence of market failure due to the peculiar nature of public goods, as well as the resulting need for public provision. But he did not go on to explore what it is in the nature of public goods that causes this difficulty to arise, evidently unaware of Hume's uncannily modern characterization of the free rider problem.[3] Nevertheless, these early insights should have sent the theory of public goods off to a running start, but such was not to be. Classical economists who followed showed little appetite for examing the economic nature of public goods. With few exceptions, they addressed the tax side of the budget only. Ricardo in particular considered public expenditures inherently wasteful, endorsing Say's dictum that "the very best of all plans of finance is to spend little."[4] John Stuart Mill gave much space to the design of an equitable tax structure but paid little or no attention to expenditure analysis.

Such was the case even though the benefit strand of equity theory could not quite escape its implicit linkage to the expenditure side. Taxation according to benefits received was a natural outgrowth of Lockean contract theory, in which civil society is formed for the protection of justly acquired property. "The subject of every state," so Adam Smith noted, "ought to contribute towards the support of government as nearly as possible in line with their respective abilities; that is, in proportion to the revenue which they respectively enjoy under the protection of the state."[5] Taxation according to benefit received thus involves the central notion of a quid pro quo, of taxation as a just price paid for services rendered. But the proper scope for such services, as indeed the role of the state, was considered as minimal. Emphasis was on how to distribute the cost of a given budget in line with the recipients' gains, rather than on how its composition and size should be determined.

Benefit theorists differed, however, in what they considered the relationship

[2] Smith (1776) p. 681.
[3] Hume (1740) Vol. III, Part ii, Section 7.
[4] Ricardo (1817) p. 159.
[5] Smith (1776) p. 777.

between benefits and income.[6] Some, including Mill, held that the benefit rule would call for regressive taxation as the poor are in greater need of protection, while others argued that the rich have more wealth to protect, thus calling for progressive rates. In either case, reference was to the *amount* of protection needed, rather than to different valuations that poor and rich would place on a given amount. Both groups also adhered to the Lockean notion that returns to effort establish a just distribution, so that redistributive taxation is ruled out. The benefit doctrine thus had an essentially conservative appeal.

Ability-to-pay theorists in turn disregarded expenditures altogether. They thought to determine a fair distribution of the tax burden quite independent of how the money is spent. The tax burden, as a matter of equity, should be distributed in line with "ability to pay." Beginning with John Stuart Mill, this was restated as requiring an imposition of equal sacrifice,[7] and subsequent refinements were added by Edgeworth and Pigou.[8] They distinguished between equal-absolute, proportional, and marginal sacrifice, with the latter doubling as an equity and welfare-maximizing rule. Pigou's formulation, moreover, introduced deadweight loss into the burden concept, thereby foreshadowing recent developments in the theory of optimal taxation. But the ability-to-pay doctrine lost professional credibility with the advent of the new welfare economics from Robbins on and its banning of cardinal utility comparisons from theoretical analysis. The practice of such comparisons, however, survived in the public mind, as did the notion that taxes should be distributed fairly.

Contrasted with the conservative appeal of the benefit doctrine, the ability-to-pay approach was favored by liberal writers who were not averse to income redistribution. Distribution of the tax burden by ability to pay was generally interpreted to call for progressive taxation, although, as Samuelson showed in an early footnote, this is by no means a foregone conclusion. All depends on how equal sacrifice is defined and on the shape of the income utility function.[9]

History

Pigou's primary concern in fiscal theory was with the design of the tax structure, in line with the ability-to-pay approach.[10] We have therefore grouped him under the prehistory caption. This grouping, however, needs qualification because his treatise also contains a brief but important chapter on expenditure theory. In this chapter, he calls for both sides of the budget to be linked by the efficiency requirement that provision for public goods should be carried to the point where marginal social benefits come to equal marginal social costs.[11] This was an advance over the

---

[6] Musgrave (1959) Chaps. 4, 5.

[7] Mill (1847) p. 805.

[8] Edgeworth (1925); Pigou (1928) Chap. 5.

[9] Samuelson (1947) p. 227.

[10] Pigou (1928) Part II.

[11] Pigou (1928) Chap. 5. The same may be said for earlier continental attempts to prescribe a proper balance between private and public outlays. Thus Schäffle's law of proportional expenditures implied a principle similar to that advanced by Pigou (Schäffle, 1873) but the needs to be covered by the state were taken to be given as group needs. Adolf Wagner similarly balanced the advantages and costs of public services (Wagner, 1883) but he left it to political science to determine the proper range of state activities.

ability-to-pay tradition as it overcame the taxation-only bias that had characterized that approach. In its abstract and normative tone, it indeed resembles the spirit of Samuelson's later contribution. But unfortunately Pigou did not go beyond stating his unexceptionable rule. He did not address the question of why certain goods need be provided through the budget, and he made no serious attempt to define the nature of public goods. As Samuelson noted, it is surprising that the author of *The Economics of Welfare* did not carry his theory of externalities to his later study of fiscal problems.[12] Nor was he aware of the new doctrine that had developed in the continental writings of the 1880s and 90s when the newly emerged doctrine of marginal utility came to be applied to public finance. Public, like private, goods, so the new argument went, should be evaluated in line with their utility to the consumer. Thereby the basis for modern public goods theory was laid and economic analysis, interpreted as the theory of efficient resource use, was expanded to nonmarket phenomena. Though beginning with Sax, the modern definition of public goods may be traced to Mazzola. Writing in 1890, he recognized the indivisibility of public services as their distinguishing characteristic, the fact that "consumption can not be divided up."[13] Since consumers differ in incomes and tastes, this indivisibility "constitutes a technical reason" why uniform pricing would leave some with more and others with less than the marginal utility that they derive.[14] Uniform pricing, therefore, would contradict society's natural tendency to use resources for maximum satisfaction. To secure it, he continues, governments charge multiple prices, "so that each pays for these goods according to his own evaluation."[15]

While Mazzola thought of the efficient tax price as resulting from the maximizing behavior of consumers, he recognized that evaluation does not come about automatically through a market process. Rather, it is entrusted to governmental agencies. When their policies are dominated by the interests of particular classes or groups, the natural equilibrium of welfare maximization is disturbed and dissatisfaction results. The equilibrating process of the competitive market is replaced by that of the political system. Though open to criticism in details, Mazzola's formulation was nevertheless an important advance. His model served as a stepping-stone for Wicksell's analysis and already contained the essential elements of Lindahl's subsequent pricing solution. Since it was dissatisfaction with this solution that thirty years later induced Samuelson's reformulation, we may observe an intriguing if discontinuous intellectual lineage from 1890 to 1954.

Wicksell, writing in 1896, accepted Mazzola's central thesis of "equality between the marginal utility of public goods and their price" as an efficiency rule. But he rejected the further contention that this result comes about when each taxpayer succeeds in maximizing his utility. Mazzola's rule as a requirement of tax policy "is really meaningless."[16] The reason lies in the "free rider" behavior, a term that came

---

[12] [1958, II, Chap. 94, p. 1233].
[13] Mazzola (1890) exerpts translated in Musgrave and Peacock (1958) p. 42.
[14] Ibid.
[15] Ibid., p. 44.
[16] Wicksell (1896) excerpts in Musgrave and Peacock (1958) p. 81.

later but a concept that was clearly grasped by Wicksell: "Since the taxpayer's own outlays on public services will have no significant effect on total supply, he will pay nothing." The necessary equality between marginal utility and tax price "can not be achieved by the action of individual taxpayers." Rather, it must be brought about by consultation between all taxpayers, a process which Mazzola did not describe. In Wicksell's view, "this is precisely the question which ought to be decided."[17]

In addressing this issue, Wicksell considers the possibility that an enlightened ruler (not unlike Samuelson's ethical observer) succeeds in implementing the general welfare, but he drops this as an unlikely solution. Majority rule under representative democracy is even more likely to fail, since the representatives will be as selfish as their constituents. The solution must be sought in a voting system in which each expenditure project is paired with alternative taxing patterns. If the expenditure project creates utility that exceeds its cost, so Wicksell argues, one of the combinations is likely to find unanimous acceptance.[18] Budget decisions should therefore be made on a unanimous basis. This will not assure that Mazzola's criterion is met, but it will provide a fair approximation. Having proposed his stern requirement of full unanimity, Wicksell then dilutes it and calls for a rule of only "approximate unanimity of decision—absolute unanimity may have to be ruled out for practical reasons."[19] This weakens Wicksell's case, especially since no definition of "approximate" is given and the nature of the "practical reason" is not described.

Wicksell also adds a "necessary, although ultimately only an apparent, exception to the principle of unanimity and voluntary consent as the basis for just taxation." This exception arises because "it is clear that justice in taxation tacitly *presupposes* (italics added) justice in the existing distribution of property[20] and income. There can be no true quid pro quo in paying for public services if what the taxpayer surrenders is not properly his. If the prevailing property order is "in open contradiction with modern concepts of law and equity, then society has both the right and duty to revise the existing property structure." But here the unanimity requirement has to be suspended "since it would obviously be asking too much to expect such revision even to be carried out if it were made dependent upon the agreement of the persons primarily involved."[21] Wicksell, at the same time, cautions against excessive interference of this sort but the essential methodological point is made: Just distribution precedes the just financing of public services and the two are viewed as distinct steps. As we shall see presently, this poses one of the fundamental points of disagreement between his and Samuelson's formulation.

We now come to Lindahl's contributions as the last step towards the completion of history. Lindahl, writing in 1919, presented what later became known as the voluntary exchange solution. Two parties, A and B, advance their offer curves for public goods, defining the maximum fraction of the total cost that they would be willing to assume at various budget sizes. An equilibrium is established at the

[17] Ibid., p. 82.
[18] Ibid., p. 90.
[19] Ibid., p. 92.
[20] Ibid., p. 108.
[21] Ibid., p. 109.

intersection of the two curves, where their marginal evaluations add up to total cost.[22] As shown later on by Bowen, the same solution may be arrived at as the intersection between the supply schedule (recording marginal cost to the community as a whole) and a hypothetical market demand schedule, in this case by vertical rather than horizontal addition of individual schedules.[23] Tax prices thus determined leave each taxpayer in a position where price ratio equals marginal rates of substitution. Social good pricing is similar to private good pricing in this respect, but the social good case combines different prices with equal quantities, while the private good case combines equal prices with different quantities.

Lindahl's pricing solution thus resembles that visualized by Mazzola and accepted as a norm by Wicksell. He differs from Wicksell in that he takes this pricing rule to come about as the result of voluntary bargaining, be it among two parties or among a number of individuals who strike successive bargains. His "standard solution" is achieved if "power is distributed evenly in relation to the existing property order."[24] If political power differs, a solution more advantageous to one or the other party will result. But in all, the political process may be expected to approximate the standard case. Following Wicksell, Lindahl notes that the solution will reflect the consequences of a given property order. For the pricing solution to be just, the property order must also be considered such, since, so he quotes Wicksell, "it would obviously be nonsense to speak of a just portion of an unjust whole."[25]

THE SAMUELSON MODEL

Such was the state of the debate in 1954 when, after a hiatus of thirty-five years, Samuelson's model appeared. There had been no mention of public expenditures in his *Foundations* and only a cursory footnote reference to taxation. The excursion into expenditure theory was undertaken, so we are told, to illustrate the usefulness of mathematical economics, rather than as the outcome of our author's long-standing and substantive concern with the problem. It was induced also by his "dim remembrance" of the Lindahl diagram in my maiden paper which, a few years earlier, had brought the voluntary exchange model and its unrealistic setting to the attention of the English (only) reading public.[26] Yet, his brief initial contribution proved to be among his most important pages.

The model is too familiar to require more than a brief summary. The problem that is posed and solved is how to allocate resources efficiently in a setting that includes public as well as private goods. Public—or, as referred to initially by Samuelson, collective consumption goods—are defined as goods for which each person's consumption is related to the total by a condition of equality, not summation, as for private goods. Given the production possibility frontier and taking individual preferences for public and private goods to be known, the set of

---

[22] Lindahl (1919 and 1928) excerpts in Musgrave and Peacock (1958) p. 169.
[23] Bowen (1948) p. 177.
[24] Musgrave and Peacock (1958) p. 172.
[25] Ibid., p. 227.
[26] [1969b, III, Chap. 172, p. 492] and Musgrave (1938).

Pareto-efficient solutions is arrived at. The efficiency conditions are shown to differ from those of private goods. For the latter, the marginal rate of transformation in production equals that of substitution in consumption, which is the same for all consumers. For public goods the marginal rate of transformation equals the sum of the marginal rates of substitution and these may differ among consumers. Given the set of efficient solutions (with each defining the mix of output between public and private goods, and the allocation of private goods among consumers), the best among them (the "bliss point," as Samuelson put it) is chosen by application of a social welfare function.[27]

This formulation differs from its precursors in important respects. The theory of public goods is now viewed as an extension of the conditions of Pareto optimality and no longer as modeling or reforming the process by which budget policy is determined. Most important, the derivation of efficiency conditions is separated from the process by which an efficient budget may in fact be arrived at. By introducing an ethical observer to whom preferences are known, the revelation issue is bypassed and the problem is solved without reference to such institutional baggage as a prevailing distribution of income, taxes, or expenditures. This is quite in line with Samuelson's earlier statement of welfare maximization in a private good setting.[28] While the competitive market may be used as an implementation device for this setting, the efficiency conditions do not derive from the existence of market institutions. Similarly, those for public goods are defined independent of budgetary or voting institutions.

In this setting, Lindahl pricing ceases to be *the* solution and becomes but a special case of the general model. As Samuelson shows in a later paper, the observer may play the Lindahl game by using a "pseudo-demand analysis" to compute the equilibrium.[29] He will begin with some particular distribution of money income, derive each individual's corresponding pseudo demand curve, and then provide for public goods in line with what people wish to buy at Lindahl prices. This solution will be efficient and reflect a point on the utility frontier. But the outcome may not be optimal. The observer then applies a set of lump-sum taxes and transfers to achieve another income distribution and repeats the experiment.[30] Doing so for all possible distributions will trace the entire utility frontier. Finally, the best point is chosen on the basis of the social welfare function. Postulating a distribution of income and playing the pricing game is a possible way of solving the problem, but a cumbersome one. The proper distribution of income has to be arrived at simultaneously with the allocation pattern and the chosen set of Lindahl prices, so that nothing is gained by introducing a distribution of money income at the beginning. The observer will save time by proceeding directly with his optimization problem. Moreover, if a distribution of income *is* introduced, the observer need not charge Lindahl prices. The prices that are charged need not equal the consumer's

---

[27] For the basic model, see [1954, II, Chap. 92; and 1955, II, Chap. 93]. For its further development, see [1958, II, Chap. 94; and 1969b, III, Chap. 172].

[28] Samuelson (1947) Chap. 8.

[29] [1969b, III, Chap. 172, p. 496].

[30] See Johansen (1965) for application of the Lindahl solution to alternative income distributions.

marginal rate of substitution. The solution will be efficient, provided only that marginal rates of substitution aggregate to that of transformation.[31]

Having separated the analytical problem of maximization sharply from that of implementation, Samuelson faults Wicksell for not drawing this distinction with sufficient clarity. In particular, he takes issue with Wicksell's proposition that just taxation must be preceded by a just distribution of income.[32] Clearly, Wicksell's proposition is mistaken if viewed within the context of Samuelson's own model. But this is not what Wicksell was after. His concern was with the mechanism of preference revelation and with improving the fiscal institutions through which this mechanism operates. It was not with the derivation of efficiency conditions in a setting that assumes preferences to be known. Once preferences are not given, a voting mechanism must be used to induce preference revelation; to do so a given distribution of income must prevail. Moreover, if the voting solution is to be optimal as well as efficient, the correct, or as Wicksell called it, the "just" distribution of income must prevail to begin with. But how can this be if, as Samuelson holds, the distribution issue must be resolved simultaneously with that of public goods allocation? In my view (although I have not persuaded Professor Samuelson of this), the circularity is broken by introducing an additional equation.[33] In the private good setting, and with preferences unknown, the competitive market may be used as a computation device. This being the case, *the proper distribution of income is that which yields the optimal result given the use of marginal cost pricing through the market system.* For the case of public goods, that distribution of money income is proper or "just" which yields the optimal solution (an efficient outcome and a distribution of welfare in line with the social welfare function) given *that* pricing rule which is approximated by the voting process. While there is more than one efficient pricing rule, I find it reasonable to postulate that the voting process should be designed to approximate Lindahl pricing. This permits parallel treatment of public and private goods prices in setting the proper distribution of (real) income, and allows the voter-consumer to think symmetrically about his or her "purchases" of public and private goods.

All this, to be sure, does not matter in Samuelson's pure model where the issues of allocation and distribution intrinsically overlap and must be resolved simultaneously. Given the omniscient referee and the global task that Samuelson assigns to him or her, there is no prior state of distribution and hence no issue of "redistribution." Allocation decisions need not be compromised by distributional concerns. As noted before, the referee may while away time by using a "pseudo demand algorithm to compute equilibrium," but all the Pareto-optimal solutions may be traced out readily by manipulating the pattern of lump-sum taxes and

---

[31] McGuire and Aaron (1969).

[32] [1969b, III, Chap. 172, p. 495]. Samuelson suggests that Wicksell confuses two concepts of justice: (1) justice in distribution so as to secure maximum bliss—the utilitarian approach, and (2) justice in permitting a person to secure optimal use of a given income—the approach implicit in considering a Lindahl price as just. I wonder whether Wicksell was indeed confused on this point. Given the need for securing preference revelation via a given distribution of income, both concepts of justice are needed and have to enter in an interdependent fashion.

[33] Musgrave (1969), p. 106.

transfers.[34] At a more realistic level, however, this ideal tax-transfer system is not available. Lump-sum redistribution in an ongoing economy is but a fiction of the theorist's imagination. Redistribution policies in the real world cause distortions, leaving the "feasible utility frontier" along which policy may move from a given initial position well inside the true frontier of the pure model. Redistribution in kind, such as expenditures on health, may then involve less distortion and hence be better than a tax-transfer scheme. In his response to Margolis, Samuelson thus disassociates himself from "the type of liberal who would insist that all redistributions take place through tax policies and transfer expenditures."[35] A second-best solution is all that there is to be had, but the reference point remains that of the pure model. Real transfers and subsidies become the counterpart to selective commodity taxation, from Pigou's query to Ramsey's theory on to today's optimal taxation theory.

This, however, is hardly the reason why transfers in kind are used so widely. In a brief departure from neoclassical tradition, Samuelson notes that "paternalistic policies may be voted upon themselves by a democratic people because they do not regard the results of spontaneous market operations as optimal."[36] I take this to recognize the existence of what I have called merit goods, a concept that has recently reappeared in relation to distribution, especially in Tobin's concept of "specific egalitarianism" and views of equity in categorical rather than simply vertical terms.[37] But these are exceptions, out of bounds for Samuelson's theory of public goods, which squarely rests on an individualistic social welfare function. The same goes for modern fiscal theory in general, including most of my own work. Whether or not marginal rates of substitution are additive is no reason why private preferences should or should not be respected. Yet, there are exceptional situations in every society where the public interest is taken to override private preferences, be it with regard to the provision of otherwise private or of public goods. Such types of interference, if this be the right term, may take budgetary form and should have their place in the body of fiscal theory rather than be excluded by definition.[38]

Turning now to the mechanism of preference revelation, Samuelson applauds Wicksell for rejecting the hypothesis that revelation can be secured through a decentralized market mechanism.[39] But he denies as naive Wicksell's proposition that an optimum will be promoted by voting upon issues that combine the tax and expenditure sides of the budget.[40] Bundle voting, to be sure, will not eliminate strategy, but in my view Wicksell's prescription retains much merit. By coupling both sides of the budget, the voter is confronted with the fact that public services involve an opportunity cost. Specification of his tax price at given service levels imposes a constraint that facilitates rational choice, and, I suspect, limits the scope

---

[34][1969b, III, Chap. 172, p. 497].
[35][1955, II, Chap. 93, p. 1232].
[36]Ibid.
[37]Musgrave (1959) p. 13; Musgrave and Musgrave (1973) p. 83. Also see Tobin (1970).
[38]For the outlines of an alternative approach see Colm (1927, 1955).
[39][1969b, III, Chap. 172, p. 501].
[40]Ibid.

for profitable misrepresentation. Indeed, better linkage of tax and expenditure decisions may well be the key to reform of legislative fiscal procedure. Samuelson's call for "corrosive nihilism" may be helpful "to puncture the bubble of hopeful thinking," but things are not all that bad.[41] The democratic process, after all, functions not too badly and it may be improved by constructive reform. Samuelson himself concedes as much.

> My doubts do not assert that passably good organization of the public household is impossible or unlikely, but merely that theorists have not as yet provided us with much analysis of these matters that has validity or plausibility. If I stimulate someone to resolve my doubts, that will make two people happy.[42]

Have these doubts been resolved by recent work on a voting system under which self-interested individuals will choose not to cheat?[43] Beginning with a prevailing distribution of income, suppose that cost shares in the budget are assigned among individuals in some arbitrary fashion and independent of their preferences, true or as revealed. Suppose that the budget is to be financed by a head tax. Individuals are then asked to record their maximum-offer schedules for various budget sizes, aggregate "demand" is determined in Bowen fashion by vertical addition, and output is set at the intersection of the aggregate demand with the supply schedule. The solution will be efficient provided that individuals will report their true demand schedules. They will be induced to do so by a tax (payable in addition to the cost share) that renders misrepresentation unprofitable. Each individual will pay a Clarke tax (named after its inventor) equal in amount to the loss of consumer surplus suffered by others because he chooses to vote rather than to abstain. This will induce him to reveal his true preferences because cheating will increase his Clarke tax by more than he can hope to gain from pushing the budget size toward his preferred level. This outcome is not surprising. If true preferences are revealed, the allocation decision will fall on the utility frontier. Cheating moves the solution inside. What A may gain from misrepresentation must fall short of what B and C lose. Misrepresentation therefore does not pay if A must pay compensation through the Clarke tax. While the proceeds are retained in the budget rather than paid out to B and C, this does not reduce the deterrent to A.

As much as I would like to, I cannot share the claim that the Clarke mechanism disposes of the revelation issue, thereby resolving the free rider problem that for centuries has haunted fiscal theory.[44] To begin with, the tax does not do away with distortions that arise from strategic behavior through the formation of coalitions. It deals with isolated cheating by individual voters only. Samuelson's call for nihilism may still hold. But there are difficulties even short of this. If cost shares are to be assigned in arbitrary fashion, net gains or losses from public services must be compensated for elsewhere in determining distributional adjustments, and voters will be aware of this. While it has been suggested that the Clarke tax approach may

---

[41] Ibid.
[42] Ibid.
[43] Clarke (1971, 1972).
[44] Tullock and Tideman (1976) p. 1145.

be used to determine Lindahl prices,[45] I see no basis for this. Moreover, the feasibility of the approach depends on the numbers involved. In the small-number case, the administrative costs are limited and the pressure imposed by the Clarke tax may be substantial. At the same time, coalition strategies are readily feasible. In the large-number case, the Clarke tax will prove very small and one wonders whether its pressure can suffice to induce voters to comply with the rather demanding task of filing their offer curves. Moreover, for the large-number case one wonders how the schedule can be collected and processed and individual Clarke taxes be assigned. It has been suggested that these difficulties might be avoided by reliance on sampling, but this seems more feasible for determining the budget size than for assigning Clarke taxes.

In all, the Clarke mechanism leaves serious problems of implementation, quite apart from the theoretically intriguing (and hence much discussed) fact that the government must somehow dispose of its Clarke tax receipts. While progress is made, it can hardly be said that the issue has been resolved. Samuelson's scepticism remains relevant, and it is a matter of regret that he himself did not undertake to lift it. Had he done so, we would undoubtedly be further in translating his theoretical vision into an operational pattern.

DESCENDANTS

Samuelson's pure theory of public expenditures has become the basis for numerous variations and extensions, some of which we note in this final section.

Polar Cases and Blended Models

Samuelson initially offered his theory of public expenditures as a "polar case model of government," to be contrasted with the traditional individualistic model of general equilibrium.[46] In subsequent writings, however, he distanced himself from the polar case concept. To be sure, the polar case did not require that the public good, while being equally available to all, should be equally useful to each consumer. On the contrary, what may be highly beneficial to A may be useless or even a social bad to B.[47] But the polar concept becomes dubious when questioning how widely the condition of equal availability to all is in fact applicable to the range of public goods and services. In response, Samuelson conceded that in many instances there exists some "element of variability in the benefit that can go to one citizen *at the expense* of some other citizen."[48] In most instances, the nature of public services reflects a "blending of the extreme antipodal models."[49] Sub-

---

[45] Ibid., p. 1156.

[46] [1955, II, Chap. 93, p. 1226].

[47] Ibid.

[48] Ibid., p. 1232. It is precisely this feature that has led me to describe the key characteristic of public consumption goods as involving nonrival consumption (Musgrave, 1969, p. 126), a term that Samuelson considers somewhat doubtful [1969b, III, Chap. 172, p. 503]. Samuelson does not, however, use the term "jointness in consumption" as characterizing the nature of public goods, a condition that is neatly distinguished from that of jointness in production [1969a, III, Chap. 168].

[49] [1955, II, Chap. 93, p. 1232].

sequently, he went further and jettisoned the "polar" public good concept altogether. Instead, he proposes a knife-edged definition of a pure private good as entering into the utility function of one particular consumer only. All the rest (that is, goods that enter two or more utility functions) falls into the public good domain by virtue of involving some consumption good externality.[50] This permits Samuelson to stress the essential analytical similarity of all externality cases, from national defense to decreasing cost industries. Yet subsequent authors have found it useful to distinguish between particular externality situations and the policy problems that they pose.

To begin with, A's consumption of x may enter B's utility function in various ways. It may do so because B enjoys A's well-being without B's own consumption intake being affected. B feels better if A consumes more milk or, generally, has a higher income. *Or*, B may benefit because A's consumption gives rise to a spillover that grants a similar benefit to B. A's inoculation reduces B's risk of infection, albeit less so than would B's own inoculation.[51] External benefits result but in diluted form. Both interactions are more or less similar formally and may be allowed for readily by the observer, but the innate difference ("psychological" utility interdependence in the one case and "physical" benefit spillover in the other) may be significant in their policy implications.[52] Moreover, the presence of dilution bears on the degree of market failure. As the degree of dilution becomes larger, it will become worthwhile for both A and B to treat x as if it were a private good and bid for it at the market. The degree of market failure is reduced and public policy now calls for a subsidy rather than total provision through the budget. Since partial externality may be viewed as the typical case, it may well be argued that a general theory of budgetary provision should be a theory of subsidy rather than one of full financing. Determining the appropriate degree of subsidy, to be sure, once more involves the problem of preference revelation and the troublesome issues of voting strategy that this implies.

Another instance, also addressed by Samuelson, arises in the case of public goods that are subject to crowding or congestion.[53] Were it not for the lumpiness factor, such goods could be provided efficiently through the market, and where divisibility can be approximated by successive units of the facility (for example, additional movie houses), provision might in fact be left to this mechanism. But where lumpiness is substantial, the charge appropriate to reducing congestion to its optimal level will hardly be that which also recovers the capital cost of the project.

A further case that has received much attention relates to public goods whose benefits are spatially limited. Such benefits are available equally to all residents of a particular area, but not (or at a lower level only) to outsiders. Thus a distinction arises between national, regional, and local public goods. This feature has been the basis for an extensive theory of local finance, at both a normative and a positive level.[54] In the normative context, local public goods theory has dealt with the

---

[50][1969b, III, Chap. 172, p. 501].
[51]Oakland (1969).
[52]The efficiency conditions for the two cases are not identical. See Roskamp (1975).
[53][1969b, III, Chap. 172, p. 510]; Oakland (1972).
[54]Tiebout (1956).

problem of optimal club size, as well as with the equilibrating process, by which a system of clubs or fiscal jurisdictions is established.[55] The resulting theory of fiscal location has been among the most productive offsprings of public goods theory, even though weakened by inadequate integration with other aspects of location theory. At the positive level, local fiscal theory has focused on location choice in response to fiscal variables as a mechanism ("voting by feet") through which preference revelation may occur. But, as Samuelson notes, the optimality of the outcome will depend on the preference configuration. Not everyone may get what he or she wants so that the optimal solution cannot be achieved without application of a "given determinate" social welfare function. Moreover, "there is a political and ethical question whether groups of like-minded individuals shall be free to run out on their social responsibilities and go off by themselves."[56] Once more there may be dimensions to fiscal theory that reach outside the neoclassical framework.

It remains to note the somewhat curious fact that contributions to the theory of public goods have focused almost entirely on consumption goods. Samuelson's original reference, as noted before, was to collective consumer goods. In subsequent papers, reference changed to public consumer goods and then simply to public goods, but the initial emphasis on consumer goods remained and had a lasting impact. Yet, public provision for capital goods is of no less importance and, especially in the context of developing countries, may well be more important. While the implications for efficiency conditions are analogous to those for consumer goods,[57] policy considerations differ. To the extent that public provision takes the form of intermediate goods that enter private production, benefit determination is simplified because the resulting cost reduction and consequent consumer responses may be measured in the market. Costs may be internalized by appropriate taxes and the free rider problem does not arise.

Public Sector Failure

Samuelson's theory of public goods, by mirror image, was a theory of market failure. Central to his argument is the proposition that there exists no decentralized market mechanism by which the optimal solution can be obtained. His pure model shows how optimal action by the public sector can remedy the failure of the market. This focus on market failure has now given way to a counteroffensive, as attention is directed at problems of public sector failure.[58] The Hegelian pendulum has swung and history is on the march again, but with a reversed course.

As one line of attack, it is argued (a) that the voting process does not yield optimal results and (b) that it involves a systematic bias towards overexpansion. Regarding (a), Samuelson may indeed be viewed as a harbinger of the new wave. While stressing the presence of market failure, he also takes a pessimistic view regarding the approximation of an optimal solution through voting. He differs, however, with

[55] Buchanan (1969).
[56] [1958, II, Chap. 94, p. 1238].
[57] For a discussion of public capital goods, see Kaizuka (1965).
[58] Among a large and rapidly growing literature, see Buchanan (1974) and Borcherding (1977).

the new school's conclusion regarding (b), that the voting process carries a systematic bias towards overexpansion.[59] Given the vagaries of strategic behavior, he finds (and I think correctly so) that the deviation from optimality may be in either direction.[60] The only basis on which there is a presumption towards overexpansion is the assumption that "transaction costs" for proponents of projects fall short of those for opponents.

However this may be, recent theorems on government failure have gone beyond voting bias and have focused on the role of bureaucracy as a third and independent factor in the fiscal process. The bureaucrat (once thought of as a civil servant) is viewed as a force whose action will distort the outcome even if preference revelation could be secured effectively through a system of (otherwise) Downesian democracy.

In sharp contrast to the classical role of bureaucracy as viewed by Max Weber,[61] the modern bureaucrat is seen as maximizing her own utility function, featuring above all the size of her bureau. Moreover, she is said to possess powerful instruments by which to accomplish her goals. Confronting the legislature with all or nothing budget requests, she pushes enactment of programs which exceed the optimal level of activity.[62] Similarly, by controlling the agenda of issues on which voters are allowed to vote, she may restrict the agenda to program levels that exceed the optimum.[63] Allowance for the role of public officials in decision making is all to the good, but I doubt the realism of the new model, including its behavioral assumptions, as well as the institutional framework in which it proceeds. Insufficient attention is paid to the existence of a budgetary process through which program choices are weighed and to the power of the electorate in imposing its will if governmental behavior moves too far out of line.

Going beyond the diagnosis of public sector failure, the new approach seeks for remedies to offset what it considers to be the built-in bias of prevailing institutions. Thereby it follows the Wicksellian tradition of focus on procedural reform. However, what I take to be questionable diagnosis also leads to questionable remedies. These involve restraining actions of various forms, including tax and/or expenditure limitations at the constitutional level, increased majority requirements, limitations as to choice of revenue sources, and so forth. As I see it, more neutral improvements in budget procedure, such as Wicksell's quest for tax and expenditure linkage and superior project evaluation, are much to be preferred.[64] Nevertheless, the new approach offers an important addition to the economics, or better, the politics, of public goods. Proceeding in the tradition of microeconomics, it may be viewed as a complement, rather than an alternative, to Samuelson's model.

Both approaches are neoclassical in spirit and may be contrasted with the quite different perspective provided by the Goldscheid-Schumpeter tradition of fiscal sociology.[65] According to the latter, the formation and functioning of fiscal

[59] Tullock (1959) and Buchanan and Tullock (1962).
[60] [1969b, III, Chap. 172, p. 501].
[61] Weber (1883), in Gerth and Mills (1946), p. 21.
[62] Niskanen (1971).
[63] MacKay and Weaver (1979).
[64] Buchanan (1974) Chap. 10, and Brennan and Buchanan (1980).
[65] Musgrave (1980).

institutions is viewed as the outcome of group interaction and as a reflection of the broader social and economic structure of society. Maximizing behavior of individuals enters but is far from the entire story. As Samuelson well recognized in retitling his second paper from "The" to "A" theory of public expenditures, fiscal theorizing may not yield a unique solution. But whatever its future course, 1954 will surely remain a landmark date in the theory of public finance.

REFERENCES

Borcherding, T. E., ed. (1977): *Budgets and Bureaucrats: The Sources of Public Sector Growth*, Durham, Duke University Press.

Bowen, Howard R. (1948): *Toward Social Economy*, New York, Rinehart.

Brennan, G. and J. M. Buchanan (1980): "The Logic of the Ricardian Equivalent Theorem," *Finanzarchiv* 38 (1).

Buchanan, James M. (1969): "An Economic Theory of Clubs," *Economica* 32 (Feb.).

———— (1974): *The Limits of Liberty*, Chicago, University of Chicago Press.

———— and Gordon Tullock (1962): *The Calculus of Consent*, Ann Arbor, University of Michigan Press.

Clarke, E. H. (1971): "Multiple Pricing of Public Goods," *Public Choice* 11 (Fall).

———— (1972): "Multiple Pricing of Public Goods: An Example," in S. Mushkin (ed.): *Public Prices for Public Products*, Washington, Urban Institute.

Colm, Gerhard (1927): *Volkswirtschaftliche Theorie der Staatsausgaben*, Tübingen, J. C. Mohr.

———— (1955): *Essays in Public Finance and Fiscal Policy*, New York, Oxford University Press.

Edgeworth, F. Y. (1925): "The Pure Theory of Taxation," *Papers Relating to Political Economy*, Vol. II, London, Royal Economic Society.

Hume, David (1740): *A Treatise of Human Nature*, III, L. A. Selby-Bigge (ed.), Oxford, Clarendon Press, 1958.

Johansen, Leif (1965): *Public Economics*, Amsterdam, North Holland.

Kaizuka, Keimei (1965): "Public Goods and Decentralization of Production," *Review of Economics and Statistics* 47 (Feb.).

Lindahl, Eric (1919, 1928): excerpts translated in R. A. Musgrave and A. Peacock, eds., *Classics in the Theory of Public Finance*, London, Macmillan, 1958.

Mackay, R. J. and C. L. Weaver (1979): "On the Mutality of Interests between Bureaus and High Demand Review Committees: A Perverse Result," *Public Choice* 34 (3-4).

Mazzola, Ugo (1890): excerpts translated in R. A. Musgrave and A. Peacock, eds.: *Classics in the Theory of Public Finance*, London, Macmillan, 1958.

McGuire, Martin C. and Henry J. Aaron (1969): "Efficiency and Equity and Optimal Supply of a Public Good," *Review of Economics and Statistics* 51 (Feb.).

Mill, John Stuart (1847): *Principles of Political Economy*, Ashley Ed., London, Longman's, 1909.

Musgrave, Richard A. (1938): "The Voluntary Exchange Theory of Public Economy," *Quarterly Journal of Economics* 53 (Feb.).

———— (1959): *The Theory of Public Finance*, New York, McGraw-Hill.

———— (1969): "Provision for Social Goods," in J. Margolis and H. Guitton, eds.: *Public Economics: An Analysis of Public Production and Consumption and their Relations to the Private Sectors: Proceedings of a Conference Held by the International Economics Associations*, London, Macmillan.

—— and Peggy B. Musgrave (1973): *Public Finance in Theory and Practice*, 3d ed., New York, McGraw-Hill.

—— (1980): "Theories of Fiscal Crisis: An Essay in Fiscal Sociology," in H. J. Aaron and M. J. Boskin, eds.: *The Economics of Taxation*, Washington, Brookings.

—— (1981): "Leviathan Cometh, or Does He?" in H. Ladd and N. Tideman, eds.: *Control of Public Expenditures*, Washington, Brookings.

Niskanen, W. (1971): *Bureaucracy and Representative Government*, Chicago, Aldine.

Oakland, William (1969): "Joint Goods," *Economica* 36 (Aug.).

—— (1972): "Congestion, Public Goods and Welfare," *Journal of Public Economics* 1 (Nov.).

Pigou, A. C. (1928): *Studies in Public Finance*, London, Macmillan.

Ricardo, David (1817): *The Principles of Political Economy and Taxation*, London, Dent, 1911.

Roskamp, Karl (1975): "Public Goods, Merit Goods, Private Goods, Pareto Optimum, and Social Optimum," *Public Finance* 30 (No. 1).

Samuelson, Paul A. (1947): *Foundations of Economic Analysis*, Cambridge, Harvard University Press.

—— (1954): "The Pure Theory of Public Expenditure," *Review of Economics and Statistics* 36 (Nov.); *Collected Scientific Papers*, II, Chap. 92.

—— (1955): "Diagrammatic Exposition of a Theory of Public Expenditure," *Review of Economics and Statistics* 37 (Nov.); *Collected Scientific Papers*, II, Chap. 93.

—— (1958): "Aspects of Public Expenditure Theories," *Review of Economics and Statistics* 40 (Nov.); *Collected Scientific Papers*, II, Chap. 94.

—— (1964): "Tax Deductibility of Economic Depreciation to Insure Invariant Valuations," *Journal of Political Economy* 72 (Dec.); *Collected Scientific Papers*, III, Chap. 179.

—— (1969a): "Contrast Between Welfare Conditions for Joint Supply and for Public Goods," *Review of Economics and Statistics* 51 (Feb.); *Collected Scientific Papers*, III, Chap. 168.

—— (1969b): "Pure Theory of Public Expenditure and Taxation," in J. Margolis and H. Guitton, eds.: *Public Economics: An Analysis of Public Production and Consumption and their Relations to the Private Sectors: Proceedings of a Conference Held by the International Economics Association*, London, Macmillan; *Collected Scientific Papers*, III, Chap. 172.

Schäffle, Albert (1873): *Das gesellschaftliches System der menschlichen Wirtschaft*, Tübingen, Germany.

Smith, Adam (1776): *The Wealth of Nations*, New York, Modern Library, 1937.

Tiebout, Charles (1956): "A Pure Theory of Local Expenditures," *Journal of Political Economy* 64 (Oct.).

Tobin, James (1970): "On Limiting the Domain of Inequality," *Journal of Law and Economics* 13 (Oct.).

Tullock, Gordon (1959): "Problems of Majority Voting," *Journal of Political Economy* 67 (Dec.).

—— and Nicholas Tideman (1976): "A New and Superior Principle of Public Choice," *Journal of Political Economy* 84 (Dec.).

Wagner, Adolf (1883): in H. Gerth and C. Mills: *From Max Weber: Essays on Sociology*, New York, Oxford University Press, 1946.

Wicksell, Knut (1896): excerpts translated in R. A. Musgrave and A. Peacock (eds.): *Classics in the Theory of Public Finance*, London, Macmillan, 1958.

MONETARY ECONOMICS*

Don Patinkin

1. Monetary theory has not been among Paul Samuelson's major concerns, yet here, too, he has made important contributions. These began with his "Note on the Demand for Money" appended to the chapter on "The Pure Theory of Consumer's Behavior" in his *Foundations of Economic Analysis* (1947, pp. 117–24). As in many of his other contributions to economic theory, Samuelson instructively relates his analysis to the earlier literature—in this case Walras' much-neglected micro-economic analysis of the demand for money. For though Walras' notion of the *encaisse désirée* had earned him a place in the history of monetary theory as a co-discoverer (together with Marshall and Wicksell) of the cash-balance approach to the quantity theory, the utility analysis from which Walras had derived his *encaisse désirée* in the fourth (1900) edition of his *Eléments d'économie politique pure* received little attention in the continental literature and was entirely ignored in the English literature.[1] And understandably so: for this analysis is as cumbersome and mechanical as it is obscure.

From this oblivion, Samuelson rescued Walras' analysis by cutting through its

---

*Without burdening them with any responsibility, I would like to thank Michael Bruno, Jacques Drèze, Stanley Fischer, Jean-Paul Fitoussi, Yoram Meyshar, and Menahem Yaari for most helpful comments and discussions. This chapter was written under a grant from the Ford Foundation, administered by the Maurice Falk Institute for Economic Research in Israel. It was completed during a visit to the European University Institute in Florence, Italy, to which I am indebted for efficient technical assistance.

[1]Including Marget's (1931, 1935) well-known discussion of Walras' monetary theory. Marget (1931, pp. 591–592; 1935, pp. 156–157) did, however, refer in a general way to Walras' earlier (and different) application of utility theory to money. And though Leser's analysis of the demand for money (1943)—referred to on p. 122, n. 21 of the *Foundations*—is based on a Walrasian utility function, it made no reference to Walras' work itself.

obscurity and deriving the demand for money balances from the utility function

$$U = U(x_1, \ldots, x_n, p_m M, p_1, \ldots, p_n),$$

subject to the budget restraint $\Sigma p_j x_j + r p_m M = I$, where the x_j represent commodities, p_j, their prices, M, the nominal quantity of money, and p_m, its price in terms of some numéraire, r the rate of interest, and I the given money income—and where $U(\;)$ is homogeneous of degree zero in all prices, including that of money. In this way his function retained the spirit (but avoided the complexities) of Walras' analysis, which had assumed that the individual derived utility not from some overall measure of real money balances, but from a vector representing the purchasing power of money over each of the "services of availability" of the individual commodities in the economy. Samuelson's exposition was also in Walras' spirit in explicitly including the imputed interest cost of money holdings as an expenditure item in the individual's budget restraint. From this maximization procedure Samuelson then derived demand functions for all goods, including nominal money holdings, homogeneous of degree zero in all prices (*including* that of money) and money income. Alternatively, the demand for nominal money holdings were shown to be homogeneous of degree one in all prices (*excluding* its own) and income.

The *Foundations* reveals other influences on Samuelson's thinking about monetary economics. Thus in more than one of his reminiscences (1969, III, Chap. 186, p. 683; 1972, IV, Chap. 278, pp. 884–86, reproduced infra), Paul has referred to his undergraduate studies in the early 1930s at the University of Chicago, where he was exposed to the teachings of Frank Knight, Jacob Viner, and Henry Simons; and in a much-appreciated personal inscription to one of the volumes of his *Collected Scientific Papers*, Paul concluded with the sentiment that we both think that "Chicago is a good place to have come from." It seems to me that this Chicago influence is also reflected in his "Note on the Demand for Money" (*Foundations*, pp. 117–24). For in it, at the height of the Keynesian influence, Samuelson rejected a monetary theory of the rate of interest. Thus, drawing support from Knight, Paul deftly refuted Hicks' contention that in a world in which there were perfectly liquid bonds, the rate of interest would be zero by observing that in such a world it would not be interest that would disappear, but money as a medium of exchange, which would be replaced by perfectly liquid interest-bearing bonds (*Foundations*, pp. 123–124). And this "real" approach to the rate of interest has characterized his subsequent discussions of the subject as well.

2. More than twenty years were to pass before Samuelson returned to questions of monetary theory. This occurred in his well-known article on "What Classical and Neoclassical Monetary Theory Really Was" (1968, III, Chap. 176), which also discussed my treatment of this question in *Money, Interest, and Prices* (1965, Chap. 8). In this article Samuelson improved and elaborated on the exposition of the *Foundations* in several ways, one of which was to make use of a budget restraint which takes as given not the individual's money income, but his supply of labor and initial endowments of assets (land, physical capital, and money balances). From this restraint and the utility function (which was essentially the same as that of the

Foundations) were then derived demand equations for all goods (including money balances deflated by the individual commodity prices) that were homogeneous of degree zero in all prices (including prices of factors of production) and the nominal value of wealth (including nominal money balances). These equations determined the equilibrium values of the real variables in the system—relative prices and real money balances. Supplementing this set of equations with one fixing the nominal supply of money then determined equilibrium absolute prices. From such a system the classical neutrality of money was readily established.

Samuelson contrasted this valid dichotomy between the determination of relative and absolute prices with the invalid one that posited a set of demand functions for commodities dependent only on—and determining—relative prices, which was supplemented by a quantity-theory equation that then determined the absolute price level. And he went on to express the view that though there were examples of economists who had presented such a dichotomy, the "best neoclassical writers did *perceive* at the intuitive level the intrinsic content of the [valid] dichotomy" (1968, III, Chap. 176, p. 534, italics in original).

As Paul himself indicated, there was no difference between us on the substantive aspects of these dichotomy-*cum*-neutrality issues. There were, however, differences with respect to the doctrinal aspects, and in a short note on this paper (Patinkin, 1972) I explained why I did not accept his view of these aspects. From Paul's reply (1972, IV, Chap. 265), I have the impression that, while the extent of our disagreement was diminished by this exchange, some differences of opinion still remained. I mention this exchange because it leads me to a general observation. Anyone who deals with the history of ideas must take account of the fact that the individuals whose writings one is studying did not generally see the full implications of everything they wrote. At the same time, and as presumptuous as it may be, anyone who deals with the history of ideas tends to project from the workings of his or her own mind in the attempt to understand how the minds of others have worked. And so I feel that at least part of the aforementioned remaining differences of opinion arise from the fact that Paul Samuelson's extraordinarily quick and encompassing mind makes him less inclined to believe that others did not see what seems so obvious to him.

Paul's 1968 article represents other characteristics of his work. Thus he carries out his analysis in terms of a stationary state, and is thus able to generalize the Archibald-Lipsey result about the irrelevance of the way a monetary increase is initially distributed in the economy. He also describes the "qualitative" aspect of money: the fact that it enables production and exchange to be carried out far more efficiently than in the case of barter (1968, III, Chap. 176, p. 531). At the same time, unlike some recent authors, he is willing to take the existence of a money serving this purpose as given, and feels no necessity to attempt a rigorous demonstration of how one of the goods in the economy eventually evolves and becomes money—a pragmatic approach with which I have the fullest sympathy. Finally, in keeping with his basic concern with welfare economics, Paul addresses himself to the question (and does so even more forcefully in a subsequent note [1969, II, Chap. 177] of whether a *laissez faire* economy will generate an amount of money (in real terms) that is optimum from the viewpoint of society. And like others before him, he neatly shows that as a result of the discrepancy between the private cost of holding money (viz., interest foregone) and the social cost (viz., zero), the real quantity of money in a *laissez faire* economy with stable prices is suboptimal.

3. I think it is fair to say that Samuelson originally conceived his profound and justly celebrated article on "An Exact Consumption-Loan Model of Interest with or without the Social Contrivance of Money" (1958, I, Chap. 21) as being primarily a contribution not to monetary economics, but to the theory of interest and to welfare economics. It is accordingly under these headings (as well as that of general-equilibrium theory) that this article is mainly discussed in this volume. Nevertheless, the overlapping-generations model presented in this article has had a seminal influence on the development of monetary theory during the past decade and continues to be a major vehicle for work in this field.[2]

My feeling, however, is that on the one hand this article makes a greater contribution to monetary economics than originally indicated by Samuelson; on the other hand, while recognizing the importance of the subsequent contributions to monetary economics that have stemmed from this article, I share the reservations of James Tobin (1980) and others about the attempt (well-illustrated by several of the papers in Kareken and Wallace [1980]) to present the overlapping-generations model as *the* basic model for the analysis of monetary phenomena.

By the first of these points I have in mind the fact that in the article itself Samuelson refers to money only as a store of value. But as Cass and Yaari (1966, pp. 465–466) later pointed out, money in this model also obviates the need for a "double coincidence of wants": in particular, it enables transactions between the younger and older generations, even though the latter cannot provide the commodities in subsequent old age which the former desire in exchange for the commodities they now provide. In this sense, then, money also serves as a medium of exchange in this model.

My reservations about the prominence given to this model in recent work in monetary theory begin with the familiar criticism that despite the fact just mentioned, this model does not capture the essence of the function of money as a medium of exchange in the real world. For this function is primarily not to make possible transactions that would otherwise be technically impossible (that is, not to create a market that would otherwise not exist), but (as Wicksell so aptly described it many years ago [*Lectures* I, pp. 63–65; II, pp. 15–18]) to carry out in a more efficient way transactions that could in principle be carried out at much greater cost in terms of time and effort by a combination of direct and indirect barter. And it would be an evasion of the issue to say that such costs also exist in the overlapping generations model, except that they are infinite there. Furthermore, though the model could undoubtedly be generalized to deal with money as a medium of exchange in the fullest sense of the term, one of its claimed advantages—namely, that is provides a rigorous explanation of the positive value of money—would then no longer be unique to it. I shall return to this point in a moment.

---

[2]Cf., for example, Lucas (1972), Grandmont and Laroque (1973), Grandmont (1980), Balasko and Shell (1981), and the articles in Kareken and Wallace (1980); see also the bibliography at end of the latter.

Second, many of the properties of what is called money in this model simply reflect the fact that it is the only asset that can be carried over from one period to another. This is the reason there is a demand for it even though it provides no direct utility—just as in the traditional Fisherine two-period model individuals have a demand for bonds (the only instrument by means of which they can carry out the lending that enables them to transfer purchasing power to the second period) even though such bonds have no direct utility. Similarly, the reason that the socially optimum real quantity of money in this model is achieved with a constant nominal quantity of money and a price level declining at the same rate that the economy is growing is not because individuals are then (in Samuelson's words) costlessly "satiated with cash" (1968, III, Chap. 176, p. 538). It is because the real rate of interest then equals the rate of growth of the economy, which is the condition for generating the socially optimum rate of savings and money is the only asset in which savings can be held. Most important of all in this context is the fact (essentially noted already by Cass and Yaari [1966]; cf. also Samuelson [1959, I, Chap. 22, p. 237]) that one could just as well carry out the analysis of the overlapping generations model on the assumption that the only durable asset consists of interest-bearing government bonds. The social optimum would then be achieved when this rate of interest equals the rate of growth of the economy. Such a model could also be regarded as an illustration of Samuelson's conclusion in the *Foundations* that in a world with perfectly liquid bonds it would not be the rate of interest that would disappear, but money, as discussed earlier.

Third, and related to my first two reservations, the fact that there is only one durable asset also means that the overlapping-generations model cannot deal with one of the basic questions of monetary theory: namely, why individuals in the real world choose to hold money when they can instead hold assets that yield a higher market rate of return. Furthermore, I would conjecture that any generalization of the model to deal with this question will have to resort to the kind of approaches that have been used in the past for this purpose: namely, to attribute to money not only the function of a store of value that can be carried over from one period to another, but also the function of providing (in one sense or another) a "liquidity service" during any given period.[3] And as already indicated, once such a generalization is carried out, the overlapping-generations model loses one of its relative advantages: in particular, its infinite time horizon is no longer necessary as a means of avoiding what Cass and Shell (1980, p. 252) have denoted as the "hot potato" problem; for even in a finite-time horizon model, in which by definition there is no demand for money in the last period so that its value then is zero, there will in earlier periods be a positive demand (and hence positive value) for money because of the liquidity services that it then provides—just as there is a positive demand for a machine that is productive for a finite period of time, even though it may depreciate in value to zero by the end of the period.

---

[3] Under this general heading I include the approach that attributes to money utility (or considers it as a factor of production) by virtue of the time and effort that it saves as contrasted with barter transactions; the Baumol-Tobin inventory-theoretic approach; the Tobin risk-aversion approach; my own stochastic-payment approach; and the like.

Since Samuelson himself has not contributed to the literature in monetary economics based on his 1958 overlapping-generations model, it shall suffice here to make these observations. Let me however say that though we should probably not draw any inferences from the fact that he has not so contributed, it may be significant that when in 1968 Samuelson explicitly analyzed the question of the socially optimum quantity of money (see above), he did not include the discussion at the end of his 1958 article in his list of earlier discussions of the question by Milton Friedman, Martin Bailey, and others (1968, III, Chap. 176, p. 538, n. 7; 1969, III, Chap. 177, p. 544, n. 3). Is this Paul's revealed preference for the way the relation of this article to monetary economics should be regarded?[4]

4. In one of his more popular writings (1967, III, Chap. 178, pp. 550–52), Paul Samuelson has described how he at one time believed that money was not important, and how he subsequently changed his mind. It is interesting to trace the way this shift has reflected itself over the past thirty-and-more years in one of Paul's major contributions to modern economics, or, more specifically, to modern public education in economics all over the world: namely, the eleven (so far!) editions of his *Economics: An Introductory Analysis*.[5] But before undertaking this task let me digress briefly on two pedagogical diagrams for which this book is noted.

The first is the circular-flow diagram, with money and goods flowing in opposite directions, which instructively illustrates the way the price system of a market economy solves the basic problems of "what, how, and for whom to produce." Here again is a reflection of Paul's studies at Chicago, for this is basically the famous "wheel-of-wealth" diagram in Frank Knight's *Economic Organization* (1933, p. 61), on which all students at Chicago were brought up. Indeed, both in the book (1951, p. 14, fn. 1) and in personal correspondence Paul has indicated this origin of the diagram.

The second diagram appears in the exposition of macroeconomic theory: namely, the "diagonal-cross" diagram (viz, the aggregate demand curve intersecting with the 45° line from the origin) by means of which generations of economic students have learned the basics of Keynesian analysis. I am not sure that Samuelson's *Economics* was the first introductory textbook to have made use of this diagram, though it may well have been. It is clear, however, that such a diagram made its first appearance in the literature in Paul's 1939 paper on "A Synthesis of the Principles of Acceleration and the Multiplier" (II, Chap. 83, pp. 1111–1112). Thus, in any event, the credit for this invaluable expository device belongs to him.[6]

---

[4] Having referred to this article, I would like to digress and note that the existence in it of a positive rate of interest in the case of a growing economy is not as paradoxical as Samuelson implies. For though the per capita income of the representative person remains constant in it, the total income of the economy which he or she represents is increasing. Hence the existence of interest in this economy can essentially be considered as an instance of Bohm-Bawerk's first cause of interest: namely, an increasing level of income (1958, I, Chap. 21, p. 469).

[5] Whose subtitle for some reason disappeared after the seventh edition (1967).

[6] This was pointed out by Bishop (1948, p. 325, n. 6). There is, however, one difference between the diagram on p. 1115 of Samuelson's 1939 article and the usual diagonal-cross diagram: in particular, Samuelson's analysis is of an economy in stationary equilibrium, in which by definition there is no net investment. Correspondingly, this diagram contains only a consumption function, and not one reflecting the aggregate of consumption and investment expenditures.

To return to my main theme, I shall trace the aforementioned shift by means of two indicators: the treatment of the quantity theory and the treatment of the role of monetary policy. In the first (1948) edition of *Economics*, the second half of the chapter entitled "Prices, Money, and Interest Rates" is largely devoted to an exposition of the quantity theory. The theory is presented as one which claims that prices are proportional to the quantity of money. A footnote alerts the reader to one of the fundamental reservations that has over the years been made with respect to this theory: namely, "that the quantity theory does not get down to the fundamental reasons why money is being created at the rate it is being created. The true direction of causation is by no means in the one-way direction from M to P" (1948, p. 291, n. 2; see also p. 292, n. 2). This is followed by a discussion in the text of two "inadequacies of the quantity theory": namely, (1) that prices are not proportional to total spending except in conditions of full employment and (2) that total spending is not proportional to the stock of money. An alternative formulation of this second inadequacy is that "*the velocity of circulation is not even approximately constant*" (1948, p. 294, italics in original). Correspondingly the equation of exchange $MV = PQ$ is dismissed as a sterile truism that in effect defines the velocity of circulation, V. The instability of V together with the insensitivity of investment to changes in the rate of interest then lead to the conclusion that monetary policy is an inadequate means of dealing with problems of deflation and unemployment ("you can lead a horse to water, but you can't make him drink"), with a supporting reference given to the Great Depression of the 1930s. At the same time Paul states that monetary policy may be more useful as a means of dealing with inflation (1948, pp. 294, 353–354).

In the second edition (1951) much the same analysis is presented, but the discussion of the quantity theory is relegated to an appendix to the chapter entitled "Money, Interest and Income" (1951, pp. 346 ff.). This appendix also includes a more detailed analysis of the instability of the velocity of circulation, in terms of the shift from *active* into *inactive* balances as the rate of interest declines.

The discussion of the quantity theory of money remains in an appendix in the third edition (1955, pp. 292 ff.). But the preface of this edition (p. vi) refers to a theme that is to become a standard feature of all subsequent editions: the "neoclassical synthesis," in which *inter alia* there is a role to be played by monetary policy as well as fiscal policy, though reliance must primarily be placed on the latter (1955, pp. 317, 360). It is also noteworthy that this increased emphasis on monetary policy is implicitly related to developments in the U.S. economy in the early 1950s (1955, pp. 315–316).

In the fourth edition (1958) the quantity theory is still in an appendix, but with two significant changes. First, the footnote that shows that $MV = PQ$ is a truism defining V is supplemented by a paragraph stating: "More important than the tautological equation of exchange is the quantity-theory hypothesis. Economists repeatedly kill it off. But it keeps coming back to life! This is not, I believe, an accident. For so long as paper money is valued only for the exchanges it helps make, doubling M *can* result in exactly the same 'real' equilibrium but with *all* P's doubled" (1958, p. 283, n. 1, italics in original). Second, the concluding footnote to the appendix recognizes the theoretical validity of the argument that in an economy with perfectly flexible prices, a continuous decline in prices can in principle generate full employment by means of the Pigou effect. Indeed, Samuelson presents this as a particular instance of the fact that "recent discussions have greatly reduced the area of disagreement between the various differing theories," while at the same time stressing that even Pigou did not recommend such a deflation as a means of actual policy (1958, p. 286, n. 1).

But a far more significant innovation of the fourth edition is the inclusion of a specific chapter devoted to a "Synthesis of Monetary Analysis and Income Analysis." Even here, however, the efficacy of an expansionary monetary policy (via its effect on the rate of interest) in stimulating investment demand in times of deep depression is considered limited, with reference again being made to the depression of the 1930s (1958, pp. 332–335). Nevertheless the chapter concludes with the statement that monetary policy has a role to play in achieving full employment in the economy (1958, pp. 340–341, 360). And a chapter with this title and this message is a standard feature of all subsequent editions of *Economics*.

In the fifth (1961) and later editions, the quantity theory returns to the text in a chapter entitled "Prices and Money" and the discussion of the Pigou effect (in expanded form) is shifted to an appendix to the chapter on the "Synthesis of Monetary Analysis and Income Analysis." At the same time the discussion of the aforementioned "two inadequacies of the quantity theory" is deleted. An undoubtedly related change is the introduction of a discussion of Milton Friedman's "sophisticated quantity theory," which contends that though V is not constant, "changes in V will either be so small or so predictable as to make one confident that dollar NNP will move in the same direction as M" (1961, p. 316). Samuelson goes on to say that "qualitatively, this is in agreement with almost any modern theory of income determination, and the only possible field for argument concerns the confidence with which one can predict the quantitative regularity of effects on NNP of changes in M."

Similarly, the chapter on the neoclassical synthesis in the fifth edition gives more weight than before to the role of monetary policy. Indeed, it concludes with the summary statements that "monetary policy by the central bank is an important way of shifting the saving and investment schedules, or the total schedule of consumption-plus-investment-plus-government spending"; and though at times of deep depression monetary policy may be of limited potency, "if stabilization policies are followed resolutely, such times should occur rarely" (1961, pp. 375–376). In the appendix to this chapter Samuelson goes on to emphasize that "there is no need to be dogmatic" about the relative advantages of the MV and $C+I+G$ approaches, and that though the "bulk of economists" is inclined towards the latter approach, "if the day ever arrives when proponents of the velocity approach can prove by their researches that theirs is the more convenient tool, pragmatic scholars will welcome all the help it can give" (1961, p. 380). And from the eighth edition (1970) onwards this sentence is followed by one which reads, "In any case, post-Keynesian and monetarists both agree that money matters much" (1970, p. 325). Correspondingly, beginning with the seventh edition (1967) we find a criticism of the "Radcliffe [Committee's] nonsequitur: 'Money alone matters' is false; ergo 'money doesn't matter'" (1967, p. 272, n. 13).

From the eighth edition (1970) onwards we also find an explicit discussion of monetarism, identified (of course) with Milton Friedman and described as an "extreme view" which contends "that essentially everything that can be done to control macroeconomic aggregates—inflationary gaps and epochs of depression or slow growth—has to be done by control of the money supply *alone*. Fiscal policy . . . per se has essentially no predictable effect on the prospects for inflation or deflation, for high employment or mass unemployment" (1970, p. 309, italics in original). This view is contrasted with that of the "eclectic majority" (which in subsequent editions Samuelson terms "the majority eclectic view of the so-called 'post Keynesian neoclassical synthesis'" (1973, p. 329; 1976, p. 331; 1980, p. 309) that "*both* fiscal and monetary policies matter much" (1970, p. 309, italics in original). Samuelson also makes it clear that he sees himself as part of this majority, and that when monetarism differs from this majority view, it is "wrong" (1970, p. 309) or "implausible" (1973, p. 329; 1976, p. 331). And though somewhat less explicit, this is also his view in the eleventh and latest edition (1980, p. 310). Indeed, in this edition, Samuelson adds to the aforementioned fallacy of the Radcliffe Committee, the "over-zealous monetarists' reverse fallacy: 'Money does matter; *ergo* money *alone* matters'" (1980, p. 270, n. 12, italics in original).

This then is the evolution of the treatment of monetary economics in Samuelson's *Economics*. It is not at all surprising that an introductory textbook should over the past thirty-odd years reflect the increasing influence of monetarism in the profession and accordingly the analytical role of M as contrasted with that of $C + I + G$. In Paul's words in the tenth edition, "Economics is not an exact science. . . . Therefore an author should present in his book a framework of analysis that can be shaded in favor of either of these two scientifically proposed models. This text has been written to make this possible" (1976, p. 331). And again in the eleventh edition, "The good author, I believe, owes the reader a fair account of the opposing contentions" (1980, p. 310). But the foregoing survey has also shown that Paul's shift toward a greater emphasis on monetary factors began to take place in the mid-1950s, well before the growing influence of monetarism had manifested itself. And, as we have seen, this shift was stimulated first by Paul's own observations of the current economic scene and subsequently by the studies of others as well. This too is the mark of Paul Samuelson: a mind free of doctrinairism and open to new ideas and evidence.

REFERENCES

Balasko, Yves and Karl Shell (1981): "The Overlapping-Generations Model. II. The Case of Pure Exchange with Money," *Journal of Economic Theory*, 24, pp. 112–142.

Bishop, Robert L. (1948): "Alternative Expansionist Fiscal Policies: A Diagrammatic Analysis," in L. A. Metzler et al., *Income, Employment and Public Policy*: *Essays in Honor of Alvin H. Hansen*, New York, W. W. Norton, pp. 317–340.

Cass, David, and Menahem E. Yaari (1966): "A Re-examination of the Pure Consumption Loans Model," *Journal of Political Economy* 74 (Aug.) pp. 353–367.

Cass, David, and Karl Shell (1980): "In Defense of a Basic Approach," in J. H. Kareken and

N. Wallace, eds., *Models of Monetary Economies*, Minneapolis, Federal Reserve Bank of Minneapolis, 1980, pp. 251–260.

Grandmont, Jean-Michel (1980): *Expectations and the Real Balance Effect*, Paris, Cepremap (Discussion Paper No. 8020).

Grandmont, Jean-Michel, and Guy Laroque (1973): "Money in the Pure Consumption Loan Model," *Journal of Economic Theory* 6 (Aug.) pp. 382–395.

Kareken, John H., and Neil Wallace, eds., (1980): *Models of Monetary Economies*, Minneapolis, Federal Reserve Bank of Minneapolis.

Knight, Frank H. (1933): *The Economic Organization*, Chicago multilith. Reprinted and repaginated; New York, Kelley (1951).

Leser, C. E. V. (1943): "The Consumer's Demand for Money," *Econometrica* 11 (April) pp. 123–140.

Lucas, Robert E., Jr. (1972): "Expectations and the Neutrality of Money," *Journal of Economic Theory* 4 (April) pp. 103–124.

Marget, A. W. (1931): "Léon Walras and the 'Cash Balance Approach' to the Problem of the Value of Money," *Journal of Political Economy* 39 (Oct.) pp. 569–600.

———— (1935): "Monetary Aspects of the Walrasian System," *Journal of Political Economy* 43 (April) pp. 145–186.

Patinkin, Don (1965): *Money, Interest, and Prices*, 2d ed., New York, Harper and Row.

———— (1972): "Samuelson on the Neoclassical Dichotomy: A Comment," *Canadian Journal of Economics* 5 (May) pp. 279–283, as reprinted in *Essays On and In the Chicago Tradition*, Durham, N.C., Duke University Press, 1981, pp. 149–153.

Samuelson, P. A. (1939): "A Synthesis of the Principle of Accleration and the Multiplier," *Journal of Political Economy* 47 (Dec.) pp. 786–797: *Collected Scientific Papers*, II, chap. 83.

———— (1947): *Foundations of Economic Analysis*, Cambridge, Mass., Harvard University Press.

————: *Economics: An Introductory Analysis*, 1st ed. (1948), 2d ed. (1951), 3d ed. (1955), 4th ed. (1958), 5th ed. (1961), 6th ed. (1964), 7th ed. (1967), 8th ed. (1970), 9th ed. (1973), 10th ed. (1976), 11th ed. (1980), New York. McGraw-Hill.

———— (1958): "An Exact Consumption-Loan Model of Interest with or without the Social Contrivance of Money, *Journal of Political Economy* 66 (Dec.) pp. 467–82; *Collected Scientific Papers*, I, chap. 21.

———— (1959): "Reply" (to A. P. Lerner, "Consumption-Loan Interest and Money"), *Journal of Political Economy* 67 (Oct.) pp. 518–22; *Collected Scientific Papers*, I, chap. 22.

———— (1967): "Money, Interest Rates, and Economic Activity: Their Interrelationship in a Market Economy," *Proceedings of a Symposium on Money, Interest Rates, and Economic Activity*, New York, American Bankers Association, pp. 40–60; *Collected Scientific Papers*, III, chap. 178.

———— (1968): "What Classical and Neoclassical Monetary Theory Really Was," *Canadian Journal of Economics* 1 (Feb.) pp. 1–15; *Collected Scientific Papers*, III, chap. 176.

———— (1969): "Nonoptimality of Moneyholding under *Laissez Faire*," *Canadian Journal of Economics* 2 (May) pp. 303–8; *Collected Scientific Papers*, III, chap. 177.

———— (1969): "The Way of an Economist," in P. A. Samuelson, ed., *International Economic Relations: Proceedings of the Third Congress of the International Economic Association*, London, Macmillan; *Collected Scientific Papers*, III, chap. 186.

———— (1972): "Samuelson on the Neoclassical Dichotomy: A Reply," *Canadian Journal of Economics* 5 (May) pp. 284–92; *Collected Scientific Papers*, IV, chap. 265.

———— (1972): "Economics in a Golden Age: A Personal Memoir," in G. Holton, ed., *The*

Twentieth-Century Sciences: *Studies in the Biography of Ideas*, New York, Norton; *Collected Scientific Papers*, IV, chap. 278. Reproduced infra.

———: *Collected Scientific Papers*, Vols. I-II (1966), edited by Joseph E. Stiglitz; Vol. III (1972), edited by Robert C. Merton; Vol. IV (1977), edited by Hiroaki Nagatani and Kate Crowley, Cambridge, Mass., M.I.T. Press.

Tobin, James (1980): "Discussion," in J. H. Kareken and N. Wallace, eds., *Models of Monetary Economies*, Minneapolis, Federal Reserve Bank of Minneapolis, 1980, pp. 83–90.

Walras, Léon (1900): *Eléments d'economie politique pure*, 4th ed., Lausaime, F. Rouge. Translated by William Jaffé: *Elements of Pure Economics*, London, Allen and Unwin, 1954.

Wicksell, Knut (1901): *Lectures on Political Economy*, Vol. I: *General Theory*, translated from the original Swedish by E. Classen, L. Robbins, ed., London, Routledge, 1934.

Wicksell, Knut (1906): *Lectures on Political Economy*, Vol. II: *Money*, translated from the original Swedish by E. Classen, L. Robbins, ed., London, Routledge, 1935.

MODERN CAPITAL THEORY

Robert M. Solow

You learn something every day. When I looked purposefully through the *Collected Scientific Papers* with modern capital theory in mind, it came as a surprise that two of Paul Samuelson's first three published papers were about the theory of capital and interest. In fact, if the subject is interpreted at all broadly, all three of these papers belong to it.

Let me take the odd one first, because it might better be discussed elsewhere in this volume (see chapter by H. S. Houthakker). It was published in 1937 [I, Chap. 20]; even given the shorter lags of those dear dead days, it must have been written when the author was barely old enough to vote. In contemporary terms, you could think of it as a contribution to the theory of life-cycle saving, though that is not the way it is presented. Imagine a consumer-saver who maximizes a lifetime sum of discounted one-period utilities, $\Sigma D^t U(x_t)$, where D is a time-preference discount factor and x_t is current expenditure on current consumption. In a perfect capital market, she or he will have to observe only the single constraint $\Sigma R_t x_t =$ constant, where now R_t is the discount factor for year t corresponding to the sequence of market interest rates. That is to say, any lifetime consumption program will be financially feasible if the present value of outlays does not exceed initial wealth, including the present value of future earnings.

For such a consumer-saver, $k^{-1} U'(x_t) = D^t / R_t$, where k is a Lagrange multiplier. R is presumably directly observable. Let us assume we know D; in the strict framework of the model this is not outlandish because, if the consumer spends the same amount x at any two times t and t', it must be that $D = (R_{t'}/R_t)^{1/(t'-t)}$. Then we can calculate $k^{-1} U'(x_t)$ for each year and plot it against x_t. Any reasonable integration will deliver the utility function $U(x)$ up to a constant of proportionality.

What is remarkable about this paper is not so much the result itself—that consistent intertemporal choice reveals the additive utility-of-wealth function—but the fervor with which its 21-year-old author disavows it. It is, he says, a cardinalistic sin against the ordinalistic holy ghost, a mere curiosity, not to be taken seriously. And, indeed, almost twenty years were to pass before it was taken seriously, or, more accurately, before this approach was taken seriously by anyone, including its author. But then it surfaced: first in the intense discussion of the Bernoulli expected-utility hypothesis—which led even our hero to entertain a cardinalistic thought—and later still in the rigorous pure-theoretical reconstruction of life-cycle theory by Cass, Yaari, et al.

FOUNDATIONS OF THE THEORY OF CAPITAL AND INTEREST

This line of thought was quite clearly a digression from the mainstream. Samuelson's next two papers were directly in the mainstream. They are not thought about much nowadays, because the ideas they state are established doctrine, so much so that they appear to us always to have been there. First let me describe what they say.

Samuelson's second published article, "Some Aspects of the Pure Theory of Capital," appeared in the *Quarterly Journal of Economics* for May 1937 [I, Chap. 17] more or less on the author's 22nd birthday. It is, in fact, a young man's article. I must explain what I mean. The 1937 paper seizes a single important idea and sees it clearly. That idea is, in essence, the logic of a perfect capital market, in which any agent can borrow or lend indefinite amounts at a parametrically given rate of interest. The important implication is that the standard greedy agent will make each instant's decisions so as to maximize the present discounted value of the flow of net revenue stemming from those decisions and the discounting at each instant of time is at the market interest rate ruling at that instant.

The paper spends a lot of time on the algebra of present values. An investment that produces the flow of net earnings $N(t)$ for $0 \leqslant t < \infty$ will be worth $V(0) = \int_0^\infty N(t)e^{-rt} \, dt$ at time zero and $V(t) = \int_t^\infty N(s)e^{-r(s-t)} \, ds$ at time t if the market interest rate is r. It follows by differentiation of this last identity that $dV/dt + N(t) = rV(t)$. This is Irving Fisher's basic arbitrage equation. Actually Fisher's name is not mentioned in the article, despite the fact that he had strongly and correctly advocated the present-value criterion in his books of 1907 and 1930. Can it be that there was a time when Samuelson had not read everything? (He does describe the "correct" maximize-present-value criterion as "an old one in the literature of the subject.")

I have written these relations as if the market rate of interest is, and is foreseen to be, a constant, namely, r. The paper shows that nothing essential changes if the interest rate is foreseen to follow, and does follow, a time-varying path $r(t)$; terms like $r(s - t)$ are replaced by $\int_t^s r(z) \, dz$.

Appendix I provides a discussion of choice of numéraire and a treatment of the algebraic relations among commodity own-rates of interest and the money-rate of interest that is as clear as anything in the subsequent literature.

All this is now pretty routine. With the advantage of forty-plus years of hindsight one wonders why it was worth saying, why it was not as plain as day to everyone who understood the algebra of present values. But in fact the important contribution of the paper is precisely to establish once and for all the point that, under *ideal* conditions, the correct criterion for the choice of investments is the maximization of present value, discounted at the market rate of interest. If, for instance, there is at time zero a one-parameter family of investment possibilities yielding flows of net revenue $N(t; \alpha)$ at time t, then the rational choice among them in a perfect capital market is to choose α so as to maximize $\int_0^\infty e^{-R(t)} N(t; \alpha)\, dt$ where $R(t) = \int_o^t r(s)\, ds$ and $r(.)$ is the instantaneous market rate of interest. Even so astute an economist as the young Kenneth Boulding had just published a paper (1935) asserting that the appropriate choice criterion was the maximization of the internal rate of return. That is: let $\rho(\alpha)$ be defined by $\int_0^\infty N(t; \alpha) e^{-\rho t}\, dt = 0$; $\rho(\alpha)$ is then the internal rate of return associated with the choice α. It is the constant interest rate that discounts the stream of net revenues associated with α to zero. Boulding's contention was that a rational investor would choose α so as to maximize ρ. Samuelson saw with the clarity of youth that it was not so, that the maximum discounted value at market rate of interest criterion was simply more advantageous to anyone with access to a perfect capital market, and he said so.

There is a subtlety here worth pursuing. I can remember discussing it with Samuelson at least twenty years ago. (I could doubt my memory, but never his. So I am glad to report that my recollection is, more or less, confirmed by an out-of-the-way footnote in 1970. [III, Chap. 151, p. 266]. A definitive treatment appeared only in 1972 and 1977 in two characteristically precise and thorough articles by John Chipman; and an equally characteristically balanced and lucid statement by Robert Dorfman turned up in working paper form while I was writing this paper. I will put the case in its simplest form.

Suppose that we redefine the investment opportunity parametrized by α to include the reinvestment of net revenues as they appear in the very same process. Obviously this redefinition makes sense only if the elementary investment process in question is subject to constant returns to scale in the sense that it can be started at any time at any scale and will yield a revenue flow proportional to the scale chosen and translated in time according to the starting date. If this reinvestment routine has been going on forever, the aggregate revenue (and therefore the aggregate reinvestment) at time t can be calculated by summing up the contributions to net revenue from the reinvestments made at each previous date. Call this aggregate revenue-cum-reinvestment $Y(t; \alpha)$; then

$$Y(t; \alpha) = \int_0^\infty Y(t - x; \alpha) N(x; \alpha)\, dx$$

(If the policy of ploughing back net revenues started at time t_0, instead of having been in force forever, only inessential complications arise from the mixed bag of previous investments inherited by the new policy at its inception. Anyway, one would usually assume that $N(x; \alpha) = 0$ for all x in excess of some finite lifetime, so the inherited initial conditions would echo for a while and gradually disappear.)

This integral equation, said to be of renewal type, has solutions that are weighted sums of exponentials $e^{g_i t}$, where the real or complex numbers g_i are roots of the equation

$$-1 + \int_o^\infty e^{-gx} N(x; \alpha)\, dx = 0$$

Observe that each g_i is an internal rate of return of the investment activity consisting of investing one unit of output in elementary process α. There will be many such roots, indeed usually infinitely many. The interesting one is the largest real internal rate of return of the process, which may be labeled $g^*(\alpha)$. There will always be at least one positive real root if the undiscounted cash flow from the process exceeds its initial cost; there will be exactly one such if, in addition, $N(x; \alpha)$ is positive for all x.

Eventually, the exponential $e^{g^* t}$ will come to dominate $Y(t)$; in other words, the policy of continuous reinvestment will eventually cause the aggregate revenue to grow (approximately) exponentially at a rate equal to the (largest real) internal rate of return of the elementary investment process chosen. If α is chosen to maximize $g^*(\alpha)$, the resulting aggregate revenue path will eventually overtake the path associated with any other choice of α. In that sense, maximizing the internal rate of return is optimal.

What would the young Samuelson (or, for that matter, the mature Samuelson) say to that? Well, of course, if rapid growth is itself desirable, and most rapid growth is most desirable, then there is little more to be said: the internal rate of return is rehabilitated as the appropriate investment criterion. But if, as we normally presume, the desirability of an investment program is simply the desirability of the best final consumption program (or dividend stream) it can support, then I would be inclined to put words into Samuelson's mouth. In the first place, a complete catalogue of possible investment activities must include not only the elementary processes, but also all processes derived from them by reinvestment decisions. So the policy of continual reinvestment of cash flows in the same elementary process is itself an eligible investment activity (and there are many others, some much more complicated). But pursuing that policy *forever* butters (exactly) no parsnips. Eventually the investment account must be liquidated, or at least some of the net revenue must be diverted, to finance a consumption program. If *eventually* entails a long preliminary period of total reinvestment, then consumption during that long preliminary period will have to be financed by borrowing. The debt thus incurred will accumulate according to the market rate of interest and will have to be paid off eventually out of the proceeds of the investment. An investment policy that concentrates on the elementary process with the largest internal rate of return is optimal, after all, only if it can eventually throw off a *true* (that is, not reinvested) cash flow, whose present value, discounted at the market rate of interest, exceeds that attainable by any other feasible policy.

An extreme case may clarify the point. Suppose the market rate of interest is constant at r, the largest internal rate of return achievable is $g^{**} = g^*(\alpha^*)$, and $g^{**} > r$. Then eventually the fortune of an investor who follows the perpetual reinvestment policy will grow like $e^{g^{**} t}$. Its present value, discounted back to time zero at the interest rate r is $e^{(g^{**}-r)t}$. Evidently the longer she or he waits, the better the feasible consumption program. In that case, of course, there is no best feasible consumption program, not even an upper bound to feasible consumption programs. For that very reason, one imagines the capital market would register a vast excess demand for credit to finance so desirable an investment, until the market rate of interest rises at least to g^{**}.

The third of these three earliest papers is in some ways my favorite, though I think it may be the least well known. "The Rate of Interest Under Ideal Conditions" [1939, I, Chap. 18] is notably un-young-Samuelsonian in appearance. It contains essentially no mathematics. What it does contain is a clear statement of the paradigm for capital theory that still strikes me as the right one, at least the right one for tranquil conditions. I call it a paradigm rather than a theory; I mean to suggest that intertemporality enters into production and consumption decisions in so many different ways that any precisely stated model is bound to be either enlightening but special or general but empty. The paradigm tells you how to go about making a theory for any useful special case that catches your eye.

Each period's interest rate must equilibrate the sum of all households' desired asset holding and the total assets of all enterprises, both optimally determined for that rate of interest. At interest rate r, each firm makes optimal (that is, present-value maximizing) production decisions and these entail the holding of fixed and working capital assets in the amount $V(r)$. Households make optimal spending and saving decisions that together entail a desired amount of wealth to be held, $W(r)$. The equilibrium interest rate solves $V(r) = W(r)$. This is clearly a static or long-period picture, so it needs to be supplemented with an account of lags, expectations, an uncertainty (and that has still not been done in a satisfying way). But it makes its point.

On the household side, the paper contains a clear discussion of what Harrod later called "hump" saving, related to life cycle. But there is a dictum on net saving, too: "The cultural values of modern society are such that there would presumably be asset accumulation at any [nonnegative? positive?] rate of interest." [I, Chap. 18, p. 195] And the paper suggests that the simplest conclusion from available evidence is that $W'(r)$ is close to zero.

On the production side, the paper says: "In general it is to be presumed that the lower the rates of interest, the more 'capital' will be employed in any process, i.e., the larger will be the present asset value, optimally determined." [p. 193] One could hardly ask for a clearer statement of the "neoclassical parable." It presumes that $V'(r) < 0$; and since V is an asset value, we appear to have found precisely the error that twenty years later became the focus of the to-do about reswitching. But have we? The sentence just quoted comes at the end of a paragraph that begins "From all this it follows that nothing definite can be said about the effect of a change in the rate of interest on asset values," And later on in the paper, this disclaimer appears: "It will be noted that the present approach does not require a definition of *capital* as a physical quantity." [p. 199]

So the presumption that $V'(r) < 0$ should probably be interpreted not as an erroneous statement about the way this model of the world must work, but as a casual statement about the way our world does work. And I think the weight of the evidence supports it, subject to all the difficulty of reading a complicated world into a simple model.

This paradigm for capital theory was not brand new in 1938. It is of a piece with the vision of Irving Fisher (1907 and 1930) and very much like the view to which Wicksell came toward the end of his life in the "Mathematical Analysis of Åkerman's Problem." Samuelson had certainly come across Fisher's work by 1938; there is a passing reference to the equilibrium condition that the "marginal rate of return over cost" be equal to the interest rate. But it seems pretty clear that he had not then fully absorbed Fisher's achievement in the integration of intertemporal relations in consumption and in production into a coherent equilibrium model. There is no sign that Samuelson in 1938 had heard about Wicksell's essay, a translation of which was published as an appendix to the *Lectures on Political Economy* in London in 1934. That essay happens to have appealed greatly to me; it presents a sort of action portrait of the old man painfully freeing himself from the limitations of the Austrian concentration on a working capital view of the world, trying to deal with fixed capital, and almost getting it right. Samuelson's 1938 article is, in a way, more akin to Wicksell than to Fisher in its almost macroeconomic statement of the paradigm.

INTERTEMPORAL EFFICIENCY AND THE TURNPIKE THEOREM

The two great sources of theorems in microeconomics have been the "law of supply and demand"—especially the limiting case of competitive equilibrium—and the principle of efficiency. They are connected, of course, by the two fundamental theorems of welfare economics. Under appropriate assumptions, competitive equilibria are efficient outcomes. And, under only slightly more restrictive conditions, every efficient outcome is supported by a set of competitive prices; that is to say, it could be realized as the competitive equilibrium corresponding to some initial distribution of endowments.

The vein of capital theory described in the preceding pages is at the supply-and-demand end of the spectrum. It has to do with the correct way to model the choices of price-taking investors and the achievement of capital-market equilibrium. The maximization is that of individual agents, and there is nothing normative about the conclusions. The ideas to be taken up now arise primarily from efficiency considerations. This time, the great stimulus to theorem finding and theorem proving came from the mathematical side, in particular from the postwar discovery and development of linear and then nonlinear programming. Although the original impetus to linear programming was primarily computational—it offered for the first time a route to the practical formulation and numerical solution of large constrained-optimization problems—that was not the aspect that struck sparks in economic theory. It was, rather, the fact that the logic of linear programming made *duality* central and explicit, and then turned up mathematical techniques—separation theorems for convex sets, for example—beautifully adapted to the study of duality. And duality, in this sense, turned out to be the natural mathematical expression of the relation between an efficient (primal) outcome and the (dual) competitive prices that support it.

No economist of our time matched Samuelson's early and sure grasp of the intuitive significance of duality considerations. Indeed *The Foundations of Economic Analysis* already stated the key idea that the value of a Lagrange multiplier has substantial meaning in any constrained maximum problem, as the increment of achievable value, in units of the thing being maximized, per incremental relaxation of the corresponding constraint. Thus if the constraint expresses the limitation on use of a scarce resource, the corresponding Lagrange multiplier measures the marginal value of a bit of extra availability of that resource, and the relation to the competitive equilibrium price of the resource is already knocking at the door.

The application of these ideas to the case of capital-using production is not entirely straightforward, but that only makes the subject more interesting. The whole point about fixed capital goods is that the historically given available stock appears as a scarce resource in the short run. But the current flow of output includes newly produced capital goods that can be accumulated over time to augment the stock. Corresponding to the stock and flow aspects on the output side are stock rents and producer prices on the dual price side. Every intertemporally efficient evolution of stocks and flows on the primal output side corresponds to an evolution of rents and prices on the dual side.

This approach to the theory of capital was laid out in two chapters of *Linear Programming and Economic Analysis* by DOSSO (John Hicks's abbreviation of Dorfman, Samuelson, and Solow), which appeared in 1958 as a RAND monograph after a long gestation period. I suppose I am hardly telling tales out of school at this late date when I say that I wrote the first drafts of Chapter 11 on "Dynamic Aspects of Linear Models" and Chapter 12 on "Efficient Paths of Capital Accumulation." In any case, as with every other chapter, that was just the beginning of a barely convergent sequence of comments and revisions. But this approach had already been sketched out by Samuelson way back in 1949 as Part III, "Dynamics and Linear Programming," of a three-part RAND Corporation memorandum under the title *Market Mechanisms and Maximization* [I, 33, esp. pp. 471–492]. I had that paper in hand when I was drafting the capital-theoretic chapters of *Linear Programming and Economic Analysis*. The two most important ideas—the fundamental intertemporal efficiency conditions and the turnpike theorem—are clearly stated in the RAND memo, though perhaps not so fully worked out as in the later version. Meanwhile, of course, Edmond Malinvaud had published his famous article, "Capital Accumulation and Efficient Allocation of Resources," in *Econometrica* in 1953, which covered some of the same ground, but with more attention to the technical problems posed by the infinity of time and less attention to the marginal equivalences and qualitative implications that concerned us.

Perhaps this is the place to mention that the whole idea for the DOSSO book grew out of the earlier RAND memo. The original plan was for Samuelson to expand the three parts of *Market Mechanisms* into a monograph. Dorfman and I joined forces only later; and even then the book took, in the Preface's masterly understatement, more time than we expected.

So much for the background; now let me try to give a nontechnical account of the concept of intertemporal efficiency. The underlying idea is quite analogous to static efficiency; the difference is what we have in mind—not alternative bundles of guns-and-butter, but alternative bundles of goods indexed not only by type but also by date. Some of the goods may be strictly for consumption purposes, some strictly capital goods or raw materials, and some can serve both purposes. There may also be nonproducible primary goods, renewable like agricultural land or nonrenewable like iron ore. Start with some initial stocks at time zero. Ordinary production theory tells us how to think about the collection of feasible production-and-consumption programs for the first day (or year or "instant"). Each of them gives rise to some collection of stocks available at time one; it will generally be different from the time-zero stocks, except for permanent resources like land. So we can repeat the process and generate the collection of feasible production-and-consumption programs for the second day. In principle, then, we can think about the feasible *sequences* of stocks and flows. The phrase "in principle" is used here, as usual, to cover a multitude of sins. Intertemporal production relations come in great variety and complexity: pure storage, aging, inventories of goods in process, machinery and buildings with wear and tear, planting, cultivating, and harvesting, the classical economists' Scots farmers' advancing of subsistence to workers, construction and transportation that takes time and uses labor and equipment. To describe the set of technologically feasible sequences in any given instance may be a task to boggle the mind. That is why it is better either to imagine it done "in principle" or to choose some simplified characterization of the production processes in question, like Ricardo's corn, Böhm-Bawerk's trees, Wicksell's axe or DOSSO's "stocks."

Among the feasible sequences, we want the efficient ones, the ones about which we can claim that there is no feasible sequence better than it in some ways and worse that it in no way. If our sequences go on forever, then presumably only the consumption flows matter: the efficient sequences are those with the property that no feasible sequence throws off more of any consumption good at any time without also throwing off less of some consumption good at some time. If we want to think about T-period sequences (which might be a good idea because the infinite sequences can bring complicated mathematical problems) then the notion of efficiency must involve the terminal stocks in the natural way.

One reasonable strategy is to define the "same" good at different times to be "different" goods. This is a way of making the intertemporal problem as much like the static problem as possible. It has been tried, beginning with Malinvaud, and it works. Under assumptions that give the feasible sets the nice geometric properties they have in the static theory of production, the duality results apply—although infinite-dimensionality can make trouble—and there are competitive prices associated with efficient outcomes. It is not the Samuelson or the DOSSO strategy, however, because it does not make contact with the economist's intuitive sense of the intertemporal nitty-gritty.

Period-by-period static efficiency is necessary for intertemporal efficiency. If

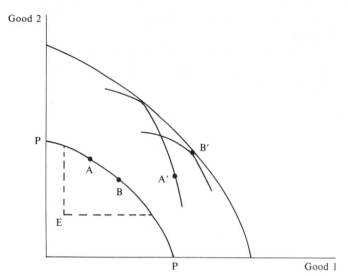

Figure 1
Two-period efficiency.

first-period production is inefficient, any sequence involving that first-period program will be inefficient because one can imagine doing the first period right and using the productive capacity thus saved to improve consumption of some good at some time. But period-by-period efficiency is not sufficient for intertemporal efficiency. This is hard to explain in words, except perhaps by not-quite-accurate analogy, but it is easy to see in Figure 1. There are two capital goods; the time-zero endowment is at E. A and B are two points on the production possibility curve for time one, so the choice of either is compatible with one-period efficiency. Each point on PP, treated as an endowment, in turn gives rise to a one-period production possibility curve; the diagram shows the ones for A (going through A') and B (going through B'). At time two the economy can accumulate enough capital to be on the outer envelope of all the one-period curves gotten by letting the time-one endowment traverse PP but cannot do better. So two-period efficiency means moving in two steps from E to that envelope. Evidently, then, the path EAA' is efficient period-by-period, but it is not intertemporally efficient because B' has more of both goods and is reachable in two periods via the intertemporally efficient path EBB'.

Corresponding to any point like A' or B' or A or B, one can draw an isoquant-like input-requirement locus showing the bundles of inputs of the two goods capable of producing the output bundle in question. The input-requirement curve for A or B must pass through E. If it passed to the northeast of E, A and B would not be producible from the initial endowment of capital goods; if it passed to the southwest of E, A and B would lie inside the production possibility curve from E. It turns out that what distinguishes an intertemporally efficient point like B' from an inefficient one like A' is that the input-requirement locus for B' is just tangent to PP at B, whereas the locus for A' cuts PP. This is where duality comes in. The slope of PP at

B is recognizable to any economist as the ratio of the (efficiency) prices of the two goods, viewed as flow outputs at time one. On the other hand the slope of the input-requirement locus for B' at B is immediately interpretable as the ratio of the (efficiency) prices of two goods viewed as stock inputs at time two. Intertemporal efficiency is equivalent to period-by-period efficiency *and* the equality of those two price ratios.

This process can be extended over more periods by letting endowments traverse the period-two envelope, drawing the production possibility curve for each, and constructing the outer envelope of those for period three. But nothing deeper than two-period efficiency arises from this process, in the sense that three-period efficiency is equivalent to period-by-period efficiency at times one, two, and three and two-period efficiency for zero-to-two and one-to-three. Overlapping two-period efficiency is all there is, with its natural interpretation in dual price terms.

There is a lot of capital theory wrapped up in this expanding envelope story. It is one of the fundamental results of the theory. For instance, the intertemporal efficiency condition, written in competitive price terms, is equivalent to Irving Fisher's equal-yield condition enforced in a perfect capital market by arbitrage between assets. So profit maximization in a full set of competitive markets for goods and assets will achieve intertemporal efficiency. And this suggests another application: In the special case that one of the goods is a nonrenewable resource whose stock can only be depleted by being used up in the production of the other good, the intertemporal efficiency condition boils down to the famous Hotelling Rule of 1931, which was rediscovered and elaborated in the 1970s in a great revival of interest in the economics of natural resources.

Now look back at Figure 1. The path EBB' is, as already noted, intertemporally efficient for its two-period horizon. It is also (or, as we shall see, it might be) the prelude to a longer intertemporally efficient path that continues on from B'. EAA' is not the prelude to a longer efficient path, but of course the path from E to A to the tangency of A's production possibility curve with the envelope is again potentially the prelude to a longer intertemporally efficient program of capital accumulation. This leads quite naturally to an important and difficult question: What does the set of three-period, four-period, . . . , T-period intertemporally efficient paths look like? Are there intertemporally efficient paths that go on forever? And how do the successively distant envelope curves behave?

This is the approach to the turnpike theorem, which was quite clearly conjectured in *Market Mechanisms and Maximization*. DOSSO went considerably further; they can hardly be said to have proved the theorem, though they elaborated the result and did point out the key saddlepoint property of the phase diagram that leads directly to a proof in continuous-time models. The first proof, in discrete time, was due to Roy Radner in 1961. Although *Linear Programming and Economic Analysis* is couched in discrete time for expository advantages, DOSSO's own thinking, even at the time, used the continuous-time formulation. (See, for instance, Samuelson and Solow, "A Complete Capital Model Involving Heterogeneous Capital Goods," [1956, I, Chap. 25].) In 1960, in "Efficient Paths of Capital Accumulation in Terms of the Calculus of Variations" [I, Chap. 26]. Samuelson

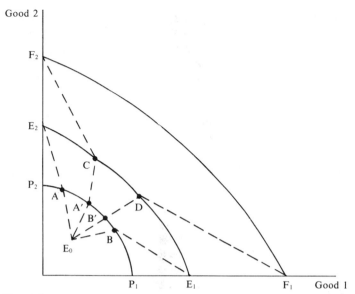

Figure 2
Efficient paths.

reworked the subject of intertemporal efficiency in the continuous-time setting, with a complete description of the saddlepoint or turnpike property amounting to a local proof. The turnpike theorem has given rise to a substantial continuing literature, including an important series of papers by Lionel McKenzie, the most recent of which (1982) gives the first complete global proof not based in any essential way on duality.

Here I try only to give a nontechnical account of the problem and its solution. One can ask if a transition like EP is the first step of a longer intertemporally efficient program. The answer is, generally no. A one-period production possibility curve with P as endowment will not contribute to the second-period envelope. This is shown more clearly in Figure 2. Look at the end-points of the two-period envelope $E_1 E_2$. Where does E_2 come from? What point on $P_1 P_2$ leads to an intertemporally efficient path from E_0 to E_2? E_2 will come from a point like A, and E_1 from a point like B. That is to say, the input-requirement locus for E_2 will be tangent to $P_1 P_2$, and similarly for E_1 and B. (I am assuming here that production of Good 2 is Good-2 intensive and Good 1, Good-1 intensive; otherwise the dotted lines would run from E_1 to A and E_2 to B.) Other points on the envelope $E_1 E_2$ come from points between A and B.

Of course the three-period envelope $F_1 F_2$ can be treated analogously. Its end-points come from points like C and D on $E_1 E_2$, which in turn must come from points like A' and B' on $P_1 P_2$, which in turn originate at E_0. And if we work back from a large-T-period envelope $Z_1 Z_2$, we can see that *any* T-period intertemporally efficient path must have passed through a very narrow gateway on $P_1 P_2$ and on all the early envelopes. The turnpike theorem says that any intertemporally efficient path, whatever its original endowment E_0 and wherever on the T-period envelope it ends up, must, if T is very large, have spent most of the intervening time growing proportionately with the stocks in or near a fixed ratio. In the diagram, any longtime-efficient path must stay very close to a ray from the origin, except perhaps near the beginning and the end of the path. Moreover, the ray in question has a special significance. It corresponds to the stock ratio that achieves the fastest rate of balanced growth the underlying technology is capable of generating. Thus it is intimately related to the famous model of an expanding economy of John von Neumann. And finally this picture tells us that very distant efficiency envelopes must be very nearly linear, with its slope representing the unchanging ratio of competitive prices of the two (or more) goods in that fastest-balanced-growth equilibrium configuration.

I have discussed this important episode in the theory of capital in terms of closed, consumptionless economies, with all output being ploughed back into the accumulation of stocks. This is consistent with the historical origins of the theory, even to the neat connection with the von Neumann model. The theory of intertemporal efficiency and the turnpike property of long efficient paths are fundamental to the theory of optimal growth in even more general contexts. For example, there is a literature on consumption turnpikes to which Samuelson contributed, along with Cass and others. Indeed, in a whole series of papers written between 1965 and 1971, he produced a number of interesting variations on the turnpike theme, including an extension to a simple case in which the social utility function is not intertemporally additive [1971, III, Chap. 140]; a discussion (jointly with Nissan Liviatan) of the case of joint production, when multiple turnpikes can arise, alternately stable and unstable [1969, III, Chap 141]; and a later (1976) paper in which the role of the turnpike is played by a special periodic motion [IV, Chap. 224]. I called this an "episode," but after twenty-seven years it might perhaps be described as a saga.

The "Cambridge Controversy"

The study of intertemporal efficiency is, as I pointed out in introducing it, part and parcel of general economics. It is a specialization to the intertemporal context of a line of reasoning that permeates static economic theory. (The turnpike theorem is more inescapably capital-theoretic. There must be an analogous result in static price theory but it would be artificial, requiring the assumption of an input-output structure that makes sense in terms of earlier-and-later but would appear rigged in other contexts.) The famous 1953 paper of Malinvaud pursues the near-identity with static price theory; differently dated commodities are treated as different commodities, and vectors of present-value prices are typographically indistinguishable from static price vectors, though of course Malinvaud is quite aware of the interest rate relations buried in changes in present-value prices.

Samuelson's approach has been a sort of hybrid. He has exploited to the hilt the educated intuitions that we all have from efficiency conditions elsewhere in economics and the dualities that accompany them. But his techniques have not been tuned to the static analogy. I do not remember any use of a separation theorem in a Samuelson proof, although of course duality appears again and again. Instead, when the context is intertemporal the argument is explicitly intertemporal. Perhaps I emphasize this more concrete way of doing business because it has influenced my own approach so much.

Ironically, then, Samuelson's initial involvement in the "Cambridge controversy"—I use the quotation marks to suggest a continuing doubt as to what the controversy was *about*—stemmed from a piece of static price theory, the nonsubstitution theorem. It is easy to see that a fixed-coefficient Leontief economy with a given supply of a single primary factor has a *linear* net-production possibility surface if it is productive at all. Clearly, then, since all marginal rates of transformation are constants determined by the technology, there is a unique set of competitive equilibrium efficiency prices—up to a normalization, of course—that does not depend on final demands. The nonsubstitution theorem shows that even if there are alternative techniques for producing each commodity, so long as they are subject to constant returns to scale, use only a single primary input, and do not involve joint production, the end result is the same. There is a unique vector of relative-efficiency prices—indeed there is a dominant choice of technique for each commodity—independent of final demand. Prices are entirely cost-determined. This result, established separately by Samuelson, Georgescu-Roegen, Koopmans, and a nice proof by Arrow, is discussed at length by Frank Hahn in another chapter in this volume. It belongs, quite properly, to general economics. It is really a statement about the cost function dual to such a technology.

So far this has nothing to do with capital theory. As soon as one thinks about time-phased production, however, a problem arises. There is an inescapable element of joint production in capital-using production, because processes typically leave some leftover capital goods as well as the final product itself. It was again a contribution of Samuelson's—again discussed by Hahn—to have seen that the nonsubstitution theorem can survive that sort of joint production: for a given rate of interest, competitive equilibrium prices are independent of final demand if they exist at all. (The last proviso is necessary because the interest rate may be too high to permit any break-even choice of technique.)

The assumptions required for the validity of the nonsubstitution theorem are pretty restrictive, especially the limitation to a single primary factor. (We have learned to live with constant returns to scale.) The significance of the theorem was thus hardly its direct applicability to the world, but rather its utility in the rigorous formulation of equilibrium models in which (competitive) prices are determined by technology alone. In capital theory, especially, there was a direct payoff. Think of the solitary primary factor as labor and choose it as numéraire, so prices are prices in wage units. Suppose there is only one consumption good. If the nonsubstitution theorem applies, then for each viable interest rate there is a unique technologically determined competitive equilibrium price of the consumption good in wage units, whose reciprocal is just the real wage. So without worrying about the demand side of the model, we can plot the competitive real wage as a function of the interest rate, as the latter ranges from zero (or minus one, for that matter) to its largest admissible value at which the real wage reaches zero or the price of the consumption good in wage units blows up to infinity. This function is easily seen to be decreasing: At higher interest rates the wage must be lower in terms of every good to allow competitive firms to break even.

Samuelson introduced this curve explicitly and described its properties first in his 1957 paper on Marx [I, Chap. 29] and again in 1959 in discussing Ricardo. He called it the factor-price frontier in 1962 in "Parable and Realism in Capital Theory: The Surrogate Production Function" [I, Chap. 28], to which I will turn in a moment. Hints of the same idea had turned up earlier in Joan Robinson's book on Marx (1956) and in a paper by David Champernowne (1960), and it had of course been used even earlier—though published only later—by Piero Sraffa. The factor-price frontier turned out to be a natural tool in the study of simple capital-theoretic models of the kind that now became the vogue. It extends straightforwardly, by the way, to many-commodity models, but only where the nonsubstitution theorem applies.

In "The Surrogate Production Function," Samuelson sets out to see how far the parable of a completely aggregated one-sector economy can be pushed. If aggregate output is a well-behaved function of inputs of labor and a previously accumulated stock of output called "capital," then constant returns to scale lets us write $y = f(j)$, where y is output per unit of labor and j is capital per unit of labor. The marginal-productivity conditions can be written $r = f'(j)$ and $w = f(j) - jf'(j)$. These two equations define w parametrically as a function of r, with j as the parameter. This is the factor-price frontier all over again for this simplest of all models. Moreoever, it is easily calculated that $dw/dr = -j$. The slope gives back the ratio of capital to labor.

Now suppose output is really produced by any of a variety of machines, each cooperating with labor. Indeed, suppose $b(x)$ machines of type x and $a(x)$ units of labor can produce either a unit of consumption good or a machine of type x. Thus $b(x)/a(x)$ measures the capital-intensity of production using machines of type x. It is crucially important here that type x production be characterized by the same capital-intensity whether engaged in producing the consumption good or producing more machines of type x. Samuelson remarks that he was alerted to the critical importance of this assumption by Piero Garegnani, after the main result had been worked out. Here is the main result. Let R be the gross rate of interest, the sum of rates of interest and depreciation. Given R, the model economy will in steady state choose the type x that yields the largest w—not out of kindness, of course, but because competition leads to cost minimization and the elimination of pure profit. In this way a factor-price frontier can be traced out, by plotting for each R the largest available w. Notice that x is changing along the factor-price frontier. If there is a continuum of types x, each point on the factor-price frontier might come from a different value of x. Nevertheless, it turns out that the slope of the factor-price frontier at any point $-dw/dR = b(x)/a(x)$ where x refers to the cost-minimizing type of machine at that particular (w, R). Thus from the *observable* factor-price frontier one could recover the corresponding ratio of capital to labor, that is, the capital-intensity $b(x)/a(x)$. It would seem reasonable then to approximate the underlying complicated technology by an aggregated production function of the simple form $f(j)$, specifically one that mimics the observed factor-price frontier. Hence the surrogate of the article's title.

It is a nice idea, but it is much too special to do the work one would like it to do. On top of all the assumptions needed for the nonsubstitution theorem, one has to add the one-in-a-million requirement that, for any type of machine, the machine-labor ratio be the same in the consumption good and machinery industries. (Otherwise any change in the composition of output, even within the same type, will change the overall machine-labor ratio.) Without this additional assumption, it is still possible to mimic the factor-price frontier with an aggregated production function, but the slope of the frontier need bear no relation to any overall capital-intensity. Then the approximation loses its point: $y = f(j)$ is no simpler than the factor-price frontier itself.

Nevertheless, in view of all the mystification that has surrounded the "Cambridge controversy," it is worth quoting the first sentence of the "Surrogate" article: "Repeatedly in writings and lectures I have insisted that capital theory can be rigorously developed without using any Clark-like concept of aggregate 'capital,' instead relying on a complete analysis of a great variety of heterogeneous physical capital goods and processes through time. . . . And I do stand by [this general approach] as the best tool for the description and understanding of economic reality, and for policy formulation and calculated guesses about the future." [I, Chap. 28, p. 325] This is neatly reminiscent of the passage quoted earlier from "The Rate of Interest under Ideal Conditions," written nearly a quarter of a century before. "But why, then, *ever* abandon the rigorous complete model?" I can hear some of our best friends say. The answer has to be: Because although exact theory may be the game, usable approximation is the prize.

Too much has been written about the reswitching question, with the result that its significance has been overblown (and misunderstood). I hesitate to add more, but reswitching has a place in the story. In models like that underlying the surrogate paper, but *without* the restrictive equal-capital-intensity condition, it can happen that a particular type or technique is cost-minimizing and therefore competitively viable at a low interest rate R_1 and again at a high interest rate R_2, whereas for interest rates between R_1 and R_2 one or more other types or techniques take over. It follows that there cannot be any one-directional correlation between the interest rate and the capital-intensity of steady-state productive technique. If there were, then the first technique would have been shown to be both more and less capital-intensive than the intermediate one(s), which would be senseless. The same example shows that the model economy could have two possible steady-state equilibria, one with a higher level of consumption per head than the other *and* with a higher interest rate. This possibility violates the standard neoclassical story, according to which the economy can pass, via an intervening period of saving-investing, from one steady state to another with a higher permanent level of consumption and a *lower* interest rate, courtesy of diminishing returns to capital. Evidently, then, the surrogate parable in which $y = f(j)$ can go wrong. It need not go wrong in any concrete case, but clearly it does not contain the whole truth.

Samuelson had the notion that universal diminishing returns, together with the assumption that every line of production involves every commodity directly or indirectly, would rule out the paradoxes of reswitching even in models with many capital goods. The role of the supplementary assumption is presumably to guarantee that diminishing returns permeate everywhere and to disallow multiple solutions. In any case, the notion is false. But sometime in 1964 Samuelson, as he wrote later, planted it in the mind of David Levhari. With such a gardener it would be hard not to grow something; in 1965 Levhari published a proof of the notion. Since the notion is false, the proof contains a slip. Counterexamples were soon produced and reswitching became an issue instead of a *curiosum*, like the Giffen good.

In the aftermath, Samuelson has written three retrospective summaries that distinguish with care what is true in the theory of capital from what is false. The first of these appeared immediately in the symposium that revealed the falseness of the false notion already described [1966, III, Chap. 148]. The second appeared in the proceedings of a conference held in Buffalo in 1974 and published in 1976 [IV, Chap. 215]. The third appeared as a comment on an article by Joan Robinson [1975, IV, Chap. 216]. In a steady state with one consumption good and many capital goods, the competitive equilibrium interest rate does measure the marginal rate of transformation of consumption-now into consumption-later. That intertemporal transformation exhibits diminishing returns if the underlying technology does so. And, under the standard assumptions for the nonsubstitution theorem, the standard properties of the factor-price frontier continue to hold. The rest is approximation or parable, practical reason rather than pure reason. Clear and thorough discussions of detail can be found in the excellent books by Christopher Bliss and Edwin Burmeister.

The puzzle about the reswitching *issue* is at a different level: How has it managed to appear as a critique of full-dress, first-principles, neoclassical capital theory that, as Samuelson has insisted, can get along without Clark-like aggregates and one-sector parables? The truth is more paradoxical still: If the notion that reswitching cannot occur with convex indecomposable technology is a false theorem of neoclassical capital theory, then the correct statement that it can occur is a true theorem—of neoclassical capital theory. The whole discussion has been conducted entirely within the framework of neoclassical theory and makes no sense in any other context. Apparently there can be smoke without fire.

A vaguer question is: Granted that the parable about high capital intensity and high steady-state consumption going along with a low interest rate is only a parable, it appears to be in the spirit of the underlying theory—what underlies the failure of the parable? The best answer I know is Bliss's: The theory gives no warrant to compare steady states. Steady states that appear to be neighboring may come at the end of histories that are not neighboring at all.

I should give the last word on this question to Joan Robinson (1975). She, too, thinks reswitching to be unimportant, but for a radically different reason. "There is no such phenomenon in real life as accumulation taking place in a given state of technical knowledge." She seems to have in mind that you never know exactly what will happen when you try something even a little different from what you have tried before. But then it is akin to saying there is no such thing in real life as a circle. True enough, but not the sort of thing to make you abandon Euclid.

FINAL WORD

I could go on. I have skipped whole topics in the theory of capital on which Samuelson has written. There is, for example, his long article with Modigliani on the "Pasinetti paradox" [1966, III, Chap. 146], but that is a detour down a road that has attracted little traffic.

There is an extraordinary series of papers worrying Schumpeter's once-famous proposition that the terminus of the process of economic development is a stationary state with zero rate of interest. The chronology is typical Samuelson (only "extraordinary" for anyone else). In 1943 the young Samuelson writes a paper on the subject—"Dynamics, Statics and the Stationary State" [I, Chap. 19]. In 1971 he returns briefly to the subject, in response to some comments by John Whitaker— "Paradoxes of Schumpeter's Zero Interest Rate" [IV, Chap. 217]. And in 1981 he produces a third, as yet unpublished, centennial paper on Schumpeter that takes yet another look at the same issue, and will in due course appear in *CSP*, Volume V. There would be some fun for me in retelling the story, if only because in the last two articles Samuelson chooses as his analytical vehicle what he always—to my perpetual pleasure—calls the "Ramsey-Solow model." (If I were a movie actress I could hope that he would frequently find occasion to refer to the "Garbo-Solow look.") But again it is a topic that no longer plays much of a role in contemporary capital theory, although once it engaged the attention of real heavyweights— Schumpeter, Knight, and Robbins, for instance. Schumpeter was a teacher of mine, too—it is at least an even-money bet that I first heard the name Samuelson from Schumpeter's lips—but he either meant less to me or I lack adequate intellectual piety.

Finally, I have not covered the celebrated consumption-loan paper of 1958 [I, Chap. 21] that introduced the two-state overlapping-generation model into economics. That has been a major innovation in the past quarter of a century; it may be no exaggeration to say that it has permitted the integration of capital theory into macroeconomics. But in view of the particular focus of the 1958 paper, it has been allocated to Kenneth Arrow's contribution to this volume.

Samuelson's work in the theory of capital shares the characteristics of his work everywhere in economics: energy, ingenuity, the distinct air—even in most technical matters—of having been written by a person and not a computing machine, a belief that economics is an important and beautiful subject, an acquaintance with everything that has ever been written on it, and, above all, that fabulous intuition for the way it has to come out. You could never hope to referee a Samuelson paper as if it were anonymous. There is a famous remark by one of the Bernoullis upon seeing an anonymous paper by Newton, something about its having the paw-print of the lion all over it. I can't remember which Bernoulli it was—but Samuelson would know.

REFERENCES

Bliss, Christopher (1975): *Capital Theory and the Distribution of Income*, Amsterdam, North-Holland.

Boulding, K. E. (1936): "The Theory of a Single Investment," *Quarterly Journal of Economics* 49 (May).

Burmeister, Edwin (1980): *Capital Theory and Dynamics*, Cambridge, Cambridge University Press.

Champernowne, D. G. (1953-54): "The Production and the Theory of Capital: A Comment," *Review of Economic Studies* 21 (No. 2).

Chipman, John (1972): "A Renewal Model of Economic Growth: The Discrete Case," in R. H. Day and S. M. Robinson, eds., *Mathematical Topics in Economic Theory and Computation*, Philadelphia, SIAM Publication.

—— (1977): "A Renewal Model of Economic Growth: The Continuous Case," *Econometrica* 45 (March).

Dorfman, R., P. A. Samuelson, and R. M. Solow (1958): *Linear Programming and Economic Analysis*, New York, McGraw-Hill.

Fisher, Irving (1907): *The Rate of Interest*, New York, Macmillan.

—— (1930): *The Theory of Interest*, New York, Macmillan.

Hotelling, Harold (1931): "The Economics of Exhaustible Resources," *Journal of Political Economy* 39 (April).

Malinvaud, Edmond (1953): "Capital Accumulation and Efficient Allocation of Resources," *Econometrica* 21 (April).

McKenzie, Lionel (1982): "A Primal Route to the Turnpike and Liapounov Stability," *Journal of Economic Theory*. 27 (June).

Radner, Roy (1961): "Prices and the Turnpike, III. Paths of Economic Growth that are Optimal with Regard only to Final States: a Turnpike Theorem," *Review of Economic Studies* 28 (Feb.).

Robinson, Joan (1975): "The Unimportance of Reswitching," *Quarterly Journal of Economics* 89 (Feb.).

—— (1956): *The Accumulation of Capital*, London, Macmillan.

Samuelson, Paul A. (1937): "A Note on Measurement of Utility," *Review of Economic Studies* 4 (Feb.); *Collected Scientific Papers*, I, Chap. 20.

—— (1937): "Some Aspects of the Pure Theory of Capital," *Quarterly Journal of Economics* 51 (May); *Collected Scientific Papers*, I, Chap. 17.

—— (1939): "The Rate of Interest under Ideal Conditions," *Quarterly Journal of Economics* 53 (Feb.); *Collected Scientific Papers*, I, Chap. 18.

—— (1943): "Dynamics, Statics, and the Stationary State," Essays in honor of Joseph Schumpeter, *Review of Economics and Statistics* 25 (Feb.); *Collected Scientific Papers*, I, Chap. 19.

—— (1947): *Foundations of Economic Analysis*, Cambridge, Harvard University Press.

—— (1949): *Market Mechanisms and Maximization*, Part I: "The Theory of Comparative Advantage"; Part II: "The Cheapest-Adequate-Diet Problem"; and Part III: "Dynamics and Linear Programming", published by the RAND Corporation; *Collected Scientific Papers*, I, Chap. 33.

—— and R. M. Solow (1956): "A Complete Capital Model Involving Heterogeneous Capital Goods," *Quarterly Journal of Economics* 60 (Nov.); *Collected Scientific Papers*, I, Chap. 25.

—— (1957): "Wages and Interest: A Modern Dissection of Marxian Ecnomic Models," *American Economic Review* 47 (Dec.); *Collected Scientific Papers*, I, Chap. 29.

—— (1958): "An Exact Consumption-Loan Model of Interest with or without the Social Contrivance of Money," *Journal of Political Economy* 66 (Dec.); *Collected Scientific Papers*, I, Chap. 21.

—— (1959): "A Modern Treatment of the Ricardian Economy: I. The Pricing of Goods and of Labor and Land Services; II. Capital and Interest Aspects of the Pricing Process," *Quarterly Journal of Economics* 73 (Feb., May); *Collected Scientific Papers*, I, Chaps. 31, 32.

—— (1960): "Efficient Paths of Capital Accumulation in Terms of the Calculus of Variations," in Kenneth J. Arrow, Samuelson Karlin, and Patrick Suppes, eds., *Mathematical Methods in the Social Sciences, 1959*, Stanford University Press; *Collected Scientific Papers*, I, Chap. 26.

—— (1962): "Parable and Realism in Capital Theory; The Surrogate Production Function," *Review of Economic Studies* 29 (June); *Collected Scientific Papers*, I, Chap. 28.

—— and Franco Modigliana (1966): "The Pasinetti Paradox in Neoclassical and More General Model," *Review of Economic Studies* 33 (Oct.); *Collected Scientific Papers*, III, Chap. 146.

—— (1966): "A Summing Up," *Quarterly Journal of Economics* 80 (Nov.); *Collected Scientific Papers*, III, Chap. 148.

—— and N. Liviatan (1969): "Notes on Turnpikes: Stable and Unstable," *Journal of Economic Theory* 1 (Dec.); *Collected Scientific Papers*, III, Chap. 141.

—— (1969): "Foreword," in S. Chakravarty, *Capital and Development Planning*, Cambridge, MIT Press, 1969; *Collected Scientific Papers*, III, Chap. 151.

—— (1971): "Turnpike Theorems Even Though Tastes Are Intertemporally Dependent," *Western Economic Journal* 9 (March); *Collected Scientific Papers*, III, Chap. 140.

—— (1971): "Paradoxes of Schumpeter's Zero Interest Rate," *Review of Economics and Statistics* 53 (Nov.); *Collected Scientific Papers*, IV, Chap. 217.

—— (1975): "Steady-State and Transient Relations: A Reply on Reswitching," *Quarterly Journal of Economics* 89 (Feb.); *Collected Scientific Papers*, IV, Chap. 216.

—— (1976): "The Periodic Turnpike Theorem," *Nonlinear Analysis, Theory, Methods and Applications* 1 (Sept.); *Collected Scientific Papers*, IV, Chap. 224.

—— (1976): "Interest Rate Determinations and Oversimplifying Parables: A Summing Up," in M. Brown, K. Sato and P. Zarembka, eds., *Essays in Modern Capital Theory*, Amsterdam, North-Holland; *Collected Scientific Papers*, IV, Chap. 215.

Sraffa, Piero (1960): *Production of Commodities by Means of Commodities*, Cambridge, Cambridge University Press.

Whitaker, J. K. (1971): "The Schumpeterian Stationary State Revisited," *Review of Economics and Statistics* 53 (Nov.).

Wicksell, Knut (1934): *Lectures on Political Economy: Vol. I: General Theory*, New York, Macmillan.

MACROECONOMICS AND FISCAL POLICY

James Tobin

THE YOUNG KEYNESIAN AT HARVARD

When the Keynesian Revolution burst upon Cambridge, Massachusetts in 1936 Paul Samuelson, all of twenty years old, had been a graduate student at Harvard for less than a year. Ten years later he recalled the invasion [1946, II, Chap. 114, p. 157].[1]

> I have always considered it a priceless advantage to have been born as an economist prior to 1936 and to have received a thorough grounding in classical economics. It is quite impossible for modern students to realize the full effect of . . . "The Keynesian Revolution" upon those of us brought up in the orthodox tradition. . . . To have been born as an economist before 1936 was a boon—yes. But not to have been born too long before!
>
> Bliss was it in that dawn to be alive
> But to be young was very heaven!

I was born a year too late, alas. I began studying economics as a Harvard sophomore in 1936, and my tutor, Spencer Pollard, blithely suggested we start by reading a new book from England. Unlike Paul, who as an undergraduate at Chicago studied under Simons, Knight, Viner, Director, and company and consorted with graduate students named Stigler, Wallis, Hart, and Friedman, I didn't really know what I was rebelling against. But maybe the classically educated old-timers like Paul didn't either, for later he often said and wrote that there was no clear, explicit, classical macromodel prior to the Keynesian challenge. Anyway, the virus that, as he recounts, so rapidly conquered the young economists of Cambridge

---

[1]Citations of Samuelson's *Collected Scientific Papers* give year of original publication, volume in roman numerals, chapter, and sometimes specific pages.

was in turn transmitted by them to us undergraduates in classes, seminars, tutorials, and common rooms. And so, though he was never formally my teacher, I began learning from Paul Samuelson in those exciting years, and I'm still at it.

Samuelson's program at Harvard was not conventional graduate study. He had anticipated much of that at Chicago, and at Harvard he was soon liberated from requirements by appointment to the Society of Fellows. He undertook the ambitious and searching formal investigation of economic theory ultimately compiled in his *Foundations*. A theorist so gifted in the calculus of optimization and market clearing and so fascinated by the elegance of neoclassical equilibrium and welfare results might have been immune to the Keynesian virus. As many general equilibrium theorists have done then and since, he might have thrown up his hands at the messy problems and untidy techniques of macroeconomics. Samuelson chose to work both sides of the street.

A big reason was certainly Cambridge itself, the American scene of intense debate over the world economic crisis and the crisis of world economics. Haberler, Hansen, Harris, Schumpeter, and Williams were in the thick of battles fought in an unceasing sequence of classes, seminars, forums, papers, and conversations. So was an unparalleled band of eager, talented, junior faculty and graduate students, among them the Sweezys, the Salants, Metzler, Goodwin, Galbraith, and Gordon. Academic economics seemed terribly important, both for understanding the Depression and for overcoming it.[2]

In this setting Samuelson became a Keynesian as well as a Walrasian, though he says [1964, II, Chap. 114] it took him and everyone else at least eighteen months and help from the equations of Hicks, Lange, Meade, and Harrod to understand the *General Theory*. A brash *enfant terrible*, Paul amazed and delighted his contemporaries and us youngsters by puncturing the classical fallacies of senior professors and unwary visitors or exposing their shaky grasp of new truth.

What if Paul had stayed at Chicago? What if he had gone to Columbia, as his Chicago mentors urged? Would he have eschewed macroeconomics? Would he have become a monetarist? Probably even he cannot be sure. My own guess is that he would sooner or later have come to terms with Keynesian macroeconomics in much the same way that he in fact did. Given his insatiable appetite for all economics, given his real-world curiosities and concerns, he was bound to give Keynes most serious attention. As a microeconomist, he was never so bewitched by the miracle of the Invisible Hand as to regard market failure as per se implausible. Moreover, his early articles display a general interest in stability of equilibrium and a generous admiration for the pragmatic pre-Keynesian dynamic models of Frisch and other European mathematical economists.

But only at Harvard could he have become friends with Alvin Hansen, the major personal association and example attracting Samuelson to Keynes and to macroeconomics. Hansen's integrity, shown by his public 180-degree change of mind about the *General Theory* at age 50, his evident conviction and seriousness of purpose, his lack of pretension, and his collegial treatment of students and junior

---

[2]Samuelson's own reminiscenes are in [1972, IV, Chap. 278].

faculty—all earned him affection, admiration, and influence among young scholars. Samuelson expresses these feelings in several tributes [1959, II, Chap. 84; 1975, IV, Chap. 287; 1976, IV, Chap. 285]. From his young friend Samuelson, Hansen asked and received theoretical and technical help and collaboration, including the famous accelerator-multiplier model, Paul's first published contribution to macroeconomics [1939, II, Chap. 82].

THE COVERAGE OF THIS CHAPTER

In this appreciation of Paul Samuelson as macroeconomist I shall concentrate on his contributions to the methodology and substance of macromodel building and to the positive and normative theory of stabilization, with emphasis on fiscal policy. This was Samuelson's own emphasis in his first twenty-five years, both in his pathbreaking early papers on multiplier statics and dynamics and in his crystallization of the neoclassical synthesis after the second world war. But at no stage was Samuelson a "fiscalist," and I shall point out the important role money and monetary policy played in his macroeconomics from the beginning. More thorough reviews of his contributions to the theory of money and finance are provided by Don Patinkin and Robert Merton elsewhere in this volume.

There are several other overlaps, reflecting connections of Samuelson's macroeconomics to his many other interests and fields of contribution. This chapter concerns income determination in the short run and stabilization policy, but these topics necessarily intersect Samuelson's work on capital theory and long-run economic growth, treated in Robert Solow's chapter. Likewise Samuelson was a student of public finance theory in general, not just fiscal macroeconomics, as will be evident both here and in Richard Musgrave's review.

Samuelson's model of intergenerational consumption loans [1958, I, Chap. 21] is treated elsewhere in this book. It has turned out to be an amazingly insightful construct, with implications for basic monetary and macroeconomic theory that have only recently begun to be fully exploited. Its overlapping-generations setup is the simplest major competitor to the classical simplifying assumption that economic agents have infinite horizons. On the differences between infinite and finite horizons turn such issues as the elasticity of the economy's ultimate demand for wealth, the absorption of saving by government deficits financed by interest-bearing debt, the displacement of capital by money, public debt, and unfunded social insurance, the long-run neutrality of inflation and monetary growth, and the optimality of monetary saturation. Both Keynes and Samuelson understood a crucial macroeconomic fact—savers and investors acquire assets that last longer than they do. I do not expatiate here on these fruits of a paper written twenty-three years ago. I simply marvel at the prescience and genius they confirm.

I cannot do justice to several well-known unusual aspects of Samuelson's voluminous writings. His feeling for economics as an evolving science with history and tradition is rare, all too rare, among modern economists. He learned the history of doctrine in every field he wrote about and wrote perceptively about the major contributions and contributors of the past. Notable for macroeconomics are his essays on Keynes and Kansen cited above, and on Wicksell [1959, II, Chap. 120]; Harris [1975, IV, Chap. 284]; Schumpeter [1951, II, Chap. 116]; and Lerner [1963, III, Chap. 183]—all marvelous examples of intellectual and personal biography. His substantive papers are full of illuminating reference to the histories of their subjects, placing his own results in perspective for the less learned reader.

What other high-powered mathematical theorist except Irving Fisher has written a running commentary on the events, outlooks, and policies of his years? As I read again a sequence of Samuelson's pieces in this genre, I saw how the Wunderkind from Gary added wisdom to logic, fortunately never sacrificing brashness to maturity. Samuelson has always been a voracious consumer and efficient distiller of the profession's research output, whether theory, empirical findings, or big-model forecasts. To a far-reaching network of informants within the profession he added over the years contacts in business, finance, and government throughout the world. His comments on current events and issues make good use of inputs from all sources. I have not tried to assess Samuelson's forecasting success, and I suspect he has been too canny to leave an easily tested record. There is the danger that inspection would reveal him to be another Sumner Slichter, who often figures in Samuelson's writings as an economist reputed for successful forecasting but by undisclosed and unreplicable methods.

A final and somewhat personal introductory comment. As a member of the Kennedy economic team, I knew, as my colleagues did, that our analysis and strategy were not nearly as "new economics" as the media label suggested. I did not know, more charitably did not remember, how much of our doctrine, as expounded for instance in the 1962 *Economic Report*, Samuelson had written down long before. To mention only two examples, Samuelson coined the concepts of potential output and its growth [1953, II, Chap. 99] and stated then that the objective of counter-cyclical policy was not just to smooth fluctuation and stabilize employment and output, but to minimize departures from full employment equilibrium and the trend of potential output. Other long-standing Samuelson contributions to our new economics will be clear in my review below of the neoclassical synthesis. By 1961 these ideas had become second nature to us, the public domain of our intellectual heritage. Samuelson was a member, one might better say coach, of that team. But he certainly didn't remind us that ideas we were so excitedly developing and propagating had appeared in his writings ten or fifteen years earlier.

THE STATICS AND DYNAMICS OF INCOME DETERMINATION

In Cambridge in the late 1930s and early 1940s Paul Samuelson undertook a fundamental inquiry into the sources of operationally meaningful propositions in economic theory. By happy chance this inquiry coincided with the ferment triggered by Keynes's *General Theory*. By still happier chance the new macroeconomics was grist for Samuelson's mill; it was the natural subject matter for developing many of the methodological points he sought to make. These concerned the properties of whole systems: the meaning of equilibrium and disequilibrium; statics, stationarity, and dynamics; stability and instability; hysteresis. According to the young

Samuelson [1941, I, Chap. 40], it was Ragnar Frisch who, a decade earlier, had engineered a "revolution of thought" in economics, one comparable to "the transition from classical to quantum mechanics." This was a shift from "statical to dynamical modes" of analysis.

It may seem paradoxical that Samuelson, given this methodological stance, found Keynesian macroeconomics a fertile field to plow. The *General Theory* itself was thoroughly in the statical mode. So were those formalizations by Hicks and others that alone, according to Samuelson's own testimony, made the book comprehensible. The paradox is, of course, resolved by his celebrated and controversial correspondence principle, summarized in his dictum "One interested only in fruitful statics must study dynamics" [*Foundations*, p. 5].

Samuelson found two sources of meaningful propositions in economic *theory*. One is that relations among observable variables reflect agents' solutions of optimization problems like maximization of utility or profits or wealth. First- and second-order conditions could then restrict signs and magnitudes in comparative static analyses, for example, of the effect of variations of taste, technology, or taxes. However, Samuelson was definitely not sanguine about the power of this principle for relations aggregated over many agents. He was therefore skeptical of its usefulness in generating systemwide propositions. Given the inevitable differences among agents, anything could happen in aggregate and still be consistent with individual optimizations. These misgivings, which foreshadow much later, the rigorous proofs of similar negative results by Sonnenschein, McFadden, Mantel, and others, contrast with a popular current fashion among macroeconomic theorists, who achieve the appearance of rigor by assuming away troublesome heterogeneities among agents. In any case, it led Samuelson to emphasize his second theoretical source of meaningful propositions, the correspondence principle.

According to the principle, a general hypothesis of dynamic stability restricts the parameters of a system of relationships [*Foundations*, p. 5]. With and only with these restrictions can meaningful comparative static propositions about the equilibrium position or motion of the system be obtained. A famous and simple example concerns the Keynesian multiplier: If and only if the marginal propensity to spend is less than one is the equilibrium stable and the multiplier formula usable for predicting the ultimate effect of an exogenous change in investment or government purchases. Initially Samuelson seemed prepared to assert stability as an empirical hypothesis, and thus in the example to say that the marginal propensity to spend must be less than one because otherwise the system would be unstable. After all, he said, unstable systems don't generate many observations—"How many times has the reader seen an egg standing upon its end?" [*Foundations*, p. 5]. I recall Joseph Schumpeter's rebuke to this line of reasoning, "Who could ever claim that capitalism is stable?"

Later, after prodding by Donald F. Gordon in 1955, Samuelson retreated, admitting that observations might be generated by a process different from the proposed model under analysis, even by a slowly divergent dynamic system, so that the quantitative information about particular parameters implied by his principle was seriously limited [1955, II, Chap. 128]. Moreover, the same static equations may be the equilibrium of a host of dynamic models, so that the stability restrictions are themselves ambiguous. The canon of consistency for theorists of course survives: Don't do comparative statics with dynamically unstable systems.

In [1941, I, Chap. 38] Samuelson illustrated the correspondence principle by applying it to several simple models. One of them was a Keynesian IS-LM model with three endogenous variables—income, interest, and investment—and three exogenous parameters—consumption, investment, and money. Like the other examples, this one was methodologically instructive. But the ambiguities in the results—even when several behavioral partial derivatives were signed a priori—also show the limitations of the method.

The young Samuelson's belief that the future of economic theory lay in Frisch's footsteps, in explicit dynamical models, and in comparative dynamics as well as in proper comparative statics, has not been confirmed in quite the way nor to the degree that he anticipated. For one thing, such systems easily become too complicated for closed analytical results. This is especially true of nonlinear systems, and Samuelson admitted he was too optimistic about the usefulness of linear models. Moreover, without and probably also with the restraints of optimizing assumptions, dynamic specifications of behavior equations contain an embarassing abundance of free parameters on whose values the model-builder has few clues. Distributed lag structures are a good example. Of course, modern computers permit a great deal of numerical analysis and simulation. Macroeconometric models are nonlinear dynamic systems, and comparative dynamics is their routine stock in trade. But for better or worse their parameter restrictions do not come from theory. They are squeezed from data by econometric estimation or are imposed by model-builders' intuitions. Whether the new dynamic economics connected with rational expectations, replacing past initial conditions with future terminal conditions, will realize the Frischian revolution remains an open question.[3]

As the years wore on, Samuelson himself tended to use the statical mode and keep the associated dynamics and stability analysis implicit. Even with respect to the multiplier, he found that the most important lessons came from Keynes's static version rather than from sequential processes of the Kahn, Robertson, or Swedish types. His neoclassical synthesis of macroeconomic theory, discussed below, is essentially a comparative static analysis of the equilibrium effects of policy variations.

In any event, Samuelson taught a generation of economists about difference equations, dynamic process analysis, and stability conditions and immensely clarified their conceptions of equilibrium, disequilibrium, and comparative statics. Most of this brilliant instruction was in the context of macroeconomics. Armed with his metatheoretical methodology, Samuelson produced a remarkable series of papers [1939, II, Chaps. 82 and 83; 1940, II, Chap. 85; 1942, II, Chap. 86; 1943, II, Chap. 90; 1948, II, Chap. 91; 1952, I, Chap. 41] ringing all the changes on investment and fiscal multipliers and laying the formal basis for Keynesian fiscal theory. He cut

[3]On the methodological issues of this paragraph see Lucas (1980).

through the confusions of the day regarding sequential processes versus equilibrium outcomes; saving-investment identities, schedules, and equilibrium equalities; exogenous tax variations versus endogenous responses of revenues; one-shot versus continued multiplicands; pump-priming versus stable multiplier scenarios. He showed that with any linear lagged spending function the ultimate multiplier for a permanent unit injection is the same as the cumulative sum of income increases due to a single unit injection. He offered as a theorem, quite relevant today, that fiscal stimulus could not pay for itself in augmented tax revenues (thus overlooking the classroom *curiosum* that this can happen in a stable model if some spending, presumably for investment, is induced by before-tax rather than after-tax income). The balanced budget multiplier escaped Samuelson's notice at first, and by his own report he was initially dubious [1943, II, Chap. 108, p. 1446]. Nevertheless, he must be counted as one of the several independent discoverers of this celebrated, probably overcelebrated, theorem, a history of which he has given [1975, IV, Chap. 274].

Perhaps more remarkable for early multiplier papers, Samuelson did not neglect other macroeconomic effects. He explained how monetary, interest, and price responses could affect the parameters, processes, and outcomes. One paper shows how interest rates will evolve during fiscal stimulus, depending on the proportions in which the additional deficit is financed by public debt, low-powered money, and high-powered money. Clarity about stocks and flows was of course characteristic of all his writings, worth noting only because of the confusions in other discussions at the time.

The accelerator-multiplier model, an analysis suggested by Hansen in connection with the 1937–1938 recession, was pathbreaking in substance and methodology. Of course it was not the first mathematical business-cycle model, but it was more closely and directly tied to current macroeconomic concepts and literary theory than earlier exercises of Frisch and others. It was the progenitor of Metzler's classic inventory-cycle models; inventories were more suitable for the acceleration principle than fixed capital. The Hansen-Samuelson model suffered from relating induced investment to movements of consumption rather than total output, a misspecification easy to remedy. All models are parables, and Samuelson always made their morals explicit. Here the lesson was that various literary theorists of the cycle were mistaken to believe that nonlinearities were necessary to explain upper and lower turning points. Samuelson did not recognize at the time the defect of linear models as cycle theories, namely that if the model parameters imply cyclical fluctuations at all they either explode or die out except for singular values of the parameters. Evidently Samuelson sided with Keynes in thinking that exogenous investment shocks rather than intrinsic mechanisms were responsible for the persistence of fluctuations. He rather discounted the durable importance of accelerator-induced investment, because it would eventually have no effect on the capital stock, compared with the more basic determinants of demand for capital emphasized by Keynes and Hansen.

These exercises in the determination of output by effective demand were carried out by a neoclassical price theorist, but he found unproblematic the failure of prices, wages, and interest rates to eliminate excess supplies. Introducing a second and more thoughtful discussion of the accelerator-multiplier model than the original version [1939, II, Chap. 83], Samuelson simply refers to frictions and imperfections as evident justifications for proceeding. Indeed Samuelson never found the existence of excess-supply disequilibrium in the labor market a surprising departure from Walrasian equilibrium worthy of defense or of theoretical investigation. Looking for the essential Keynesian contribution ten years after the *General Theory* [II, chap. 114], he singled out not nominal wage stickiness but Keynes's insight that capital markets would not be cleared by interest rates, asset valuations, and other financial adjustments without movements of real income.

Probably for similar reasons, Samuelson could never muster much enthusiasm for the controversy about the Pigou or real-balance effect, the riposte to the claim of the *General Theory* that involuntary unemployment could characterize a true equilibrium in the classical sense [1963, II, Chap. 115]. Evidently Samuelson agreed all along that in principle competitive markets could not be in Walrasian market-clearing equilibrium with excess supplies of labor. He has been much interested, as a matter of pure theory and the logic of Walrasian systems, in the issues raised by Patinkin concerning the neutrality of outside money—or moneys, including government debts—and the classical dichotomy [1968, III, Chap. 176]. Samuelson certainly recognized a wealth effect on demand, emphasizing very early the link from asset revaluation to consumption as a more powerful effect of monetary policy than that of interest rates on investment. But he cites Pigou and quotes a 1935–1936 remark of Leontief—"If wages are low enough, this dime in my hand will employ everyone in the nation"—more as curious examples of a principle carried to uninteresting extreme that as serious macroeconomic argument [1964, II, Chap. 115, p. 1536]. Samuelson did not regard the actual economy as perfectly competitive. He thought frictions and imperfections made automatic market adjustment slower than the volatile fluctuations of investment demand associated with Keynes's "state of long-term expectation." He commented, again long before expected price inflation or deflation was so central a theoretical issue and practical concern, that such expectations are quite possibly more important determinants of aggregate real demand than are price levels [1940, II, Chap. 88].

From early postwar years on, Samuelson was skeptical that full employment and price stability were compatible objectives in the absence of good luck or wage and price controls.[4] It did not occur to him to define full employment by the unemployment rate consistent with price or inflation stability. He certainly regarded Keynesian fiscal policies, and monetary policies, too, as two-sided weapons, to be used against excess demand as well as excess supply. His article with Solow [1960, II, Chap. 102], suggesting that Phillips curves represent tradeoffs for policymakers, has been much maligned, cited as the prototypical example of Keynesian error of the 1960s. Actually it is quite guarded and sophisticated in distinguishing long-run effects from short-run and worrying about expectations induced by policies and experience. It certainly does not say that expansion of

---

[4] An early example is [1953, II, Chap. 99, pp. 1294–5, 1307].

monetary demand can purchase any desired rate of employment and capacity utilization indefinitely at finite cost in inflation.

Samuelson's early macroeconomic writings concern the demand side of fiscal policy. Many of his later writings concern the supply side and therefore have particular relevance today. His contributions to public finance are reviewed elsewhere in this volume. Therefore, I shall simply note that in the 1950s and 1960s Samuelson clearly analyzed the effects of accelerated depreciation, investment tax credits, preferential treatment of capital gains, and deductibility of interest. A 1964 paper [III, Chap. 179] proves the neutrality of proportional taxation on accrual of true economic income to capital, with respect to rates of return. Regarding concessions going beyond such neutrality he said, "If we call spades spades, let's call bribes bribes," even if we decide as a matter of national policy to offer them. He could repeat verbatim in 1981 much earlier testimony to this effect.

THE NEOCLASSICAL SYNTHESIS

Paul Samuelson's greatest contribution to macroeconomics was the neoclassical synthesis, of which he was the principal architect [1951, II, Chap. 98; 1953, II, Chap. 99; 1955, II, Chap. 100; 1963, II, Chap. 115]. Thie *Weltanschauung* reconciled the classical and Keynesian strands of his thinking and that of many of his contemporaries. It became orthodox doctrine for a generation of economists and for many of their students. Certainly in the profession it was the mainstream Keynesian tradition in North America.

Of course there has always been strong dissent in both directions. From the older Cambridge, Joan Robinson and her colleagues and disciples attacked the synthesis as a heretical perversion of Keynes's true message. American post-Keynesians echo the charge. This battle is intimately entangled with the war of two Cambridges over capital and growth theory, reviewed elsewhere by Robert Solow.

On the other side of Samuelson's middle ground, Walrasians have always questioned the basic consistency of the market failures assumed or alleged in Keynesian theory with rational behavior. Recently this challenge has dramatically regained professional attention and support from the new classical macroeconomics and the theory of rational expectations. Robert Lucas, the leader of this counterrevolution, pays Samuelson and his partners in crime the high compliment of making the neoclassical synthesis the heresy become orthodoxy that Lucas is rebelling against.[5]

As I interpret it, Samuelson's exposition of the neoclassical synthesis contains both positive and normative propositions. The positive propositions, baldly stated, are as follows:

Market-clearing equilibrium provides a tolerably good description of long-term trends. Market adjustments *and countercyclical policies* will over the decades keep macroeconomic outcomes close to full employment on average; anyway, there will be no tendency for relative margins of underutilization to rise secularly. In this

[5]Lucas (1980).

sense, long-run growth tracks equilibrium supplies of labor, capital, natural resources, and—most decisive for labor productivity and living standards in Samuelson's view—knowledge.

These tracks are fairly smooth and cannot account for observed short-run volatility in economic performance. Fluctuations about the trends reflect mainly shocks to aggregate effective demand, to which prices, wages, and interest rates cannot and do not respond rapidly enough to preserve equilibrium. Movements of output and income are therefore intrinsic to the economy's responses to shocks, and in the absence of stabilizing policies the mechanisms of quantity adjustment can produce cumulative swings of large amplitude.

At bottom these short-run disequilibria reflect adjustment costs and lags, market imperfections, and discrepancies of information and expectation. The shocks that generate cyclical fluctuations may be governmental in origin, but there are many other sources as well. As noted above, Samuelson accepted Keynes's view that investment, dependent on business expectations and confidence regarding a long and uncertain future, was naturally erratic. For this combination of reasons, there is plenty of room for fiscal and monetary measures of stabilization to hold the economy closer to its equilibrium path.

The neoclassical synthesis cleansed Keynesian economics of some mistakes of content, context, or emphasis, mistakes not so much intrinsic to the *General Theory* as Depression-bound simplifications and extrapolations by Keynes's followers in the thirties and forties. Among these were:

1 The view that consumption demand would inevitably become weaker with the advance of productivity and the secular-stagnation pessimism to which it led. Samuelson anticipated [1943, II, Chap. 108] the agonizing postwar reappraisal of the consumption function, arguing that upward shifts in the short-run function would prevent secular decline of the average propensity to consume;

2 The view that monetary policy was inconsequential because of very high interest elasticity of demand for money or very low interest elasticity of investment;

3 The connected view, certainly not Keynes's own but inherited from the accelerator and perpetuated by Harrod-Domar growth theory, that capital-output ratios are frozen. Samuelson was at pains to disavow both this extreme and the "implicit 'classical' axiom that motivated investment is *indefinitely expansible or contractable* so that whatever people try to save will always be fully invested" [1946, II, Chap. 114, p. 1523];

4 The exclusive stress on government purchases, like public works, as vehicles of fiscal stimulus. Of course Samuelson had long recognized tax and transfer multipliers;

5 The assumption of textbook convenience that nominal prices or wage rates or both would remain constant in the face of fluctuations of aggregate demand—all that is really needed is that they are not perfectly flexible.

The normative and policy propositions follow easily, and in Samuelson's mind they were the most important part of the message. After all, as much as he relished all aspects of economics, he loved welfare economics most of all. Neoclassical welfare calculus, he found, far from being rendered irrelevant by Keynesian economics, applies not only to resource allocation in equilibrium but also to the choice of measures to restore and maintain full employment. Essentially resources are scarce even when some are temporarily unemployed. There are always socially valuable ways to employ them; make-work projects—like Keynes's burying coins for treasure seekers to dig up—are always unnecessary and wasteful.

The size of government and the amount of public consumptions and investments should be in principle determined by equating their returns in social utility on the margin with the values of the private uses of resources they displace. Fiscal and monetary policy can always generate the private purchasing power to reemploy the resources in private consumption and investment, which thus become the opportunity cost of exhaustive public expenditures. This principle—Samuelson called it the new look [1955, II, Chap. 100]—is consistent with the use of fiscal policy, discretionary or built-in, for stabilization, because stimulus can be provided or withdrawn by adjusting taxes and transfers as well as purchases. Samuelson was careful to point out [1951, II, Chap. 98], taking issue with a number of proposed formulas for countercyclical policy, that the principle does not imply that government purchases should be cyclically constant at their optimal levels for an economy in sustained macroequilibrium. If recession or depression reflects weakening of the marginal efficiency of private investment or of the marginal utility of current private consumption, then it is a proper social response to channel some of the released resources into public programs whose marginal social values remain high. The reverse would be true in booms.

Furthermore, Samuelson argued, monetary and fiscal measures are within wide limits substitute techniques of stabilization. Their mixture can be adjusted to achieve socially desired allocations of output, as between consumption and investment. Rational stabilization policy does not consist, as many Keynesian enthusiasts continued to believe even after the Depression, in throwing all instruments together into high or reverse gear. It consists in choosing, among those combinations that achieve stabilization objectives, one that also meets social criteria of allocational efficiency. If these criteria dictate, as they appeared to in 1961 and again in 1981, shifting the composition of output in favor of capital formation, this can be achieved without changing overall macroeconomic balance by combining tighter fiscal policy with easier monetary policy. In the 1960s application of this recipe was largely inhibited by interest rate floors designed to stem gold outflows. In the 1980s it is inhibited by official dedication to monetarist and supply-side nostrums.

It is relevant to the 1981 bandwagon rush to offer tax concessions to encourage private saving and business investment that Samuelson added distributional equity to the goals of stabilization and allocation that could be achieved by judicious choice of fiscal and monetary measures. We don't have to suffer extremes of inequality in order to achieve full employment and high capital intensity. Neither does prosperity require that we channel purchasing power to workers and to the poor, as underconsumptionists before and after Keynes contended. In summary, Samuelson told Congress [1955, II, Chap. 100, p. 1330].

A community can have full employment, can at the same time have the rate of capital formation it wants, and can accomplish all this compatibly with the degree of income-redistributing taxation it ethically desires.

Samuelson consistently recognized that the one goal that fiscal and monetary policies may be unable to marry, probably permanently, with full employment is price stability. Even so, he surely overstated the case. In a more elaborate exposition Samuelson would recognize the limits on substitutions among policy instruments imposed by economic behavior and by other constraints or goals such as international trade and capital movement.

To my mind his optimism is nevertheless much closer to the truth than the reverse doctrines popular in 1981, that prosperity and progress are impossible without smaller government and greater inequality. But then I am a partner in crime, so dubbed in a cherished inscription by PAS on the flyleaf of Volume I, and I think the neoclassical synthesis was the great achievement of postwar macroeconomic theorizing.

REFERENCES

Lucas, Robert E., Jr. (1980): "Methods and Problems in Business Cycle Theory," *Rational Expectations*, A Seminar Sponsored by the American Enterprise Institute for Public Policy Research, *Journal of Money, Credit and Banking* vol. 2, (Nov.).

Samuelson, Paul A. (1939): "Interactions between the Multiplier Analysis and the Principle of Accleration," *Review of Economics and Statistics* 21 (May); *Collected Scientific Papers*, II, chap. 82.

—— (1939): "A Synthesis of the Principle of Acceleration and the Multiplier," *Journal of Political Economy* 48 (Dec.); *Collected Scientific Papers*, II, chap. 83.

—— (1940): "The Theory of Pump-Priming Reexamined," *American Economic Review* 30 (Sept.); *Collected Scientific Papers*, II, chap. 85.

—— (1941): "Concerning Say's Law," *Econometrica* 9 (April); *Collected Scientific Papers*, II, chap. 88.

—— (1941): "The Stability of Equilibrium: Comparative Statics and Dynamics," *Econometrica* 9 (April); *Collected Scientific Papers*, I, chap. 38.

—— (1942): "The Stability of Equilibrium: Linear and Nonlinear Systems," *Econometrica* 10 (Jan.); *Collected Scientific Papers*, I, chap. 40.

—— (1942): "Fiscal Policy and Income Determination," *Quarterly Journal of Economics* 56 (Aug.); *Collected Scientific Papers*, II, chap. 86.

—— (1943): "Full Employment after the War," in S. E. Harris, ed., *Postwar Economic Problems*, New York, McGraw-Hill; *Collected Scientific Papers*, II, chap. 108.

—— (1943): "A Fundamental Multiplier Identity," *Econometrica* 11 (July–Oct.); *Collected Scientific Papers*, II, chap. 90.

—— (1948): "The Simple Mathematics of Income Determination," in L. A. Metzler et al., *Income, Employment and Public Policy: Essays in Honor of Alvin Hansen*, New York, Norton; *Collected Scientific Papers*, II, chap. 91.

—— (1948): "Dynamic Process Analysis," in Howard Ellis, ed., *A Survey of Contemporary Economics*, vol. I, Philadelphia, Blakiston; *Collected Scientific Papers*, I, chap. 41.

—— (1951): "Principles and Rules in Modern Fiscal Policy: A Neo-Classical Reformulation," in *Money, Trade and Economic Growth: Essays in Honor of John Henry Williams*, New York, Macmillan; *Collected Scientific Papers*, II, chap. 98.

—— (1951): "Schumpeter as a Teacher and Economic Theorist," *Review of Economics and Statistics* 33 (May); *Collected Scientific Papers*, II, chap. 116.

—— (1953): "Full Employment versus Progress and Other Economic Goals," in Max Millikan, ed., *Income Stabilization for a Developing Economy*, New Haven, Yale University Press; *Collected Scientific Papers*, II, chap. 99.

—— (1955): "Comment on 'Professor Samuelson on Operationalism in Economic Theory,' by Donald F. Gordon," *Quarterly Journal of Economics* 69 (May); *Collected Scientific Papers*, II, chap. 128.

—— (1956): "The New Look in Tax and Fiscal Policy" in Joint Committee on the Economic Report, 84th Congress, 1st Session, *Federal Tax Policy for Economic Growth and Stability* (Nov. 9, 1955), Washington, U. S. Government Printing Office; *Collected Scientific Papers*, II, chap. 100.

—— (1959): Book review of Torsten Gardlund, *The Life of Knut Wicksell* in *Review of Economics and Statistics* 41 (Feb.); *Collected Scientific Papers*, II, chap. 120.

—— (1959): "Alvin Hansen and the Interactions between the Multiplier Analysis and the Principle of Acceleration," *Review of Economics and Statistics* 41 (May); *Collected Scientific Papers*, II, chap. 84.

—— (1960): with R. M. Solow, "Analytical Aspects of Anti-Inflation Policy," *American Economic Review* 50 (May); *Collected Scientific Papers*, II, chap. 102.

—— (1964): "The General Theory," in Robert Lekachman, ed., *Keynes' General Theory: Reports of Three Decades*, New York, St. Martin's Press; *Collected Scientific Papers*, II, chap. 114.

ON RICARDO
AND MARX

C. C. von Weizsäcker

Samuelson's 1957 paper on Marx [10] and his 1959 paper on Ricardo [11] belong to his most widely read contributions to economics, and, in my opinion, rightly so. Clearly, he had predecessors in the analytic investigation of Ricardo and Marx. Thus, he could build on the contribution of Böhm-Bawerk, Bortkiewicz, Viner, Sweezy, Robinson, Stigler, Winternitz, Schumpeter, Seton, Meek, Kaldor, and others. But Samuelson's papers for the first time systematically exploit modern activity analysis to investigate the consistency of Ricardo's and Marx's main theories. Samuelson has, of course, been a major force in the modern revolution of allocation and price theory. Of the main contributors to this revolution he was the only one to take the time to use the new tools for the purposes of Dogmengeschichte. He thereby gave definite answers to controversial questions of great interest. By and large his answers show that in Ricardo as well as in Marx there are important inconsistencies. Theirs is a pre-Walrasian world. If we agree with Schumpeter that Walras was the greatest economic theorist of all time [18, p. 827], we should expect inconsistencies in any pre-Walrasian system intended to explain at least as much and indeed more than the Walrasian system does.

On rereading Samuelson's 1957 and 1959 Marx and Ricardo papers for the purpose of writing this article, the importance of Walras became clearer to me than it was before. The basic mistake made by Ricardo and Marx was not to distinguish clearly between exogenous data and endogenous variables. The inconsistencies shown by Samuelson in Marx and Ricardo can, it seems to me, all be explained by this mistake. The strict methodology of distinguishing between data and variables requires a theory of behaviour of the elements of the system, that is, of the individuals. But this theory did not exist before marginal-utility theory was developed by Gossen, Jevons, Menger, and Walras.

The Ricardo (1959) paper and the Marx (1957) paper belong together. They use the same basic model to handle different questions. The Ricardo paper, although published later, will be discussed first.

A year before Samuelson's article appeared, Stigler published his analysis of Ricardo's "93% Labor Theory of Value" [21]. This article definitely settled the question whether or not Ricardo believed in a labour theory of value in the strict sense. Indeed, the main purpose of that article was to explain why the obviously erroneous opinion that Ricardo did propose such a theory could have survived for so long. Ricardo accepted deviations from proportionality between labour content and prices of goods to the extent that they were due to differences in capital intensity of production. Prices were derived by Ricardo from costs including the prevailing rate of return on capital and did not include a land cost component. He believed this theory to be true even in the presence of land rents. By looking at production relations on marginal (no rent) land, Ricardo thought he could exclude land as an ingredient of value.

This fallacy is analyzed and corrected by Samuelson with two different models. One model assumes a fixed amount of homogeneous land. The other model considers heterogeneous land. Both models are striking: the first, because Samuelson succeeds not only in refuting Ricardo but also in turning his theory upside down: he develops a land theory of value, where the land content of products determines their relative prices. The other model is an interesting forerunner to recent advances in location theory.

If one accepts, as Ricardo does, the Malthus theory of population and labour supply, it is possible to determine the long-run wage of labour in terms of the minimum commodity basket needed for the worker's subsistence and reproduction. Consider now an economy with a limited and fixed amount of homogeneous land. Assume for the moment that no capital is required in the production process. Suppose that the economy is in a Malthusian long-run equilibrium: population has grown up to the point where the wage rate equals the subsistence wage. The surplus of labour productivity over the subsistence wage is the land rent that land owners obtain. The land and labour content of each good can now be computed, using the Leontief input-output coefficients prevailing in equilibrium. Now, reduce labour to land in the following way: equate the total land content of labour with the total land content of labour's means of subsistence. The total land content of a commodity is the land content already computed plus the total land content equivalent of its labour content. This gives a system of linear equations for the total land content of all commodities, which can be solved. It then turns out that in this Malthusian long-run equilibrium prices are proportional to their total land content: a land theory of value.

This result of Samuelson is not frequently quoted in the literature, perhaps because for present day mainstream economics it highlights a methodological rather than a substantive point. The methodological point is this: To explain the values of goods, that is, to explain endogenous variables, means to reduce them to something, which is exogenously given. What is exogenously given in this Ricardian model is the quantity of land. The long-run supply of labour is endogenous in

Ricardo's system, and thus can itself be reduced to exogenous land. A labour theory of value would better be deduced from an exogenously given supply of labour in a model with an abundance of land.

In the second part of the Ricardo paper Samuelson introduces capital and profit. Again exploiting the Ricardian theory of the long-run trend in the profit rate, Samuelson arrives at a modified land theory of value. Assuming, as Ricardo does, that the rate of profit falls until it reaches a definite long-run equilibrium level, this long-run equilibrium with a Malthus-Ricardo subsistence wage and a Ricardo minimum profit rate is again characterized by prices which do not vary with changes in demand pattern of landowners. Here, the prices are no longer strictly proportional to the land content of the goods. But it remains true that they can be computed without knowledge of demand functions of capitalists and landowners. The demand of workers is given by the subsistence basket.

In an appendix to the Ricardo paper Samuelson treats the case of differential rent due to heterogeneous land. It is a very elegant programming formulation using the duality theorem in linear programming. Samuelson shows thereby that the problem of equilibrium differential rent is much more intricate than could be solved with the analytical techniques available to Ricardo. He shows in particular that Ricardo's attempt to save his (rate of return modified) labour theory of value fails. Not only is demand important in setting the extensive margin in land use. In addition, as a rule, marginal land will only be used for a small subset of commodities so that most commodities do not have land rent-free costs, which might correspond to modified labour contents. The use of different types of land for different products will be regulated by the principle of comparative advantage, and Samuelson wonders why Ricardo, the inventor of comparative advantage, did not apply the idea to his theory of land rent.

The elegant programming formulation of the theory of differential rent seems to me to be an important contribution to location theory. Recent results concerning the von-Thünen model are quite similar in spirit to the Samuelson setup for studying differential rent.[1]

The paper "Wages and Interest: A Modern Dissection of Marxian Economic Models," published in 1957, applies modern activity analysis to the Marxian system. It was not greeted with enthusiasm by Marxists. Yet, as far as I am aware, they were not able to refute the inconsistencies shown to be the consequence of Marx's propositions as interpreted and formalized by Samuelson. Other than agreeing, the only way open to them was to claim that Samuelson had misinterpreted Marx. Whether or not this is the case, Samuelson's article is important because his interpretation of Marx certainly corresponds to the interpretation of many—perhaps naive—readers of *Das Kapital*.

When I read *Das Kapital* in 1960/61, I was not aware of Samuelson's article. Without then having so clearly formalized my interpretation of Marx and thus my

---

[1]See, for example, Schweizer and Varaiya [19]; Schweizer [20].

impression of inconsistencies. I still could later say that it completely agreed with Samuelson's interpretation. I believe anyone sufficiently capable of old-fashioned forms of logical thinking reads Marx similarly. The reader trained in Hegel's logic perhaps has a different access to Marx.

In the Marx article Samuelson developed the analytical instrument of the wage-profit curve that he himself later called the factor price frontier. This instrument, probably independently developed later by others like Sraffa, substantially influenced capital theory in the last two decades. In this article, Samuelson used it—indeed it seems to have been designed for that purpose—to show the inconsistency of the three Marxian propositions about capitalism: 1) capitalism produces substantial technical progress, 2) under capitalist conditions the real wage rate does not rise, 3) the rate of profit has a tendency to fall. Marx believed that competition dictated to individual capitalists and workers the laws that govern the capitalist system. It is in this spirit when Samuelson writes (in his footnote 9):

> Rewriting (11) as $w/p_2 = \phi$ $(r; a, b)$, and now letting (a, b) be variable as a result of technological change, the competitive Invisible Hand can be proved to select (a, b) so that $w/p_2 = \phi$ (r) = maximum of ϕ $(r; a, b)$ with respect to (a, b). Similarly, $r = \phi^{-1}$ (w/p_2) = maximum of ϕ^{-1} $(w/p_2; a, b)$ with respect to (a, b). Always $\phi'(r) < 0$. I believe this to be a new theorem. Of course, it is a prosaic mathematical fact, not a Dr. Pangloss teleology.

In other words, changes in production methods are only introduced if they not only allow surplus value to rise but if they also actually raise the return on the capital invested. To the extent that technical change opens up new production opportunities, the capitalist system will only make use of them if—given the real wage—they imply a higher rate of profit. Although he did not see the logical consequences for his law of a declining profit rate, Marx comes close to saying exactly this. In volume III (chapter 15, section IV) Marx offers a numerical example to make his point. His point here is that under capitalist conditions it is not necessarily the case that a reduction in required labour will induce capitalists to introduce a new machine. They will only do it if it will raise their rate of profit. His numerical example is this: 18 shillings of constant capital and 2 shillings of variable capital (wages), implying costs of 20 shillings, produce 22 shillings output (in value, and as Marx here assumes, also in price terms). The rate of profit on the capital invested is $2:20 = 10$ percent. Now, a machine is invented, which reduces the required direct labour by one half, but requires more constant capital, so that constant capital is now 19 shillings and variable capital is 1 shilling. The value (that is, the labour requirement) of the output has declined from 22 shillings to 21 shillings. But the capitalist has no incentive to introduce the new machine, because his or her profit does not rise. (Apart from this valid point supporting the Samuelson theorem, the passage also shows that Marx did occasionally get confused regarding values and production prices.)

There is probably no better place than the Samuelson papers on Ricardo and Marx, if one looks for examples of the advantages of mathematical models, for keeping one's thinking clear.

THE TRANSFORMATION PROBLEM

In his 1971 survey of the literature on the transformation problem,[2] Samuelson draws the consequences from the availability of modern analytical tools for the problem of transforming Marxian labour values into Marxian (and bourgeois) production prices:

> I should perhaps explain in the beginning why the words 'so-called transformation problem' appear in the title. As the present survey shows, better descriptive words than 'the transformation problem' would be provided by 'the problem of comparing and contrasting the mutually-exclusive alternatives of 'values' and 'prices'. For when you cut through the maze of algebra and come to understand what is going on, you discover that the 'transformation algorithm' is precisely of the following form: 'Contemplate two alternative and discordant systems. Write down one. Now transform by taking an eraser and rubbing it out. Then fill in the other one. Voilà! You have completed your transformation algorithm.'

The modern techniques allow us to compute classical natural prices or, the same thing, Marxian production prices, without ever computing Marxian values. Indeed, to do the latter simply is a detour. It was different, I believe, when Marx wrote or when Ricardo wrote. Neither Ricardo nor Marx could advance the state of knowledge concerning natural price beyond Adam Smith unless they proceeded as Ricardo and Marx did. Without a clear formalized concept of Walras-Leontief input-output coefficients or analogous Austrian (Böhm-Bawerkian) formalizations of production and without the instrument of solving linear equations, they had to proceed along the route of approximation. Their first approximation is the labour theory of value. Then Ricardo refines this approximation, and Marx follows him very closely by pointing to the different capital intensities. As Bortkiewicz and others then pointed out, this second approximation is still not sufficient. All these approximations are no longer needed if modern techniques are available.

The need to take this particular detour is supported by the fact that basically Böhm-Bawerk's method of using simple interest rather than compound interest boils down to essentially the same approximation as the one used by Ricardo and Marx. I have tried to show this elsewhere [23]. Indeed, the Clark-Ramsey-Solow macroeconomic production function is again closely related to this approximation.

Samuelson's survey on the transformation problem received criticism from Bronfenbrenner, Baumol, and Morishima basically on the point that Marx's labour theory of value was not simply a theory of price, but the foundation for his whole theory of capitalism.[3] Samuelson's answer, I think, is appropriate: We have to distinguish between Marx, the contributor to rigorous economic analysis, and the Marx whose "philosophy was, in secular, non-theistic language, a new and radical step forward in the tradition of prophetic Messianism," as Erich Fromm put it [3, p. 3].

---

[2][13]; See also [12].
[3][2], [15], [1], [16], [5].

This distinction cuts both ways. The labour theory of value is neither needed for the young Marx's ideas about alienation and historical materialism, nor does it help to introduce the viewpoint of historical materialism into rigorous economic theory. Similarly, as Samuelson points out, the Marxian concept of exploitation can be formulated merely in terms of the relation between necessary labour and totally expended labour in a capitalist system. The labour theory of value is not at all needed to formulate this concept of exploitation or to show the existence of exploitation in capitalism under the assumptions made by Marx. The "Fundamental Marxian Theorem," as Morishima calls it, states that the existence of a positive profit rate (in constant price terms) and the existence of exploitation in the Marxian sense are equivalent. It can be shown to hold given certain assumptions.[4] The proof does not have to involve any reference to Marxian labour values.

Both Samuelson and Morishima show that for a stationary system with a zero profit rate the equivalence of labour values and production prices. This can be done by means of the now well-known duality relations between quantities and prices in Leontief and more general systems. This duality relation has been used in a more general way in a joint article by the present author and Samuelson [14]. There we introduce the concept of synchronized labour costs of commodities, by which we mean the labour requirements of consumption goods in a system growing at a predetermined rate g per unit of time. For a given supply of labour, growing at this rate g through time, these synchronized labour costs are indications of the steady state opportunity costs of a given consumption good in terms of any other consumption good. By the duality theorems of capital theory it can be shown that these synchronized labour costs are equal to the production prices that prevail if the rate of profit r is equal to the rate of growth g. Moreover, a society trying to maximize steady state consumption will find an appropriate production technology in a market system, provided the rate of profit is equal to the rate of growth. This is the well-known golden rule. We thus see that production prices at positive profit rates have greater relevance for planning problems, say in a planned socialist economy, than would have Marxian labour values.

Marx's labour theory of value, one can thus conclude, no longer serves a useful purpose. In its time it was probably a necessary analytical instrument and it is, as Morishima stresses, a precursor of modern duality relations of capital theory.[5] Having had a function in the past, it must no longer confuse us today, and it can now be disposed of. This is particularly true because, in addition to the "number one issue," the transformation problem,[6] there exists the problem number two, the problem of reducing different kinds of labour to simple labour. The neoclassical revolution clearly has shown that the reduction problem cannot be solved, unless a

---

[4]These assumptions are more restrictive than Morishima would like to have it: cf. von Weizsäcker [22], and Morishima [6], where Morishima obviously misunderstands my argument. The same is true of Robinson [9].

[5][4]. But Morishima also agrees that his fundamental Marxian theorem is independent of the labour theory of value [7].

[6]Cf. [17]. In appreciating Marx as a mathematical economist, Samuelson rightly calls the transformation problem the number one issue in the technical discussions about Marx.

mere tautology is called a solution. This was so clear from the beginning of the orthodox critique of Marx that nobody bothered to write about it at any length.

The reduction problem cuts much deeper into the Marxian theory of exploitation than the transformation problem. The models discussing the transformation problem use a homogeneous labour input, which allows computation of necessary labour, time and so forth, and thus allows the construction of a Marxian exploitation concept—even without use of the Marxian labour theory of value. But labour time becomes a theoretically shaky measure in models of competitive capitalism with heterogeneous labour. There is no way around concepts like disutility of labour, scarcity rents of skills, and the implicit wage of the selfemployed. A measure of exploitation by labour time expended is no longer reasonable under such circumstances.[7] Are other exploitation theories possible? I don't know. Nobody in the Marxist camp has really tried, perhaps because, as Robinson put it, Marxism is the opium of the Marxists [8].

Neo-Marxism draws its inspiration from Marx, the messianic prophet of humanism, the philosopher of alienation, commodity fetishism, and false consciousness, the sociologist of the class struggle, but definitely not from Marx, the mathematical economist. To the extent that Neo-Marxism produces scientifically interesting propositions, they are never derived from the labour theory of value or the quantified model of exploitation. Despite Marx's criticism of the trend, the division of labour has been intensified since his time, in East and West alike. Thus, unless the students quarrel with their professors, Marx is no longer widely read in the economics departments. Marx the prophet is not read, because "this is not economics." (I believe this to be a grave mistake.) Marx the mathematical economist is not read, because it is thought to be analytically no longer relevant (with which I basically agree). Samuelson has read both Marx the prophet and philosopher and Marx the mathematical economist. He honoured a precursor of himself, a great mathematical economist, by investigating in detail the relevance of his work for present day economic theory.

REFERENCES

Baumal, W. J. (1974): "The Transformation of Values: What Marx 'Really' Meant (An Interpretation)," and "Comment," *Journal of Economic Literature* 12 (March).

Bronfenbrenner, M. (1973): "Samuelson, Marx, and their Latest Critics," *Journal of Economic Literature* 11 (March).

Fromm, E. (1961): *Marx's Concept of Man*, New York, F. Ungar.

Morishima, M. (1973): *Marx's Economics: A Dual Theory of Value and Growth*, London, Cambridge University Press.

——— (1974): "The Fundamental Marxian Theorem: A Reply to Samuelson," *Journal of Economic Literature*, 12 (March).

——— (1974): "Marx's Economies: A Comment on C. C. von Weizsäcker's Article," *Economic Journal* 84 (June).

[7]This is a somewhat ironic result, given the fact that any concept of exploitation based on labour time calculations probably would imply empirically that the degree of exploitation in the Marxist Soviet Union is quite high.

———— (1974): "Marx in the Light of Modern Economic Theory, *Econometrica* 42 (July).

Robinson, J. (1953): *On Re-Reading Marx*, Cambridge, Students' Bookshops.

———— (1975): "Value before Capitalism," *Kyklos* 28 (Fasc. 1).

Samuelson, Paul A. (1957): "Ways and Interest: A Modern Dissection of Marxian Economic Models," *American Economic Review* 47 (Dec.); *Collected Scientific Papers*, I, chap. 29.

———— (1959): "A Modern Treatment of the Ricardian Economy, *Quarterly Journal of Economics* 73 (Feb. and May); *Collected Scientific Papers*, I, chaps. 31 and 32.

———— (1970): "The Transformation from Marxian 'Values' to Competitive 'Prices': A Process of Rejection and Replacement, *Proceedings of the National Academy of Sciences* 67 (Sept.); *Collected Scientific Papers*, III, chap. 154.

———— (1971): "Understanding the Marxian Notion of Exploitation: A Summary of the So-Called Transformation Problem Between Marxian Values and Competitive Prices," *Journal of Economic Literature* 9 (June); *Collected Scientific Papers*, III, chap. 153.

———— and C. C. von Weizsäcker (1971): "A New Labor Theory of Value for Rational Planning Through Use of the Bourgeouise Profit Rate," *Proceedings of the National Academy of Sciences* 68 (June); *Collected Scientific Papers*, III, chap. 155.

———— (1973): "Reply on Marxian Matters," *Journal of Economic Literature* 11 (March); *Collected Scientific Papers*, IV, chap. 22.

———— (1974): "Insight and Detour in the Theory of Exploitation: A Reply to Baumol," and "Rejoinder, Melin Unclothed, A Final Word," *Journal of Economic Literature*, 12 (March); *Collected Scientific Papers*, IV, chaps. 229 and 230.

———— (1974): "Marx as Mathematical Economist," in G. Horwich and P. A. Samuelson (eds.), *Trade, Stability and Macroeconomics: Essays in Honor of Lloyd A. Metzler*, New York, Academic Press; *Collected Scientific Papers*, IV, chap. 225.

Schumpeter, J. A. (1967): *History of Economic Analysis*, 6th Ed., London, Oxford University Press.

Schweizer, U. and P. Varauja (1976, 1977): "The Spatial Structure of Production with a Leontief Technology I and II," *Regional Science and Urban Economics* 6 and 7.

———— (1978): "A Spatial Version of the Nonsubstitution Theorem," *Journal of Economic Theory* 19 (Dec.).

Stigler, G. (1958): "Ricardo and the 93% Labor Theory of Value," *American Economic Review* 48 (June).

von Weizsäcker, C. C. (1973): "Morishima on Marx," *Economic Journal* 83 (Dec.).

———— (1977): "Organic Composition of Capital and Average Period of Production," *Revue d'Economie Politique* 87 (March–April).